THE KEVIN SHOW

ALSO BY MARY PILON

The Monopolists: Obsession, Fury, and the Scandal Behind
the World's Favorite Board Game

THE
KEVIN
SHOW

AN OLYMPIC ATHLETE'S BATTLE WITH

MENTAL ILLNESS

MARY PILON

BLOOMSBURY PUBLISHING
NEW YORK · LONDON · OXFORD · NEW DELHI · SYDNEY

BLOOMSBURY PUBLISHING
Bloomsbury Publishing Inc.
1385 Broadway, New York, NY 10018, USA

BLOOMSBURY, BLOOMSBURY PUBLISHING, and the Diana logo are trademarks of
Bloomsbury Publishing Plc

First published in the United States 2018

Bloomsbury Publishing Plc does not have any control over, or responsibility for, any third-party
websites referred to or in this book. All internet addresses given in this book were correct at the
time of going to press. The author and publisher regret any inconvenience caused if addresses have
changed or sites have ceased to exist, but can accept no responsibility for any such changes.

ISBN: HB: 978-1-63286-682-0; eBook: 978-1-63286-684-4

Library of Congress Cataloging-in-Publication Data is available

2 4 6 8 10 9 7 5 3 1

Typeset by Westchester Publishing Services
Printed and bound in the U.S.A. by Berryville Graphics Inc., Berryville, Virginia

To find out more about our authors and books visit www.bloomsbury.com
and sign up for our newsletters.

Bloomsbury books may be purchased for business or promotional use. For information on bulk
purchases please contact Macmillan Corporate and Premium Sales Department
at specialmarkets@macmillan.com.

For Dad

CAST

KEVIN HALL

sailor, patient, case study, surveillance subject, star of The Show

AMANDA

Kevin's love interest

GORDON

Kevin's father

SUSANNE

Kevin's mother

KRISTINA

Kevin's younger sister

THE DIRECTOR

the guide of The Show

With several guest appearances along the way.

CONTENTS

*I think that melancholia is the beginning and a part of
mania . . . The development of a mania is really a worsening of
the disease (melancholia) rather than a change into another
disease . . . In most of them (melancholics) the sadness became better
after various lengths of time and changed into happiness;
the patients then developed a mania.*
—ARETAEUS OF CAPPADOCIA (First Century CE)

*Our wills and fates do so contrary run
That our devices still are overthrown;
Our thoughts are ours, their ends none of our own.*
—WILLIAM SHAKESPEARE, *Hamlet* (1603)

*Good morning, and in case I don't see ya, good afternoon,
good evening, and good night!*
—JIM CARREY in *The Truman Show* (1998)
Screenplay by ANDREW NICCOL

KEVIN

As Kevin Hall stood onboard the *Artemis*, a 72-foot catamaran, trying to help his teammates dredge Andrew Simpson's body out of the water, he wasn't entirely sure if the scene unfolding before him was really happening or not.

Dressed in a sleek black wetsuit plated with metal and a knife strapped to his calf, Kevin was one of eleven professional sailors moving with the swift, tense alacrity that only emergencies can trigger. Capsized boats are an inevitable part of sailing, but most boats weren't this boat—one of the largest and fastest sailing vessels in the world, made of a carbon fiber that turned into a plank of daggers when shattered. The sound of the boat breaking had cracked the air just seconds before, as if the sailors had been standing in a forest and all the trees around them had snapped at once. Yet only moments before that, Kevin and his teammates had been skimming comfortably along in San Francisco Bay. This wasn't supposed to be happening.

With his shaved head and athletic build, Kevin bore a strong resemblance to his teammates. Their fitness and physical similarity evoked military or comic book heroes more than it did a sport on water. Still, the day was supposed to end with going back to shore, maybe having a meal and some jokes. Not with a visit to the coroner.

Andrew "Bart" Simpson, whose body might or might not have been in the water, was a stocky British Olympic gold medalist with short, spiky chestnut hair and a wide smile. Universally loved by his teammates, he, like Kevin and many of the others on the *Artemis*, had a wife and children. One of the world's best sailors, Simpson knew what to do in emergencies, which made his being trapped underwater for ten minutes all the more incomprehensible. The $140-million *Artemis* was supposed to be a technological wonder, so it made no sense to anyone onboard that it had crumpled so quickly into a taco shell, trapping Simpson in its fold.

When they had started their test run more than three months out from the first race of the America's Cup, light charcoal skies and moderate winds had made the patch of water between Alcatraz and Treasure Island less intimidating than usual. The city was wrapped around them in a sheath of familiarity, as it was just another weekday when those on land were at work, in school, and otherwise going about their lives. A few errant boats carrying tourists chugged to and fro in the distance. Tiny specks of cars puttered across crowded bridges. Seagulls surveyed the scene and whisked overhead. Organizers of the America's Cup had touted this very city-meets-sea quality of San Francisco as one reason why the Bay Area was a perfect stage for the event—a place where the boats would be visible to those on land. It wasn't immediately clear to Kevin how much of this capsize was viewable from the shore. Thank goodness they had only been on a test run and that a full crowd and the press weren't watching. That wouldn't be the case for much longer, but Kevin couldn't think that far ahead, as catastrophes have a jarring way of bringing one smack into the present.

Finally, Kevin and his teammates were able to pull Simpson's soggy two hundred pounds out of the water and onto a floating backboard. They began performing CPR. The San Francisco Police Department's Marine 7 unit pulled up to the site of the crash in a white police boat that was dwarfed by the *Artemis*. The cops observed the red hulls, or main bodies, of the boat completely flipped over, the white letters spelling out ARTEMIS upside down, and a tall, black wing-sail twisted into a knot of trash floating against San Francisco's skyline. Or, in sailing parlance, a boat that had "turtled," the rounded shells meant to be underwater instead facing the sky.

The emergency responders began to perform CPR, one officer cutting open Simpson's wet suit so he could apply a defibrillator to his chest. They pushed, the sailors waiting for Simpson to breathe, to show some sign of life. But Simpson was dead. He was thirty-six years old.

For all of their years of disaster training, the crew now realized that nothing could have prepared them for the death of a man onboard, a freakish occurrence in their sport. Kevin and his teammates were in a state of shock, wondering how what should have been a simple practice run had turned tragic. Sailing is a moody sport—even top sailors can't compete without a wind, yet they'll also delay a competition if there's too much of it—but the conditions that day were mild. And months of preparation and millions of dollars had gone into the design of the *Artemis*, a vessel that had stunned other sailors with its foils and gadgets and that had seemed almost to fly over the water. Kevin suddenly felt lost. What had happened? Who, if anyone, was to blame? And why had Simpson, of all the sailors on the boat, been the one to die? Kevin had known Simpson for years, their sailing careers often overlapping, intersecting, and running in parallel. Simpson had something that Kevin and some of the other men on board the *Artemis* did not—an Olympic gold medal—and he represented something that all of the men on board aspired to be: a champion athlete and family man with a kind heart and generous spirit, seemingly unfazed by the success that he had attained.

Kevin thought about all this and more as the emergency workers took Simpson's body away and everyone went home. In the days that followed, part of him wanted to talk to his teammates about what had happened, but part of him dared not. Because, if he was honest, he still wasn't entirely sure that the crash and Simpson's death had really happened. It seemed too horrifying to be real. And for a few moments, there had been that flash.

The Director. Cameras. Actors. Scripts.

Kevin wondered: Had it all just been part of The Show?

PART I

MEET KEVIN HALL

Go, go, go, said the bird: human kind
Cannot bear very much reality.
Time past and time future
What might have been and what has been
Point to one end, which is always present.
　　　　—T. S. ELIOT, "Burnt Norton"

We do not know our own souls, let alone the souls of others.
Human beings do not go hand in hand the whole stretch of the
way. There is a virgin forest in each; a snowfield where even the
print of birds' feet is unknown. Here we go alone, and like it
better so. Always to have sympathy, always to be accompanied,
always to be understood would be intolerable.
　　　　—VIRGINIA WOOLF, "On Being Ill"

I can't find being born in the diagnostic manual.
　　　　—FRANZ WRIGHT, "Pediatric Suicide"

KEVIN

ALTHOUGH HE WAS born on land, Kevin was more at home on water.

To those standing on the shore in Ventura, California, it could be a peculiar sight: a six-year-old boy, noticeably smaller than the other young sailors around him, maneuvering a sailboat with the confidence of one far beyond his years, all on his own. From the moment he first approached the water the year before, Kevin understood that sailing was a large-scale, nautical game of chess, a sport that combined an obsession with detail with a feel for the wind. Here, on the water, he could be independent, on his own, at one with his surroundings, and far away from the expectations and hoop jumping of school, home.

Kevin had confidence radiating through every pore. He had the kind of tanned skin and blond hair, the product of an untold number of hours out in the sun, that is distinct to many children of European ancestry living in Southern California. His face was bedecked with a constellation of freckles, and his hair was straight and dutifully parted in the same direction as his slightly curled smile.

Some talents are born. Others are made. It's possible that Kevin Hall was both. From his mother, Susanne, he had inherited a natural feel for the water; from his father, Gordon, an aptitude for math and the ability to interpret and apply data to a sport. Both are critical for sailing success, and within days of his first sail, Kevin was engaged in a positive feedback loop: he sailed and won, and then received praise for winning, which made him want to sail (and win) more. Kevin wasn't especially well coordinated, but he was an active child who loved climbing trees and playing sports. Like many children, he began to dream of going to the Olympics one day, an aspiration to Wheaties-box-inspired fame. Sailing wasn't the most popular event at the Games, but it had been part of the Olympics since their modern inception in 1896. And for good reason: for centuries, sailing had spoken to the most primal competitive instincts, as well as humankind's relationship with the water, technology, and, of course, grueling physical prowess.

To watch the home movies of the Hall family is to see a depiction of Southern California's many promises: sun-soaked days, majestic Pacific shores, suburban ease, and the spaciousness of a swath of America where days easily blend into months and years. Kevin was the son of two doctors who had relocated there to live that idyllic life where careers and children could bloom together. "The future always looks good in the golden land," Joan Didion wrote of California in 1966, just three years before Kevin was born. "Because no one remembers the past." In California, more than anywhere else in America, she went on, people are "trying to find a new life style, trying to find it in the only places they know to look: the movies and the newspapers."

It was hard to blame the Hall family for drinking it all in, especially since everything seemed to be going their way.

SUSANNE

WHEN SUSANNE WATCHED Kevin on the water, she couldn't help but think of her father. It was strange to think that just after he died, her son had started developing confidence in the very sport his grandfather had loved, almost as if some baton had been passed.

So much had happened over the past few years since she first left Canada—it was staggering to think about. Susanne had been only twenty-two years old when she and Gordon married in 1964. Concerned at the time about the looming possibility that Gordon might be drafted to the war in Vietnam, they had decided to both volunteer together to serve, even though Susanne was a Canadian by birth. The three years they spent stationed in Germany were some of the best of their lives, as they were relatively carefree and their time there was full of European travel.

Kevin was born in Germany in 1969, just after man walked on the moon. Susanne stayed home with him that first year, but she longed to get back to work and eventually did. After a short posting to Africa, she and her husband moved back to the United States in 1971, settling in Rockford, Illinois, where Gordon had grown up. Kevin's sister, Kristina, was born there that same year.

As a girl growing up in eastern Canada, Susanne had learned to sail from her father, spending hours and hours on the water with him as he taught her and her two sisters how to understand the wind and command a boat, even though sailing was a chiefly male pursuit at the time. Susanne carried what she had learned from her father into her academic life. When she entered medical school at McGill University in the 1960s, she was one of only a handful of women in a class of more than a hundred.

Living in the Midwest, where the land feels as flat and vast as an ocean, yet knowing she was nowhere near the shore, somehow made Susanne feel oddly claustrophobic. It had been years since she had had meaningful access to a boat, but now, back stateside and staying not far from Gordon's family in Illinois, she found herself yearning for it. On a whim, she and Gordon booked a trip to California for a medical symposium, and while out there, to secure a tax write-off for the trip, Gordon signed up for a job interview. Susanne had been to California only once before, for a brief visit, but as she sat at the pool while her husband was at the interview, gazing at the clear, crisp skies above her and the islands in the distance, she fell in love with the Pacific coast and the idea of raising her children in a place where they could sail even more than she had as a child.

Within weeks, she and Gordon had bought a boat (before a house) and quickly found that they had the entire infrastructure they would need to relocate their family of four to Ventura, California. Located northwest of Los Angeles, Ventura had sprouted in the mid-nineteenth century around a Spanish Catholic mission, and had boomed in the post–World War II years into a quilt of single-family homes overtaking an agriculturally rich land.

Their home was situated beyond the farming roots, however, and rested on the water, a ranch-style house on a small, street-like canal that curled out into the ocean. The road was well paved and lined with sixties-style California architecture, colorful houses with white trim, accompanied by palm trees and clean, well-maintained cars. The Halls had a boat dock in their backyard, as did all of their neighbors. Easy canal access gave the Halls' neighborhood a nautical yet suburban vibe—life on the water, but just off Highway 101.

Gordon had his position as a doctor lined up, but soaring malpractice insurance costs made Susanne's reentry into medicine impractical. Gordon and Susanne backed a successful boat, which led to expanding their investment in the boat industry and Susanne becoming a yacht broker, a job akin to that of a real estate agent but centered on boats rather than buildings. Susanne would help those looking for a boat to purchase, as well as list and represent boats for those looking to sell, and receive a commission for her services. Like real estate, the boat business has its inherent ebbs and flows, as it is a high-stakes line of work that can be susceptible to greater economic trends.

Susanne missed medicine but was thrilled with the reentry of sailing into her life. If only her father were still alive to see it. But sadly, six months before their move to Ventura in July 1975, he died and would never have the chance to see his daughter's reconnection with, or his grandson's love for, the water.

GORDON

EVERY NIGHT AS they sat around the dinner table, Gordon impressed upon his children the responsibility that came with the advantages of their environment. He regularly made a point of telling Kevin and Kristina that they were the offspring of two intelligent, well-to-do parents, and they were exceptional by many metrics. They got good grades, lived in a good neighborhood, and were exposed to things that as children, Gordon and Susanne could only have imagined. Success mattered in the Hall family, but it was to be earned, not taken for granted.

Gordon took great pleasure in Kevin's progress on the water, and he spent most of his weekends driving his son and his boat to competitions in the area. Whenever Kevin won a regatta, Gordon proudly placed his medal, trophy, or other award on the Hall family mantel, where a model ship rested on the corner. The titles included back-to-back wins in the U.S. Youth Camps, an unheard-of feat in the sport. They were titles that confirmed Kevin wasn't just a winner in the eyes of his parents; rather, he was the one everyone else was looking to try and defeat.

Before long, Kevin's sailing effectively became a part-time job for Gordon—and for Susanne as well. Kevin's parents embraced the duty, happy to encourage their son in something that he was not only talented at, but appeared to be enjoying. Neither parent wanted Kevin or his sister to feel forced into sailing, so when Kristina didn't take to the sport, and, after a short time, she quit, they didn't object.

Gordon delighted in the sport of sailing, but he loved the natural high that came with regatta competition even more. Unlike Susanne, who had grown up around boats, the sailing world was new to him, and he learned about it through the prism of his wife and son. In college, he had been a competitive marksman, but sailing resonated with him more than shooting ever had. He loved the strategy, the planning, and the pursuit of perfection involved and spent countless hours studying the minutiae

Kevin Hall as a teenager (courtesy Hall family)

of the sport. Gordon believed that the world was a zero-sum game of winners and losers, and the goal, of course, was to be a winner. Focus was paramount.

Kevin, meanwhile, maintained his targets on the water, but he also had a voracious appetite for reading, particularly fiction. On his bookshelf were several volumes by C. S. Lewis, including *The Chronicles of Narnia*. "There are no ordinary people," wrote Lewis, a notion that reverberated with father and son, but for different reasons. Like many children, Kevin absorbed the messianic world of Lewis, the notion that one could save the world. His father was far more practical, finding such notions living where they belonged: in pages of storybooks that were intended to sit on shelves.

Starting with Kevin's earliest regattas, Gordon talked to his son over and over about the virtue of being gracious in victory, of exchanging the friendly handshake at the end of an event no matter who had won. Because Kevin was competing in singlehanded sailing, in which a crew of one commands the boat, the competition came not just from opponents, but from setting his own personal bests, a class of sailing that structurally was more like individual events in swimming or track. Kevin liked just about all of the kids he sailed with and against, so for him, that wasn't a difficult task. Sure, Kevin's first few months on the water saw some tears. Any child's would, Gordon figured.

Gordon also tried to talk to Kevin about whether he was doing his best, and when Kevin won, he asked him, had it been just luck or had he really put his whole self into the race? Gordon could see that Kevin was starting to internalize that question, that feeling of wondering whether, truthfully, he was sailing to his full potential or not. All told, Gordon felt that Kevin had a healthy attitude about winning, which was

Kevin Hall (courtesy Hall family)

no easy task when people started throwing terms like "child prodigy" around.

The family's dinner conversations revolved around sailing strategy and tactics that Kevin could deploy before heading out to his weekend competitions. Kristina enjoyed playing Atari with her brother and goofing around with him when their parents weren't around, but she wasn't much interested in talking about sailing, or about any competitive pursuit, really. Yet she was forced to spend hours in the car, either en route to do a boat deal or for Kevin's competitions, across state lines. With compassion, Gordon echoed a refrain to his daughter repeated by countless parents through the ages: Life isn't fair.

KEVIN

KEVIN KNEW THAT his father and mother loved him whether he won or lost—Gordon and Susanne told him that repeatedly. Still, when he did lose, a sense of shame washed over him, a deep feeling that he had let his family and himself down. His losses were rare, but even so, the specter of defeat was always hanging over him, an invisible, unwanted companion in otherwise clear waters.

As a teenager, Kevin continued to soar in the sport. His many lessons on the water now included discussions of how to deal with capsizes, which were to be expected: how to protect himself from injury if a vessel somehow became unmanageable, and how to safely get back on a boat if it flipped. He learned how to navigate storm conditions and to appreciate the virtues of wearing a life jacket, his coaches dutifully weaving together sailing's teachings with bigger life lessons, one practice at a time.

Kevin defeated dozens of other sailors in his age category, winning various regional titles, and at fifteen, he became a local news sensation as the youngest sailor ever to win the United States Junior Singlehanded Nationals. What's more, he defended his title again a second time the following year. While most kids were merely studying for their SATs, Kevin had proved himself the best in the nation at something—twice. (And the best in the world, too.)

At the rate he was going, the idea of making the Olympic sailing team someday started to seem possible.

SUSANNE

THERE WAS A problem, a secret, looming—two, really—that Susanne didn't want to tell her children, or anyone else, about. She and Gordon could save lives, but they knew very little about how to run a business. The balance sheet of their boat brokerage company was unpredictable, and they were constantly improvising, with questions like "Which debt do we pay first?" floating in the air one month after another. Sure, they had made some savvy decisions, like becoming the first backers of the original line of 100 Olson 30s, a bet that had paid off financially and helped them quickly establish a profile as serious dealers. Yet the success, however grand, had felt short-lived when the economy went into a slump in the early 1980s and the super-wealthy stopped splurging on luxury items like yachts. The Halls' business, which had also afforded Kevin access to boats he wouldn't have been able to sail otherwise, began to buckle. With it, so did Susanne and Gordon's marriage.

At first, Susanne had thought it was a simple case of two people growing apart. They had been so young when they married. But as the years went by, the differences between their personalities grew vast. Small arguments became big ones, whether related to the boat business, parenting, or current events. They tried their hardest to keep their acrimony away from Kevin's and Kristina's eyes, and they didn't tell them anything until they felt their divorce was certain. At times, Susanne wondered if she should have seen things coming more, but she also knew that raising two children was more of a priority than resting in regret. Her marriage felt like a failure, a thought that was arresting and painful and was the last thing she wanted to discuss at length with anyone, particularly her children.

As Gordon and Susanne divvied up their debts and assets (it felt like more of the former than the latter), they argued about where Kevin should go to school. Gordon thought that the sailing program at the U.S. Naval Academy in Annapolis would offer Kevin the best opportunities, or perhaps he could stay in state. But Susanne felt that her son's creative side would be more fulfilled at Brown University, where he could both receive a prestigious Ivy League education and be able to sail with some of the best college-age sailors in the world. Kevin circumvented the parental squabble by applying for early admission to Brown, and was accepted. While his parents were arguing, he had made up his own mind.

When Susanne told Kevin that she and his father were separating, he, like many teenage boys when confronted with emotional issues, didn't seem interested in discussing it at length. His childhood dream of going to the Olympics and being a professional sailor seemed to be inching closer and occupying more of his mind. Brown's highly regarded sailing program seemed a clear step toward the winners' podium, as it had fed several stars to the Olympics through the years. Family problems receded to the background of Kevin's mind, his future more in the foreground—at least for now.

KEVIN

BEFORE HEADING OFF to Brown, Kevin had spent his junior year in France as a high school exchange student. He loved the French language, and some parts of his brain felt freer operating in it, as if through French

Gordon, Susanne, Kristina, and Kevin Hall (courtesy Hall family)

he had unlocked some sort of secret code. In French literature, he encountered the same kind of magic and fantasy that he had loved in the C. S. Lewis and other books he had read as a child, along with the puzzle and joy of translating from one world to another.

While in France, Kevin sailed in regattas around Europe and began to dream and think in French, a breakthrough for anyone studying a second language. He lived with a French family whom his parents had met through the boat business and the family treated him both like one of their own and like a special guest.

When Susanne stood waving Kevin off to France, a preview of the college separation soon to come, he seemed fine, all smiles. She, however, was choked up. With her husband and son gone, and Kristina hers to

Kevin and Gordon Hall (courtesy Hall family)

raise on her own, the outwardly perfect suburban life that she had known for twenty years had, in just a couple of months, completely disintegrated.

There would be even more debilitating news awaiting her just ahead.

KRISTINA

SEPARATING? WHAT WERE her parents talking about? The news seemed to be coming out of nowhere.

Of course they weren't going to use the word "divorce," because saying "divorce" would have been admitting failure, something she didn't think either of her parents was capable of doing. Nor did it surprise her that neither her mother nor her father raised their voices when explaining their plans, a hallmark of West Coast passive aggression. Her family of four was gone—Kevin to Brown, her father to Big Bear, California, a nearly three-hour drive away, and her mom to Montreal and Los Angeles, where she was going to return to school to dust off her medical credentials and hopefully go back to work and repay some of the debts from the boat business. Kristina would be left with some supervision in the family house in Ventura, with her mother dropping in occasionally to check up on her. Susanne didn't like the idea of leaving her child for long periods, but felt she had no choice. Kristina would be going off to college soon and was going to have to get used to being on her own.

It was bad enough, Kristina thought, that for years and years she had been dragged along to regattas and forced to suffer through seemingly endless hours of tedious and irrelevant conversation about boats and winning. But now her father wasn't even going to be around at all? Kevin had benefited from a picture-perfect two-parent household, but Kristina was graduating into a different reality.

KEVIN

Upon arriving at Brown University in the fall of 1987, Kevin quickly blended in with the school's thicket of overachievers. The school was made up of a collection of austere brick and modern buildings spread over nearly 150 lush acres in Providence, Rhode Island, connected by stretches of sprawling green spaces and a tangle of sidewalks. It maintained a musty Ivy League air, but its students and faculty also prided themselves on an attitude of crunch, with Frisbees flying through the air and political debates taking place right and left. It had an open curriculum, giving students more freedom to pursue their own academic interests; they were encouraged to create their own major if it didn't already exist. A culture of brainy wandering was encouraged from the top down.

It wasn't long before Kevin started calling his father with questions and concerns about cheating in sports. In college sailing, the boats were small and underpowered, meaning they had little sail compared to the boat and weight of the team. But they could be rolled in a certain way—a wiggling of the rudder and the hull back and forth—that was illegal but nudged the boat forward, sometimes resulting in a win. Anyone caught rolling a boat was penalized in the competition, but like a lot of cheating in sports, it was easy to get away with. Before college, Kevin had spent his entire life learning and obeying rules and felt good about doing so. Now he faced the question of whether he should play honestly and compromise his results, or push the gray to suit himself with the other athletes and accept that this was part of what competing at the Ivy League level entailed. He told his father that he felt torn over what to do. Where was the line about what was legitimate and what wasn't? Which side of it should Kevin be on?

For Kevin even to ask such a question before college would have been unthinkable, and a moot point besides, as he usually won by such a wide margin that cheating wouldn't have changed the outcome anyway. Gordon answered his son's queries by saying that this kind of dilemma was the stuff of which character was made. Kevin listened to that advice and told his Brown teammates that he would never lower himself to cheating. If others beat him dishonestly, so be it. At least he would be able to sleep at night.

Cheating or not, Brown's sailing team was on the ascent, with some of Kevin's competitors from the junior circuit now sailing with him every day as teammates. Coach Brad Dellenbaugh had built up the sailing program over several years into one of the nation's best and had carefully recruited a broad base of young athletes, including women. The women were not only on the team but truly incorporated into Brown's coed squads, with women and men sailing and competing together on a single boat. Brown's team also boasted many young women who went on to sail at the Olympics, a triumph in that Title IX, which had expanded opportunities for women in sports, had only been passed in 1972. With such a talent-thick roster, there were times when the team's own practice races were more competitive than the intercollegiate regattas.

Like many student athletes, the young sailors had a strict schedule that kept them busy with practices during the week, competitions on the weekend, and a full load of coursework beyond that. There was a team meeting every Wednesday evening, often at ten or eleven at night because that was the only time when all of the athletes could make it. They were often the last students in the dining hall, having returned from the water just as the staff was cleaning up.

A lot of things can't be controlled in sailing, a sport that is often about the seeming paradox of preparing for the unpredictable, but Kevin was determined to take charge of whatever he could. He was among the most disciplined sailors on the team, meticulously thinking through everything from his workout schedule to what meals he was going to eat to when and for how long he was going to sleep. To his teammates, he seemed extremely organized and focused, but not strict or serious. He laughed often and enjoyed discussing movies, books, and Bob Dylan song lyrics. To all outward appearances, Kevin seemed to be flourishing in his new collegiate life, embedded in engrossing classes, challenging sailing, and new friends, all far away from the noise of his parents' divorce.

Yet stress began to mount on Kevin in his upper-class years. He spent November and December of his junior year bingeing on caffeine late into the night, studying texts tied to his seemingly opposed majors—French literature and math. As he edged closer to graduation, he began to feel the pressure of the question that hangs over so many anxious undergraduates: What the hell comes after college? One part of Kevin's brain was immersed in French literature, concerned with themes of love, race, language, class, passion, and the creative life. The other part was consumed with his second love, math, with its geometric patterns, spatial relationships, and elegant formulae, a more analytical and practical field. Part of Kevin wanted to run away and become a poet, but then there was sailing and his dream of making it to the Olympics, which now seemed out of reach, not because of his abilities, but because of the financial logistics involved. To get the training he needed for that level of sailing, he would have to find a way to turn his sport into a paying full-time job.

In school, Kevin was a student who didn't raise his hand often, but when he did, he tried to have a pointed, intelligent comment ready. He turned his work in on time, attended class consistently and punctually, and asked his professors questions during their office hours. Math had come to him easily in high school, but in college, he felt intimidated by the whiz kids around him, including one who drew colored pencil renderings of complex algebraic equations. He felt an obligation to his father to slog through the difficult coursework, as his father wanted him to get a degree in something that he deemed more practical than French literature.

In that major, Kevin's studies centered on Marguerite Duras, an edgy novelist and filmmaker whose work dealt with sexuality, politics, love, and death. Brown offered a whole class devoted just to her works, for which Kevin eagerly signed up. As he inhaled its reading list, he found himself particularly interested in what she wrote about her inner life, a theme that was discussed often in the course. It was Duras who quipped, "Very early in my life, it was too late" and, "It's not that you have to achieve anything, it's that you have to get away from where you are." In math, Kevin enrolled in two upper-level courses: topology, the branch of mathematics concerned with continuous deformations, surfaces that bend but don't tear; and differential geometry, which uses calculus and algebra to study complex problems. His already fertile mind was ingesting new and more existential information than it ever had before, at a time when his brain, like those of most college students, still maintained some of the sponginess of adolescence.

Kevin's junior year also marked his first full season of training under U.S. Sailing Team coaches, the very people who helped prepare Americans for the Olympics. These coaches paid close attention to the top sailors in the collegiate pipeline, a critical feeder system for a country that continuously pushed up against sailing powerhouse Great Britain and other countries such as Norway, Spain, and France for medals. By plucking a few stars like Kevin for the training program, the coaches could gain a better understanding of how they performed on the water, while the young sailors learned the different nuances of the Olympic sailing classes and the rigor of preparation needed to compete at that level.

Kevin's selection as part of the U.S. Olympic training schema was exciting, but it pulled him away from Brown's sailing team and the routine to which he had grown accustomed. Undoubtedly, some of his Brown teammates who were not chosen by the Olympic coaches resented Kevin's opportunity, but if they had to be honest about it, they probably didn't miss the occasional bouts of arrogance he'd shown while on the team. He understood that he was talented on the water and had few qualms about discussing his shot at the Olympics, which he regarded more as a matter of when and how than if.

What friends Kevin had, for the most part, were from sailing. His high school and college years had been almost entirely devoted to the sport, allowing him little time for socializing outside of it. As he walked around Brown's campus that fall, he suddenly felt socially maladjusted, the idea of "hanging out" with no stated purpose never really having entered his head before college. Then he came down with a bad case of herpes zoster, more commonly known as shingles, and had to spend time in the infirmary with a fever and rash that kept him out of classes. Overwhelmed by the effort of keeping up with the most challenging pile of coursework he'd had yet, Kevin realized, for the first time in his life, that he probably would fail at something.

The parts of the body that trigger anxiety and excitement are similar on a physiological level, and in Kevin they were locked in an intense dance. He began to talk faster, enjoy music more, forgo sleep, and he started feeling euphoric in a way that he had imagined only hallucinogenic drugs could induce. He showed up to his French seminar one day with a boom box over his shoulder and insisted on playing two songs for the class, "Blood and Fire" by the Indigo Girls and another by a French artist. In scrambled sentences and wild gestures, Kevin tried to convey to the class that he felt the music was related to the works they were studying. No one else saw the connection, but because the songs took up only a few minutes of class time, the professor let him play them before politely regaining control of the room.

Kevin was dating a young woman named Meg, a student at the University of New Hampshire, about a two-hour drive north of Providence, and one day he suggested meeting up in Boston, a convenient halfway point. Meg thought that sounded like a good idea.

What she didn't realize was that Kevin was not traveling to Boston only to see her—he was also bent on carrying out a mission. The Director was sending him there, and once he arrived, would tell him what to do, where to go, and how to carry out a plan that would help create world peace and harmony. The Director was less of a voice, Kevin would say later, than a vapor of energy, a sense of will that came from another place surrounding Planet Earth. It was a presence, a way of thinking that was more important than Kevin's life on the water, more important than his finals, more important than his social world.

Manic and thrilled, Kevin boarded a bus bound for Boston. In his mind, things couldn't have been clearer. He was ready and an audience was eagerly tuning in. It was time to be in The Show.

PART II

THE HIGHS

Genius and lunacy are well-known next-door neighbors.
—Vincent Van Gogh's doctor

And Something's odd—within—
That person that I was—
And this One—do not feel the same—
Could it be Madness—this?
—Emily Dickinson, "Fascicle 15" (1862)

But Reality makes me gag
So I'm dreaming
—Kevin Hall

KEVIN

As he boarded the bus in Providence, Kevin felt electric. The microphones were hot, the cameras were rolling, his worldwide audience was tuning in. Kevin knew exactly where he was supposed to go. Forces he couldn't see, but strongly felt, were propelling him. He had an important mission: he had to save the world. More specifically, he had to teach the world to sing by the age of twenty-one, much like the song lyric from R.E.M. that had belted from Michael Stipe's mouth into Kevin's ear and kept floating around his mind.

Passengers on the Boston-bound bus that afternoon would have seen him as a fit, blond-haired college student clad in a T-shirt, jean jacket, and scarf—too scant a wardrobe for a New England winter day. Beyond that, nothing out of the ordinary. As the bus roared down the highway, Kevin surveyed his fellow passengers. He thought they looked like characters from the works of Marguerite Duras that he had studied in his French classes. This gave Kevin an exhilarating high, making him feel as though he was in the right place at the right time. He was able to see connections that most people couldn't—a gift from a source beyond.

Saving the world was going to take a team, an "army for good," made up of people from politics, media, music, Hollywood, art, business, the military, and, to some degree, sports. That's where Kevin came in. Everyone was watching him, the prodigious tillerman on the water, to see if he was going to be able to contribute his part. He had been groomed since childhood for The Show and now the plan was rolling. Kevin couldn't have been more excited. Finally, the chaos of his life was making sense.

The Director, Kevin knew, was sending him to Boston to fulfill his duties as a social coordinator. He had to help stage a "love-in" kind of thing, a big, fundraising-style concert like Live Aid, which had raised money for the famine in Ethiopia. Similarly, his show could utilize satellites, cable television, and other new technology to make the world feel smaller by linking people together so that every single television set in the world could tune in, thus creating political awareness and helping raise money for the needy. The Berlin Wall had fallen just a month before, signaling the end of the Cold War and making the idea of throwing a world-scale party seem positive and plausible.

If Kevin could apply the determination he showed on the water to this project, no arena would be too large for him to handle. Kevin was the hero of The Show, the one making it all happen, and any and all displays of valiance and risk taking would be welcome. On television, people did all sorts of crazy things and lived. So could he.

About an hour later, in the early evening, the bus arrived in Boston's South Station, a large, loud, dirty, gray terminal in the city's downtown. Kevin stepped outside and quickly became fascinated by the numbers on the tops and sides of the taxicabs lined up out front and zooming by. It was now clear to him that his math skills were central to the role he was to play on The Show. Meg was not there, nor did Kevin make any attempt to call her in New Hampshire.

He walked straight out into traffic, unconcerned with the cacophony of honks and yells as cab drivers darted about to avoid hitting him. His mind was focused on the sequences, patterns, and puzzles in the digits glowing on the taxicabs. They were trying to tell him something, but he couldn't quite make out what it was. The Director must be testing him, seeing if he was the right choice to be the star.

Kevin mulled all this over as he walked away from the gray bus depot and through Boston's winding colonial streets, eventually entering a cozy sports bar that he was convinced was the same as the setting of the hit television show *Cheers*. (It was not.) He sat down and ordered a Samuel Adams—the local favorite on tap—and a burger, French fries, and onion rings. The bartender asked if he was sure he wanted both French fries and onion rings, unaware that Kevin needed the X (fries) and O (rings) shapes for the patterns he was planning to make on the tabletop. All this, too, was a sign. It would all make sense once the concert had manifested.

When his meal of fried goods arrived, Kevin noticed that even the food on The Show tasted better than ordinary cuisine. He had eaten plenty of French fries and onion rings before, but these were more delicious than any he had ever consumed. His taste buds were bursting.

Next, Kevin noticed that the bar had phone booths, and at a signal from the Director, he walked into one so he could call Michael Jackson's and Madonna's agents. He left his wallet behind on the table, just in case the bartender needed it to settle his check while he was on the phone. No representatives for either Michael Jackson or Madonna were available, so Kevin returned to his seat and his spread of food. His wallet was still there, but it would have been fine with him if it hadn't been, as Kevin figured that money didn't matter on The Show anyway. All costs would be taken care of by the Director.

A bartender noticed Kevin's peculiar behavior and asked if he was okay. Kevin said he was fine.

He paid his check and headed out into the night.

In the wintry weather, still with only his jean jacket against the chill, Kevin walked around Boston's winding downtown canyons, a blend of colonial buildings and the boxy constructions of the decade, feeling exhilarated about the upcoming concert and his role in it. Whenever he heard music coming from a car radio or a nearby bar or restaurant, he felt as though the playlist was being perfectly coordinated from above. He heard songs from bands like Journey and Boston, the latter an obvious reference to his new surroundings, and riffed along with some of them, sure of his purpose in life.

Kevin turned a corner and found himself standing in front of the Pine Street Inn, a homeless shelter housed in a brick building on Harrison Ave. Three years earlier, a homeless man had frozen to death on the street just two blocks from the shelter, prompting its staff to do more street outreach programs at night, offering food, blankets, and warm clothing. One of these efforts was under way as Kevin strolled up, observing a collection of people bundled in unwashed clothing lingering out front, waiting.

Kevin examined this all-too-common tragic urban scene and thought, *of course*. Those people were *real*, and precisely the kind of people his benefit concert was going to help. Yet at the same time, Kevin also wondered if the homeless people before him were actors playing parts. Whoever they were, those running The Show wanted him to be there precisely at that moment in the night "for the world to see how close to *that* reality each life can be for a person," as Kevin later put it. He felt as though he was Dan Aykroyd's character in the 1983 movie *Trading Places*, a modern-day take on the Mark Twain tale *The Prince and the Pauper* in which a wealthy commodities broker (Aykroyd) and a homeless man (played by Eddie Murphy) switch roles when they're unknowingly made the subjects of a wager. In Kevin's version, he, the affluent child of two doctors who had sailed at an Ivy League school, had swapped places with an alternate version of himself. Kevin reasoned that spending time at the homeless shelter would be a fantastic opportunity for him to develop a greater sense of compassion for others and a deeper understanding of what his mission was with the concert. The cameras were still rolling and everyone was still watching to see what Kevin would do next.

He entered through a front door, observed the lines of huddled souls waiting for food inside, and sat down at one of the tables. He splayed the contents of his wallet before him: his credit cards, fake ID, yacht club card, U.S. Sailing Team card, Brown student ID, and pilot's license, which he had earned as a teenager under his father's tutelage. As he fanned them out on the table, he tried to mimic the coolness of a dealer in Las Vegas at a poker table, the small tokens a royal flush of his identity. Kevin also felt, inexplicably, that this display of cards demonstrated to the world how all lives were interconnected.

Curious about the appearance of an enthusiastic, clean-cut college kid at the homeless shelter, a social worker sat down and began asking Kevin some questions, whereupon he became agitated. Everything had felt right to him until this moment, but the social worker was making him feel as though someone was trying to unplug him, as if he was in the wrong part of the scene at the wrong time. This was supposed to be about unity, after all, so why couldn't the social worker see that Kevin, he, and everyone around them were all one?

Mid-conversation, Kevin bolted out the door, once again leaving his wallet on the table. Later, he couldn't quite remember his excuse for leaving, but thought that it had something to do with Madonna's or Michael Jackson's agent waiting for him outside.

The night had become more frigid, yet Kevin continued wandering, still clad in his thin jean jacket. He felt no need for sleep. He had a concert to plan. Seeing a sturdy-looking drainpipe, he climbed it, jumped down, and then climbed another. He found puzzles and patterns in every path he took. Downtown Boston was his adult-sized jungle gym, ripe for his discovery and play. He thought about all the people watching him, the cameras broadcasting his every action to the world, and wondered if his audience was as pleased with being alive as he was. He hoped so. Passing electronics stores, he saw television sets and wondered if he could pull out their cables, change their channels, and move his feed somehow. But he couldn't, so he continued to roam. The anxiety of the Olympics, his math classes at Brown, and his inchoate plans for life after college felt blissfully far away.

As the sun began to rise, Kevin passed by people who resembled celebrities and more characters from Duras novels. He quietly followed one or two of them in hopes of getting another clue about what his next step should be in executing his mission.

Antiques stores suddenly caught Kevin's interest, as did the idea of trying to retrace Paul Revere's famous night ride. When businesses opened their doors and flipped their CLOSED signs to OPEN, Kevin poked his head inside and asked friendly clerks questions about the historical periods of their wares. A Flemish telescope caught his eye. If he bought it, he thought, replicas could be made, and the store would become a landmark. He was, after all, helping to plan one of the greatest humanitarian events of all time, so it only made sense that people would bid for the rights to manufacture replicas of whatever items he bought. This boom would also carry over to the books Kevin was reading and the music he was listening to in The Show. It pleased him to know that he was not only sharing arts with the masses, but creating a mini-economy: the perfect private-public partnership.

Soon Kevin found himself in Beacon Hill, a historic neighborhood lined with narrow cobblestone sidewalks, brick buildings, and replicas of old-fashioned gas lamps. "A hill that's also a beacon? *Perfect!*" Kevin thought. The Director was clearly at work.

Kevin made his way into a park. A squirrel bounded by and stopped right in front of him, another sign that he was on the right path to getting the concert off the ground. Everything was locking in perfectly.

He saw a tree just right for climbing, easily scaled it with his fit limbs, and from its branches yelled muddled quotes from Shakespeare to those who walked by, words that might have been mistaken by some as heckling. One passerby was a pleasant-looking young woman, who looked as if she was off to college classes or maybe work.

Thinking back to when he had read *Hamlet* in high school, Kevin reasoned that she must be Ophelia, the daughter of Polonius and love interest of Prince Hamlet. "Ophelia was instructed by her father to be wary of a false love from Hamlet," Kevin had written in his high school paper about the play, "and when she realizes that their love is true, it is too late. Hamlet, his head full of thoughts of revenge opposed to ideas of justice, becomes irresponsible and is deemed crazy by his peers."

Now in Boston a few years later, here was Ophelia, Kevin thought, and true to her part, she was wary of false love. She must be a plotline within The Show. They were to act out a scene together—Shakespeare was all about the play within a play—and then, afterward, Kevin could get back to concert planning. Carefully perched in the tree, he waited for her to walk by, and as she approached, he saw the perfect moment to jump. With a thud, he landed right in front of her.

Ophelia! Kevin said. *I'm so glad it's you! You're here!*

She responded with a look. Not the kind of look that Kevin had in mind. Maybe she wasn't the right woman to play Ophelia in the scene after all.

He ascended the tree again, this time throwing off his watch, feeling fresh and clean in the chilly Boston morning. He loved how deliciously vivid everything felt now that he was in The Show: the music more harmonious, the food more savory, the breeze more refreshing, even the bark under his fingertips more crisp and satisfying. In so many ways, it felt as though things couldn't possibly get any better.

Then the cops showed up. But he couldn't be in trouble, Kevin reasoned. They must just be actors playing cops, sent in, as Kevin had been, to take part in The Show. Maybe they could all go find Ophelia *together*.

KRISTINA

HER MOM HAD to be joking.

Kevin, missing?

Kristina couldn't keep track of her brother's whereabouts even in the most ordinary of circumstances. He was usually off at some sailing regatta, *winning* some sailing regatta.

Of course, Kevin would take *this* weekend to once again be the focus of their parents' attention. This was supposed to have been *her* time, a break from her first semester at the University of California, Santa Cruz. For weeks, the plan had been for Kristina to have a nice birthday celebration with her mother, who had flown in for the occasion. Now, in mere seconds, even though he was on the other side of the country (or at least had last been seen there), he had hijacked the narrative.

Kristina couldn't say that she was surprised by her mother's reaction to the news about Kevin, as it seemed totally out of his normal behavior pattern. Her parents had always seemed consumed with his sailing career and either unaware of or indifferent to the fact that while she was living on her own in Ventura, she was engaging in more than her share of partying. It hadn't gone over very well that she had racked up $20,000 or so in credit card debt *before* college, filling up not only her own gas tank but those of her friends, too. If anyone in the family was likely to go missing, it was she.

Kristina always wore a bright smile along with her brown shoulder-length hair, but she often wondered if she was a hippie who had long been separated from her tribe, a free spirit wrongly born into and trapped in the cookie-cutter suburbs of Southern California. She felt more attuned to the counterculture of Northern California than to the bleached hair and tanned skin ideals of her home due south.

In college, she explored the live music scene, including a concert at the UCSC cafeteria where some guy who identified himself as "Eyeball" handed her LSD, which she had already experimented with some in high school. Of even more significance, she had attended her first Grateful Dead show, and as she watched the band play its rock-folk-psychedelic-blues, she felt its music seep into her being in all of the right, deepest ways. The Dead community embraced her regardless of where she had been or where she was thinking of going, a stand-in for the family she felt she had lacked in high school and was still missing in college. While everyone had been off at sailing regattas when she was a child and teen-ager, she had been back home with a babysitter or on her own. With the Dead crew, everyone was together all the time, in a space that felt bliss-fully without expectations of achievement or judgment.

Nevertheless, Kristina felt scared. Kevin was usually in motion, but it seemed wildly out of character for him to go completely missing, and she wondered what possible reason he could have had. The details were fuzzy, but her mother said something about his being in Boston, not Providence, and the possibility that she might have to fly there to see what was going on. Unsure what to do, Kristina decided to go to a party that night, leaving her mother behind to try to sort things out. Nor was it likely a good time to mention that she had acquired a new, thirty-something boyfriend whom she had met at a wilderness program.

A few hours and a few bites of pot brownie later, Kristina came back to her dorm room. Her mother told her that they had found Kevin, but that he had done something that involved the cops and was in some sort of hospital. He was alive, but something was off. Her mother needed to leave for Boston as soon as possible.

Kristina and Kevin Hall (courtesy Hall family)

Kristina shrugged. She was glad her brother was safe, but resentful that her birthday weekend with her mother was a bust.

Some twenty-seven hundred miles separated her from Kevin, but in some peculiar way, nothing, really, had changed.

SUSANNE

BY THE TIME Susanne's plane arrived in New England, Kevin was in the Human Resource Institute in Brookline, Massachusetts, heavily sedated, his face streaked with a well-worn drool path. Susanne's brain volleyed back and forth between being a doctor and being Kevin's mom as she tried to figure out what had gone wrong, and why, and what to do about it.

She learned that after being picked up in the park by the cops, Kevin had been taken to an emergency room and then transferred to the institute, one of the Boston area's leading facilities for the compassionate treatment of mental illnesses. From the outside, its brick and beige building could easily have been mistaken for a school. Four stories tall, and half a block wide, it had symmetrical rectangular windows lined up in neat rows and an inviting staircase with a metal rail, as orderly as the description of what her son had been through wasn't.

Years later, Susanne wouldn't be able to recall who called her about Kevin or what the specifics of the conversation were. Maybe the shock blocked it all out. But she did remember flying from California to Boston, in a jarring transition from spending what she had hoped would be a relaxing time with one child to a frantic time with another. Whatever was wrong with Kevin felt completely beyond her scope as a parent, with even the best-case scenario seeming horrible. What had Kevin gotten himself into, and what, if anything, could she have done, or do, differently to avert what was already a disaster?

As Kevin lay in his hospital bed, Susanne tried to ask him questions, but his responses made no sense, just a slurred jumble of words and phrases as his mind roamed in the fog of delusion, the effects of medication mixed with reality's thaw. Susanne knew that although tests and EEGs were being run, there was no promise that they would provide the black-and-white certainty of a diagnosis she so desperately craved.

It now felt miraculous that Kevin had managed to tell the doctors how to contact his family in California. Apparently, too, he had asked them to let him lie on the floor, a wish that they hadn't granted. Now, he was going on and on about rivers being like wheels, with no beginning and no end.

Amazingly, the police had brought no criminal charges against him, a privilege not often afforded to those exhibiting such erratic behavior. The irony was not lost on Kevin, whose delusion had itself focused on socio-economic concerns, but the reality of his being treated preferentially because he was white, young, male, and cleanly dressed would continue to baffle him, long after the drugs set in. Although the minds of those experiencing psychosis shared similarities, the societal framework of discrimination surrounding those brains, either based on skin color, gender, class, or some combination of all of those factors, yielded far different outcomes.

Susanne wondered if someone had slipped a drug of some kind into one of Kevin's drinks, assuming that like any college student, Kevin indulged in partying from time to time. When his tests for drugs came back negative, she discarded that theory and wondered if his derangement could have been caused by the aftershocks of the case of shingles he'd had just a few weeks ago. Or Lyme disease? Encephalitis? For years, she had seen patients come in and out of her care, many of them children or young people, and she knew that it didn't take much to throw the delicate balance of the human mind and body into chaos. It was one of the great marvels of life that it all worked as often and as well as it did.

Gordon arrived, and he and Susanne met with Kevin's doctors, who told them that their son was suffering from manic depression—also known as bipolar disorder, the preferred term for the condition today. They told him that it wasn't likely to go away anytime soon, if at all.

Unlike those with unipolar depression, people with bipolar disorder experience periods of mania alternating with, or mixed with, periods of depression. When they're down, people with the disorder are lethargic, slow to react, and apathetic, and they may have difficulty concentrating. When they're up, they may experience a state of frenzy marked by erratic, exuberant, grandiose, sometimes paranoid behavior. Psychologists' understanding of it was still relatively nascent in the late 1980s, and at the time, the term "bipolar disorder" was only beginning to gain traction as a more scientific alternative to "manic depression," which psychiatrists had used in decades prior.

Nor was Kevin alone. Estimates vary, but anywhere from 3 million to 6 million American adults, or between 1 percent and 2.6 percent of the American adult population, live with bipolar disorder. Its diagnosis often comes in the college years, as was the case for Kevin, and the average age of onset is eighteen. Unlike unipolar depression, which may make its symptoms known much earlier, it often hits young people whom society regards as adults, even though their brains and personalities will continue to develop dramatically until their midtwenties. Women and men are equally likely to develop it, and researchers have found that those of color are significantly more likely to be misdiagnosed, or not to receive proper treatment and services.

Kay Redfield Jamison, a physician who herself has been diagnosed with bipolar disorder and is one of the foremost authorities on the subject, writes in *Touched with Fire* that those with the disorder "usually have an inflated self-esteem, as well as a certainty of conviction about the correctness and importance of their ideas. This grandiosity can contribute to poor judgment, which, in turn, often results in chaotic patterns of personal and professional relationships." It's common for those who are manic, she says, to engage in impulse spending, reckless driving, impulsive sexual encounters, volatile outbursts, and other questionable behaviors. People with bipolar disorder may also be more prone to misuse drugs and alcohol and to become addicted to those substances.

In spite of the stigma that still hangs over discussing mental health diagnoses, many highly successful people through time have lived with bipolar disorder and can lead robust professional and personal lives: the actress Carrie Fisher, author Sherman Alexie, comedian Russell Brand, singer Demi Lovato, singer Rosemary Clooney, comedian Stephen Fry, novelist Graham Greene, politician Patrick Kennedy, artist Edvard Munch, journalist Jane Pauley, musician Lou Reed, businessman Ted Turner, and artist Vincent Van Gogh, among a long list of others.

Although it would be easy to romanticize the relationship between bipolar disorder and professional, particularly creative, success, the reality is that many have triumphed by overcoming their affliction, not because of it. They have fought to make that success happen every single day, the very act of creating being an act of resistance, with or without medication. For some, though, bipolar disorder played a role in the tragic ending of their lives: the authors Virginia Woolf and Ernest Hemingway, Nirvana lead singer Kurt Cobain, the activist Abbie Hoffman, to name a few. So, too, have some made the extremes of the disorder part of their work: the raw lyrics of Cobain, the violent swirls on Van Gogh's canvases, the cerebral prose of Woolf's novels and essays. Books, paintings, and songs are brains on paper, canvas, and in verse, and these individuals' work continues to be a gift to those who suffer and seek community, as well as to those hoping to gain insight into their minds, peering in from a window outside. Bipolar disorder's consequences, if untreated, can be catastrophic. Numbers vary, but the lifetime rate of attempted suicide for those with no history of a mental disorder is less than 1 percent; for those with a major depressive illness, it's 18 percent; and for those suffering from manic depression, it's 24 percent or greater.

Susanne and Gordon had both seen various psychiatric disorders in their careers, and they knew that their son's condition couldn't be treated with a few days of bed rest and antibiotics. Nor would it ever go away completely—it would follow him for the rest of his life. As they sat in the hospital trying to understand what was happening to Kevin, they were baffled. The predisposition for bipolar disorder is believed to be genetic, but there was no known history of it on either side of Kevin's family.

Kevin's parents also knew that the history of psychiatric care and incarceration are interwoven. For generations, those with mental illnesses have been ostracized and in some cases outright abused, locked in institutions far from the public eye. It would be impossible to count the number of jobs, intimate relationships, friendships, or other ties that have been severed after a disclosure of bipolar disorder, or any other mental illness, but the repercussions for talking about it were real. One 2006 survey found that a quarter of people thought depression was "a sign of personal weakness" and would not employ someone with it. Thirty percent said they would not vote for a politician if they knew he or she had depression, and 25 percent said that they considered people with schizophrenia to be dangerous. Yet a quarter of the first thirty-seven U.S. presidents had been afflicted by mental illness during their time in office. Though there is no shortage in pop culture of depictions of the mentally ill wielding axes, research consistently shows that those who have been diagnosed with a psychiatric disorder are far more likely to be victims of violent crime than perpetrators of it. Nor is it uncommon for psychologists to confuse manic depression with schizophrenia, a vastly different diagnosis and treatment protocol.

Kevin's parents and doctors focused on medication, an approach in tune with the ideas of the period. At the time, it was widely thought that a pill could fix many mental woes, and Gordon especially latched onto that appealing possibility. A few months after Kevin's Boston episode, Prozac appeared on the cover of *Newsweek* magazine as the "breakthrough drug for depression." In a country of fast cars and fast food, fast cures for mental illness seemed just around the corner, the swallowing of a pill as simple as using the once newfangled oven known as a microwave. Maybe the time consuming practice of psychotherapy was not necessary, or less so, in a world of such magic pills.

Attitudes may have changed, but mood cycles have been documented for thousands of years, the English word "melancholia" deriving from the Greek words for "black" and "bile"; the ancient Greeks believed that mania was brought about by a rise of foul substance. Persian thinkers identified bipolar disorder as a separate disorder from mania and schizophrenia around A.D. 1000, and Chinese authors described bipolar disorder in the 1500s. In 1903, Carl Jung established modern diagnostic criteria for the disorder, laying a foundation that is still in use today. The term "manic depression" entered the *Diagnostic and Statistical Manual*, psychology's bible, in 1952.

"The illness," Jamison wrote of bipolar disorder, "encompasses the extremes of the human experience."

KEVIN

THEY SAID THE words to him, *bipolar disorder.* But at first, they were just that—words.

There was some comfort in the clarity of a diagnosis, as now Kevin knew what he was suffering from and that it had a name. With that, too, came the overwhelming task of trying to understand the ailment and everything destined to come with it. For Kevin, it felt as though he had suddenly been thrust into a frightening mystery that was taking place in his head. He had to give himself a crash course in bipolar disorder, the same way he had to cram for a mathematics exam. Unlike math, though, this problem didn't make any sense to him. He could also make the case that he had what felt like a spiritual emergency, or even a mystical awakening, and instead of trying to understand it, everyone was slapping some label on it. Whether intentional or not, everyone's message to him seemed to be "You're broken. Let's fix it."

Kevin's parents had thought that by nurturing their son through childhood and adolescence, by ensuring that he was healthy and happy, they had more than cleared the way for him to become a successful young man. They simply didn't understand how this could be happening to their son. Doctors gave Kevin heavy doses of lithium to bring him down from the high of The Show. A common treatment for bipolar disorder at the time, lithium had been reintroduced into popular use after World War II when an Australian psychiatrist began using it on patients and reporting some successful results, but also some patient deaths. It received FDA approval in the United States in the 1970s, and while many patients complained of side effects, including numbness, it saved lives; by some measures, it reduced the suicide attempt rate of those with bipolar disorder sevenfold.

As Kevin's mania subsided into a new, heavier sadness and the tedium of everyday life, he assessed his situation and the people around him at the hospital in Brookline from a still-askew but dead-on-target point of view. "They gave me chemical suppressants," Kevin wrote in his journal. "They gave me physical depressants like cigarette smoke and contradictions." Kevin's doctor was Russian, and Kevin wondered how the man could ever understand him unless the two of them first discussed George Orwell's 1945 dystopian allegory *Animal Farm*. Kevin still couldn't sleep. He jotted down a muddle of words and numbers. He visited the hospital's music room.

Creative thinkers who suffer from bipolar disorder, unipolar depression, and other mental ailments are often granted some leeway by certain parts of society, the volatility of their moods almost expected as a tax to be paid for the flow of their ideas, but athletes are offered far less flexibility. Much less is known about the way in which bipolar disorder impacts athletes than is known about the way it impacts artists, who may suffer from it at a significantly higher rate than the general population. Not until

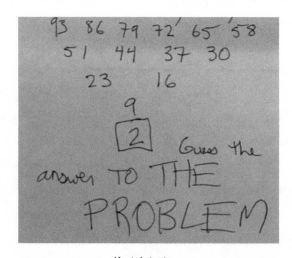

Kevin's jottings

years after Kevin was diagnosed would research find that in some cases, elite athletes are more prone to depression and anxiety than those in the general population. Being an athlete requires high levels of confidence and self-esteem, a belief that the seemingly impossible is in fact possible. It's a narrative of the self that can push the bounds of human potential but also set dangerously high expectations.

"We are what we pretend to be," Kurt Vonnegut wrote, "so we must be careful about what we pretend to be." Kevin had not only pretended to be an elite athlete before his diagnosis, he had actually been one. Now that self-confidence was shaken, and he wondered if he would ever get it back. Athletes also learn not only to be fast and accurate, but to remain calm while doing so, and they have been shown to be able to predict the movements of their opponents by picking up on subliminal cues that others fail to notice. For years those skills had come naturally to Kevin, but now he wondered if he still had them. Or even if they had mattered in the first place.

As Kevin's mania faded, the real-life consequences of his life on The Show became apparent. Doctors allowed him use of the phone and he called one of his French literature professors back in Providence. He explained, in French, that he had had a manic episode, that it had involved Duras, and that he might miss some classes because he was institutionalized.

His French professor was surprised, as the story Kevin told her felt discordant with the bright, precocious sailor she had come to know in her class. This was certainly the first time that a student had called her from a psychiatric ward, and if she'd had to pick which of her students would have been most likely to do so, Kevin wouldn't have made the list. And the coursework from her class had been part of his delusion? Had he been on drugs? For whatever it was worth, his French sounded great.

Kevin's girlfriend, Meg, having been called by Kevin's parents, arrived at the hospital to find him throwing his clothes around the room. Kevin told her that he was "pretending he was flexible" and proceeded to lie on the floor and giggle at his defiance of hospital conventions. She sat down beside him and held him as a kaleidoscope of thoughts about the king of England rushed through his head. Kevin wondered if they were clues.

Kevin leaned in toward Meg, indicating that he had something he wanted to say. She leant her ear.

It was all going to be okay, he assured her. He didn't have to go to the Olympics and win a gold medal anymore. He had a much more important thing to do with his life.

Now he was the star of The Show.

GORDON

FROM THE MOMENT his phone rang in the middle of the night with the news that Kevin had experienced a psychotic break, Gordon felt as if he was living in a nightmare. The last few days had been a blur of getting on the plane, arriving in Boston, shuttling to a hospital, and sitting uncomfortably with his ex-wife as they tried to figure out what had happened and what on earth they were going to do about it.

Gordon could tell that Kevin being in the middle between his parents was making him tense. It was fraying Gordon's nerves, too. Even though he and Susanne tried to be amicable after the divorce and maintain a sense of civility, there was no masking the awkwardness between them. Neither of them wanted to spend a lot of time with the other; it had been a long time since they had done so.

Tense or not, however, they all needed to agree on what had to be done to get him back to school, to the water, and to his life.

Since the divorce, Gordon had been living in Big Bear, a small, picturesque town in California's San Bernardino Valley, a couple of hours' drive from Los Angeles, with his new partner, Meimei. Like Gordon and Susanne, she was a doctor. Gordon reasoned that their home, in the resort destination and near a lake and skiing, could be a restful retreat for Kevin. He could stay with them over the upcoming Christmas holidays while he recuperated, Gordon said, and he would adjust his work schedule to tend to him.

Gordon had hoped that the interlude would give him the opportunity to help his son, but now, as Kevin sulked around the house, clearly depressed about what had happened, feeling lonely and ostracized, it was hard not to feel like nothing more than a helpless observer. Even the most minor of Gordon's suggestions—that Kevin join him and Meimei for a meal, go with him to the grocery store, accompany him for a drive— seemed to fall on deaf ears. The few times that Kevin did try to express himself, his words didn't make any sense.

Gordon had arrived in Boston after Kevin's mania had passed, finding just a sedated version of his son, so he didn't fully understand what Kevin meant when he complained about his medication bringing him down. Wasn't it making him feel better? Gordon wondered. Wasn't it effective? This slug-like version of Kevin dragging himself around the house was like some strange inverse of the active sailor son he had always known. Gordon wondered how much of Kevin's lethargy was due to depression and how much to the medication, a line that seemed impossible to draw.

At some point, mental health experts had given the Hall family a spreadsheet entitled "Relapse Prevention." It laid out tips for preventing another episode, including taking pills at the same time every day, doing daily exercises, planning small tasks, and eating meals consistently. Someone in the family had read that each episode could mar Kevin's brain (a notion that was later dispelled) and they began to worry that if he had another, or multiple episodes, that important parts of what made Kevin *Kevin* could erode. Kevin, too, shared concerns about the lifelong implications.

There was the white spiral-bound guidebook entitled "Becoming Your Own Therapist," in which Kevin drew large swirls across its sterile pages, his spirals akin to those on the poster of Alfred Hitchcock's film *Vertigo*. On one of the worksheets headed THOUGHTS, he jotted down "Being Jesus" and then added, "They'll never believe me." That guy said he was the center of the world two thousand years ago, Kevin thought, and he is still praised widely today. Yet when Kevin had his own revelations, why was he institutionalized? On the Fear Form, he said that he was most worried about missing schoolwork and about one of his team-mates thinking he was too big for their boat, a reference to the anxiety that sailors have about making weight. Similar to wrestlers and weight-lifters, sailors may need to fall within certain weight categories, both as individuals and as a team. A fluctuation of a few pounds could not only impact a single person's weigh-in, but also carry implications for the entire crew and other members' weights, as those pounds were divvied up between a total number for the boat. Yet dieting was not enough, as the sport required a grueling amount of muscle strength honed in the weight room to best power the boat.

As Gordon watched Kevin struggle, he came to the conclusion that his son's manic break had been caused by the combined pressure of school and sports. Gordon was upbeat about Kevin's being able to recover and get his life back together soon. As Kevin packed his bags to head back to Providence, Gordon thought that the worst was over.

He was wrong.

KRISTINA

THERE WERE GOOD places to do mushrooms and then there were great places to do mushrooms. The Magic Kingdom of Disneyland in Anaheim, California, was the latter, or so Kristina and her friends had been told. They intended to find out for themselves.

As they entered the amusement park, swirling forms and colors rolled all around them—a spectacle of furry, familiar childhood characters, the pleasing sight of Cinderella's castle, cakelike storefronts along Main Street USA, and the optimistic air and shine of Tomorrowland. But as the crew of friends made their way toward Frontierland, Kristina could feel her hallucinogenic trip teetering south.

She passed out. She remembered a white light and the feeling of falling backward through a tunnel. Was this death?

When she came to a few seconds later, she found herself at the foot of Splash Mountain, her friends furiously fanning her and trying to find help. A fireman who happened to be vacationing nearby came to her aid, as did a nurse. Kristina and her friends lied and said that it was the heat that had made her faint, nor did anyone push them for a backstory. No one mentioned the mushrooms.

She was escorted to an island of grass in the parking lot outside, beneath a sign that read THE HAPPIEST PLACE ON EARTH. And there she and her friends spent eight hours, mushroom time, that is, so that she could recover.

As she lay facing the park's gates, Kristina thought about all that had happened during the last few weeks—her mother's aborted birthday visit, her brother's hospitalization—and wondered when her parents would start treating her like an adult. It felt as if they were always protecting her, always withholding information, even though she was already in college.

Then, with a flash of clarity, Kristina realized that she couldn't die, she couldn't be out of it, she couldn't be incapable, she had to act like a grownup. Her family needed her.

KEVIN

AS HE WALKED the pathways of Brown's campus, now lined with the skeletal trees and slush of winter, Kevin still felt unsettled. Without sailing, what, if anything, was he? How was he going to spend the seemingly vast sprawl of years that would unfold after he tossed his mortarboard into the air? His fellow math major students still intimidated him to no end, and how could he tell his parents that he had a promising future with a degree in . . . French literature?

As he grudgingly and reluctantly processed his diagnosis, he still wasn't sure where the other Kevin, the one from The Show, had come from or whether or not he was coming back. A handful of his close friends knew about his hospitalization, but they rarely mentioned it and Kevin wasn't too eager to discuss it, either. Kevin was back, and that's all that seemed to matter.

His other teammates didn't know the specifics of his bipolar diagnosis, or even that it was psychiatric in nature, but they did know that something was off and they were curious, more in an academic sense than in a gossipy one. Kevin had carved out a reputation as the teammate who was the first one to arrive, the last one to leave, and as a focused, driven student. He had been protective of, and behaved like an older brother to,

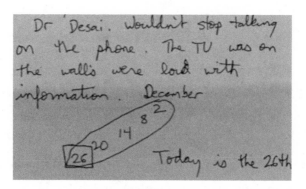

Kevin's journal

his younger teammates, and they felt a deep sense of wanting to return the favor. They had eagerly helped him out however they could while he was away—favors like moving his parked car and helping him get information about homework assignments so that he would feel welcome and calm upon his return.

He appreciated these gestures and made a point of telling his friends so, trying to create an outward sense of having returned to his pre-Boston routine. Privately, Kevin was trying to reconcile his new, manic identity with the version of him that was back on campus. In a mix of French and English, he wrote in his journal:

> . . . l'évidence that I am crazy, that I need help, that I must be
> ripped away from my friends at Pine St. Inn Shelter. Taken
> where? To the station. I think it was the police station. I know it
> was room 102. No, it was room 101 and me and my worst fears.
> 1989. The song remained the same in my head since Orwell wrote
> his warnings on the WALL and on the black and blue board of
> my mind . . . Perhaps I have waited all my life for this day.
> Perhaps I have waited all of many lives.

AMANDA

DURING HER FRESHMAN year at Brown University, Amanda Rosenberg stared at the back of Kevin's neck in physics class. She knew in that instant, based on his neck alone, that she wanted to date him.

Watching the way he carried himself in the lab, Amanda suspected that he was an upperclassman, and perhaps an athlete. He looked fit, blue-eyed, freckled, West Coast, all-American—a contrast to the Upper East Side New York Jewish culture she had grown up in. Tall, with long blonde hair, Amanda had thrived in her environment but was eager to break with it. She was more of a daddy's girl than her mother's daughter; unlike her mother, an actress before she married a doctor, Amanda was deeply interested in physics. Quantum mechanics, in particular, drew her interest, the idea that even the smallest things—atoms, subatomic parti-cles, things we can't see with our naked eyes—could help explain how the universe worked. The details of photons, relativity, and electromag-netic fields intoxicated her, as did the work of the quantum physicist Richard Feynman, whom Amanda viewed as a rock star. Feynman posited that "nature as She is—absurd" and Amanda studied how quantum mechanics rested on something of a seesaw. The closer someone got to nailing down one measurement, he said, the less precise another measure-ment tied to the same particle must become.

Some version of that uncertainty principle may have been in play in her physics class, Amanda thought as she watched the man with the strong neck.

Despite gender norms dictating that men typically make the first move, Amanda decided that she would be bold. She stood up from the stool and walked over, a woman on a mission to ask a guy to be her lab partner.

KEVIN

HAVING RECENTLY BEEN dumped by Meg in the aftermath of the Boston episode, Kevin saw no need for having a partner, romantic or otherwise. When the rest of the class had quickly paired off to work together, leaving him on his own, it had seemed to him a fitting symbol of his loneliness and heartbreak, reinforcing his suspicion that he was not meant for collaboration. It all felt so pointless. Why bother to find a partner in the first place? Kevin could work solo.

By this time, Kevin had somehow set aside some of the heavy disappointment he had felt every day in Big Bear: that he hadn't been saving the world at all, that he'd done nothing but create confusion and stress and medical bills for his family. Nonetheless, part of him still wondered if the Director was going to come back for another episode, even if Kevin was taking one Haldol (an antipsychotic) and lithium dose after another. Part of him now wondered how he could ever bring it up without getting locked up again. By comparison, everyday life, even on a good day, felt humdrum and void of meaning.

Kevin continued not to tell most of his friends or acquaintances much about what had happened in Boston or the reason for his hiatus in Big Bear. If they did inquire, "I was out sick," or something to that effect, usually satisfied what little curiosity they had. When Kevin had gone out for ice cream with one cute girl from his math class, he had felt comfortable enough to tell her that he'd needed a break following a big mental breakdown. She replied that the experience sounded like the acid trip she'd recently taken. Kevin couldn't argue with her about that.

Deflated on the inside, Kevin was surprised when a tall, blonde, and assertive classmate approached his table during physics class. With a pretty face and confident demeanor, she introduced herself as Amanda and seemed as functional and calm as Kevin wasn't, his insecurity magnified by her presence.

She asked if he had a partner.

No.

Did he want to pair off with her?

Kevin mumbled something about working alone.

She didn't push him and she set about doing the assignment on her own.

He couldn't blame her. He had manic tendencies, which in his eyes didn't exactly make him the most dateable man on campus.

Amanda was undeterred. She returned to physics class the next day with a new weapon: denim short-shorts. Her low-cut shirt and red lipstick probably didn't hurt, either. She walked over to his table and asked him once again if he wanted to be her lab partner.

This time, he was more receptive.

Later, Kevin would describe this second coming of Amanda in the physics lab in ecstatic terms. "Something clicked, the ahhooogah! horn sounded and my eyes launched out of their sockets, as my feet started winding up with the 'Yabba Dabba Do' sound to run after the only one of us in the room who wasn't a cartoon of a physics student." Through the oxytocin cloud, Kevin was wary of becoming involved, plagued by questions about where their relationship could possibly go. Kevin figured that things between the two of them could end in one of two ways: (1) eventual breakup and subsequent grief, or (2) a serious relationship with him, a bipolar guy. He felt like he had more baggage than an airport, even at his young age, and the idea of their becoming a couple felt pointless in a way that had nothing to do with his attraction for her.

"Sad as it seems, human beings have always been unhappy with who they are," writes the naturalist Diane Ackerman. "Even the most comely of us feel like eternally ugly ducklings who yearn to be transformed into swans. One of the bad jokes of evolution is that we have evolved brains, which can imagine a state of perfection we cannot achieve."

Not long after meeting his new lab partner, Kevin felt a pain in his testicle and a lump, no larger than a marble.

He went to a doctor to get it checked out, but didn't think much of it.

GORDON

GORDON WAS REELING. First, the news that his son had bipolar disorder. And now he had an acute pain in his testicle? As a doctor, he thought of the symptoms and wondered if it could be cancer. How was that possible? In 1990, the testicular cancer rate was 5.1 cases per every 100,000, or roughly 0.0051 percent. Although it was also a young man's disease, most common among those age twenty to thirty-nine, awareness of it was low and the taboos around it were high. Where on earth had this come from? Gordon couldn't think of any members of his family who had testicular cancer, or even a scare of it. It made no sense that his healthy, champion athlete of a son could have not one, but two significant ways in which his body was at war with itself.

Gordon took comfort in the numbers. If it was testicular cancer, the survival rates were high—90 percent or more. He checked around at his hospital and found a urology surgeon with an open slot for operating the morning after Kevin was due to return home.

Gordon knew that when Kevin awoke from surgery, he would look down and find a four-inch incision below his stomach and a prosthetic left testicle where his old one had been. His ability to produce biological children would be impaired, but not erased, as the remaining testicle typically still produces sperm. Banking sperm was relatively affordable and easy, not nearly as invasive as freezing and storing eggs. It seemed like a no-brainer that Kevin would want to do it, just in case.

But banking sperm was far from Kevin's twenty-one-year-old mind. He didn't even seem to be very concerned to learn that the growth in his testicle had been malignant. The doctors had removed it and all traces of the cancer.

Kevin wanted to know what day it was. And how many days he had until his next race.

AMANDA

SOFT CANDLELIGHT, EXPOSED brick, and white linen tablecloths— such was the ambiance of 3 Steeple Street, a restaurant nestled along the Moshassuck River near campus. The warm interior was a welcome contrast to the New England November unfolding outside the window around them and finally, after a couple of months of flirtation in physics class, her lab partner had asked her out on a date. Amanda tried not to look impressed when Kevin showed the waitress an authentic ID and ordered white wine. As he slipped the glass surreptitiously to her across the table, the newness of the moment, of each other, astounded them both.

Amanda's crush on Kevin was so overpowering that she struggled to remember the name of anyone else in their physics class, or even their faces. They simply didn't seem relevant and Kevin drew so much of her attention that there didn't seem to be much room for anything else. For his part, Kevin noticed that Amanda was wearing a heavy stainless steel watch, a distinctive accessory that was hard to miss. Amanda explained that it was her father's, and that he was a doctor in New York, and that in many ways she had felt closer to him growing up than to her mother. Talking about doctors seemed a bit strange to her as she tried to reconcile the youthful athlete sitting across from her with a patient who had just gone through cancer treatment. He had volunteered some information to her about his ordeal, but she held off on asking him more questions about it.

The wine kept flowing, as did the conversation. After dinner, Kevin invited Amanda to his place to listen to a recording of *Peter and the Wolf*, the Soviet composer Sergei Prokofiev's children's story narrated and told with the instruments of an orchestra: the flute bird, the oboe duck, the bassoon grandfather, the French horn wolf. "What kind of bird are you if you can't fly?" the little bird argues with a duck. "What kind of bird are you if you can't swim?" answers the duck. Even if by outward appearances many of Kevin's Brown classmates viewed him as an academically successful student-athlete, he connected with the existential identity themes.

It was there, with the strings of Peter struggling with the wolf dancing around their ears, that Amanda began to see the physical implications of Kevin's recent cancer surgery—scars that were fresh and would be with him for the rest of his life. So much of Amanda's experience up to that time with her family, in the pressure cooker of a private all-girls school, during her first few weeks at college, had felt dull compared to the feeling she now experienced with Kevin. Yet as they held each other on his flannel sheets, she felt a remarkable sense of optimism.

Not to mention the strange, new thrill of being in the presence of a man in crisis.

KEVIN

THREE WEEKS AFTER surgery, Kevin was back on the water, much to the amazement of his teammates. They were in awe, viewing Kevin as a superb, fiercely determined athlete who was being tested in ways they couldn't even begin to imagine.

With his junior year sailing with the Olympic coaches over, Kevin had returned to Brown's team roster as a senior. His goal now was to make a bid at the Singlehanded Nationals at the National Collegiate Athletic Association (NCAA) championships—big talk, everyone thought, despite their admiration for him. In his freshman and sophomore years, he had come in second place in the championships. Having taken his junior year off to train with the Olympians, this year was his final shot at the title.

Kevin took comfort in returning to his team and training regimen, but was still behind his normal routine after surgery and before Nationals and facing an incredible time crunch. Most sailing injuries were bruises, sprains, or occurred in the lower back, with maybe a knee injury here or there. But coming back from cancer was unheard of. Kevin's coaches and doctors were the first to admit that preparing a cancer survivor for a shot at an NCAA title was a new experience for them, too. Nobody was expecting him to compete at all, let alone perform well. What was worse for Kevin was the specter of failure to win the title, one he felt he should have already won.

Privately, Kevin grappled with the repercussions of having had cancer, including wondering if he had made a mistake by not banking sperm. He still had a hard time seeing the point of it. He had one testicle left, after all, and plenty of time, as he confronted questions of fatherhood that most of his teammates barely thought about, if it all. Then there were Kevin's concerns about whether he should have biological children at all. The more he researched cancer and bipolar disorder, the more he worried about passing either or both along in his genes.

With the competition looming just a couple of weeks away, Kevin asked his doctors questions about whether he would be able to do sit-ups and workouts with sutures. His school and sailing were layered on top of monthly blood tests and regular CAT scans that doctors said were still necessary to ensure that the disease was under control. His medical brain trust was wary, and told Kevin that it was crucial for him to augment his workouts slowly and pay close attention to what his body was telling him. He didn't fully ingest their advice and began working out as he saw fit alongside his teammates. Slowly, but surely, Kevin was worming his way back onto competitive waters. Surgery in October and competition in November didn't seem crazy to him, even if those around him were aghast.

By the time Kevin arrived at the NCAA sailing competition at Gull Lake in Kalamazoo, Michigan, he felt both locked into the sport and somehow detached from it, as though he was on autopilot, just coasting through the movements of competing for the 1990 title. Some of his detachment was due to the medication, and some to his desire to deny the pain of cancer and bipolar disorder and focus on the one thing that had always brought him happiness: achievement on the water.

Kevin yearned for the NCAA title, but those around him hedged their expectations. They were just excited he was alive and while Kevin's fitness rebound astonished them, they also knew how hard it was to win a collegiate title under even the best circumstances. With his mother and teammates watching, Kevin soared across the large oval of water, located west of Detroit and south of Grand Rapids. It was freezing in the biting kind of way one finds only in the Midwest in November, a relentless frigidity that many locals endure with a stoic smile.

Much to everyone's astonishment, Kevin, the bipolar cancer survivor, charged into second place.

He couldn't have felt more ashamed.

SUSANNE

KEVIN HAD NOT only competed but conquered. Watching him glide across the water in the distance, Susanne was elated. For him to have come so close to winning the title after what he had been through shocked her and his teammates.

Susanne rushed to tell Kevin after the race how proud she was of him, and she meant it. But neither her words nor his accomplishment seemed to be sinking in. Kevin's shoulders were slumped, his post-regatta demeanor melancholy. There seemed to be nothing she or anyone else could say to reverse his disappointment at winning second place. There's some research that indicates bronze medalists are actually happier than silver medalists, the thinking being that they're less likely than a silver medalist to engage in counterfactual thinking, or dwelling on what might have been. They're happy to have made it to the podium. That wasn't dissimilar from how Susanne viewed Kevin's NCAA performance: getting to the competition, especially after the mania, the depression, cancer, *was* the accomplishment.

Frustrated, confused, and saddened, Susanne kept smiling and hoped that Kevin would shake it off.

KEVIN

KEVIN ENDED UP winning a collegiate title at the NCAA championships as part of Brown's overall sailing team. Even though he hadn't won first place in the Singlehandeds, his points from that race had contributed to the win. Technically speaking, he had a collegiate title, even if it wasn't the one he set out to snag.

Nevertheless, a sense of imposter syndrome washed over Kevin—the feeling that he was a fraud, that his success to this point was undeserved and had come about through luck rather than real ability. He also feared that if he could not repeat his success, he could be exposed for being incompetent, false before the world. Researchers first observed imposter syndrome in high-performing women in collegiate and professional environments who felt unable to take ownership of their successes and abilities. Sports provide fertile ground for imposter syndrome for women and men as well, with champions working their whole lives to earn a specific title. If attained, it can feel unreal, undeserved, and a winner may have to defend her prowess against others on a regular basis and in a realm in which success is measured in clear, but arbitrary, metrics. Then there's the risk of the sudden loss of self-esteem that comes with feeling that they have failed to live up to an idealized image.

Kevin was still young enough to try to fill out his sailing résumé with America's Cup wins, and, most coveted of all, an Olympic gold medal. Maybe those victories would feel different, he thought, the crowning achievements of a perfect career, well-earned titles that promised the satisfaction of knowing one had reached the zenith of one's sport and earned a place in history.

Meanwhile, Kevin read whatever books and academic articles he could find about bipolar disorder, researching it as he would a French literature paper or math theorem. It was comforting to know that he wasn't alone, but he struggled with the idea of possible brilliance. Was he on track to become the athletic version of Ernest Hemingway? Or was he just one of many ordinary people who was merely trying to get through the day? Many of the memoirs and books he read romanticized mania, portraying it as a world that only certain people could access, people who were members of some sort of elite club. In an odd way, that portrayal made the weight of pursuing the Olympics feel that much heavier for Kevin. If he was a sailing savant, did that mean he had more space in which to be crazy, as it was the price to pay for being a high achiever? But without the inspired performances on the water, then who was he? Was he just crazy? And if so, what did that mean?

Increasingly, the parallels between the worlds in books and the plotlines of The Show were clear and soothing to Kevin. He eased into fiction the way one eases into a comfortable reclining chair, the voices of authors he had never met seeming to blend with the nuances of the strange world he was introduced to in Boston. James Joyce, Vladimir Nabokov, and Thomas Pynchon were among his favorite authors, speaking to him directly in a way those immediately connected to his world couldn't. He thought of Pynchon's novel *Gravity's Rainbow*, which centers on several characters' quest to find the secret of a mysterious "black device." Kevin wondered whether, like the book, a fusion of science, philosophy, and culture, he wasn't on a similar multidisciplinary quest at times, and like the hunt for the black device, the stakes were just as high: saving the world.

Kevin graduated from Brown in 1991 with two majors, math and French literature—a reflection, he was the first to say, of his bipolar brain. Math spoke to his love of practicality and precision, French to his escapist, contortionist side. He thought of Joseph Campbell, who wrote of his soul being in a state of unrest as his inner and outer worlds failed to reconcile themselves. It was easy to recite Campbellian platitudes about following one's bliss, but far more complicated to figure out how to execute that in a day-to-day manner.

Amanda still had three more years of schooling to complete, but she and Kevin remained a serious couple. So serious that Amanda's family pressed Kevin on the question that befalls many a college student: What was he going to do with himself after graduating?

Kevin had to think about his long-term plan. To him, the idea of making a living at sailing seemed a far-off dream with no clear path to reach it. Meanwhile, Amanda had some catching up to do in Providence. She was normally an A student, but her grades had slipped her freshman year.

She knew whom to blame for that.

•

Kevin landed some work coaching and moved into a small apartment in Bristol, Rhode Island, to finish up a thesis he'd started while at Brown, an ambitious analysis of the love letters of Marguerite Duras and Beethoven. Kevin argued that Beethoven's famous "Immortal Beloved" letter wasn't written for a particular recipient, but was rather directed at love itself, an epic missive against loneliness and sorrow. As he wove in the words of Duras, he wrote that those who wondered to whom Beethoven was addressing his letter had missed the point—it was about Beethoven combating alienation, about the identity of the sender rather than the recipient. Kevin had already been awarded his degree, so the thesis wasn't required, but he was eager to finish it and discussed it at length during office hours with one of his favorite professors. She admired his gusto, but privately worried about whether his writing the paper was a good idea, given his earlier breakdown. Nonetheless, Kevin insisted that he felt fine and that the research and writing was invigorating to him.

With team and collegiate sailing behind him, Kevin could now focus on a new sailing challenge: the Finn, a single-person boat and one of the several classes of boats in the Olympics. The Finn suited him well, being among the most physical and tactical of the Olympic classes. Debuting at the Helsinki Olympics in 1952, it was a finesse game, much like surfing, but necessitated strength and raw power. Finn sailors tried to bulk up their weight with as much muscle as possible. The weight helped the feathery craft move, earning those athletes the nickname "gorillas on the water."

To prepare for sailing in the Finn class, Kevin built up to a weight of 210 to 220 pounds of mostly muscle on his six-foot frame, a far cry from his resting weight of 175 pounds. In junior and collegiate sailing, Kevin had focused on general fitness, as had his sailing peers, but the level of precision required for Olympic competition was completely new for him, with each pound and workout counting for an opportunity that came only once every four years. Kevin's shifting in and out of sailing classes meant that his weight yo-yoed, further knotting up his already complicated relationship with his body. His bipolar disorder medication had the propensity to add bloat, and like most human beings, Kevin struggled at times to maintain willpower over his diet. Half or even all of a pizza seemed

The Finn class (Wikimedia Commons)

more substantial than a slice, even though he knew the risks of indulging in junk foods. Whenever he succumbed to a food binge, the loss of control scared him and made him question whether his medications were working as intended. Or whether what he was feeling was what everyone else felt and was therefore whatever "normal" was supposed to be. He deconstructed the issue over and over again in his mind, wondering if he had some sort of eating disorder to add to his already thick medical chart, or if overeating was a manifestation of his mania, an exuberance for the sweet or savory. Then again, maybe he was just a hungry athlete, or it was some kind of side effect of the meds. Then the guilt of overeating arrived and triggered a cycle of regret that he knew all too well. It seemed as if whenever one arena of his life was on the upswing, another, even a seemingly simple one like nutrition, plummeted. He could never win.

Although his doctors had told him to avoid caffeine, as it might trigger a manic episode, Kevin began to drink one cup after another. It had been more than a year since his episode in Boston. Maybe it had been a one-time event, after all.

That would turn out to be wishful thinking.

•

With his French thesis completed, Kevin and several young sailors gathered at Logan Airport in Boston to head to Japan. Kevin was eager to compete again, this time at the Japanese-American Intercollegiate Goodwill Games, a competition that brought together top collegiate-level teams from around the world, part of Japan's broader efforts to bolster its sailing culture prior to the America's Cup.

The competition didn't go as well as Kevin had hoped, however. Sailing with a female teammate from Brown, he came in fourth place. It seemed to Kevin that he hadn't had enough time to practice with his partner in their boat, yet during the competition, he had been completely immersed in the process, unconcerned with whether they were winning or not. There simply hadn't been time for those thoughts in the moment.

After the competition was over, the group of young sailors headed out to let loose on Tokyo's fast, bright streets for some celebratory drinking and sightseeing. Things with the group seemed relatively tame, but Kevin, with what he felt was his lack of preparation for the race replaying in his mind, could feel the presence of the Director, back from Boston, nearby. He was summoning Kevin into The Show.

At the end of the evening, Kevin headed back to the hotel with his friends. They bade each other good night, everyone assuming that Kevin, like the rest of them, would go up to his hotel room and sleep until morning, when they were due to catch their flight back to the United States.

The Director had other ideas.

•

Kevin crossed Tokyo's loud, clustered, traffic-jammed streets with his eyes closed. Instead of marveling at the remarkable luck he was having in not getting seriously injured or killed, he was reasoning that there was a silent army of people on hand protecting and supporting him. The Director wouldn't want to kill off his lead actor. Once again Kevin was being selected for a special mission. The traffic felt as if it was choreographed around him in an elegant ballet. The cameras were rolling.

It's unclear the order in which Kevin went wandering about Tokyo, but at some point, he found a basketball and began dribbling it, seeing his behavior as a form of performance art connected to the popularity of the NBA back home. As he examined the ball's patriotic palate of red, white, and blue coloring, it seemed to him like a remarkable coincidence as an American abroad. Beautiful, even. How did people know? Perhaps they were The Show's sponsors. A big part of Kevin's mission in The Show was becoming clear: it was up to him to manipulate the global economy for altruistic purposes.

Kevin came upon a truck parked on the street and tried to open the door. It was unlocked, which was well-executed staging. He sat in the driver's seat, flipped down a sun visor and, to his surprise, there were the keys to the ignition. The Director must have found out that Kevin was a fan of *Terminator 2*, a film in which Arnold Schwarzenegger also found a truck, opened its door, and flipped down a sun visor to find the ignition keys. If that wasn't a sign of being on The Show, Kevin didn't know what was. Maybe it wasn't a surprise, rather, a true feeling of synchronicity.

He began driving around recklessly, thinking about another popular Schwarzenegger science-fiction film of the moment, *Total Recall*. As he jerked the wheel to and fro, he considered the tale of a construction worker who battles with his memories and wonders about those who are trying to control them. Kevin felt sure that there were hidden messages in that film that would tell him who he was supposed to be in The Show's Tokyo episode. He wondered if Amanda, back stateside, had been selected for The Show as well, and if she was being groomed to be his leading lady. Surely the appearance of a smart, blonde, beautiful college sweetheart in his life was no coincidence, but a strategic casting move for future episodes.

After driving around for a while, Kevin parked the truck, leaving the keys in the ignition, and walked around. He reached a building with computers inside and a sign reading GENIUS SCHOOL. Much to his dismay, the building was locked. Then, as he had done in Boston, he became fascinated with climbing poles, walls, and whatever else could be scaled. He shed his shirt and sailing shoes and made his way to the Tokyo Imperial Palace, a popular tourist destination. The Director had chosen this site for Kevin's coronation, of course.

Kevin wandered the imperial grounds, clad in nothing but his sweat pants. He was in awe of the palace's dramatic pointed roof, its lush land-scape of meticulously manicured trees and grass, its waterside placement, and its central white edifice, a building that was majestic and exotic, unlike anything to be found in Ventura or Providence. Kevin marveled at the site's history, tranquility, and regal nature, and that it was ensconced by flickering billboard screens, signage in a language he couldn't read, bright and edgy fashion and spikey hair, all seemingly so futuristic compared to anything he had seen in the United States. Real estate in Tokyo had recently sold for as much as $139,000 a square foot, making the land even more valuable than prime real estate back home and a fitting location for a scene in The Show.

It was there, on the pricey, revered site, that the police came.

•

Although Kevin's French-speaking abilities were sound, his Japanese language skills were nonexistent. One officer after another passed Kevin around at the local police station, confounded by the language barrier, as well as the circumstances in which the clean-cut American young man had been found. Somehow he was ultimately released from police custody without being charged, but once outside, Kevin realized that he couldn't remember where his hotel was. Finally, though, still feeling as if he were on The Show, he found his way back, just as his teammates were leaving for the airport.

On the bus with them, Kevin looked out the window and began to quietly cry. The Show was becoming confusing, and suddenly it felt as though he was no longer in control. Any free will he had was lost, the future was scripted beyond his control, and the past reeked of having been manufactured, a lie. Yet at the same time, the world reverberated with overwhelming beauty. No one around him, in spite of their best intentions, seemed to get it, or the jarring juxtaposition of it all, nor did Kevin know where to even begin.

As the young sailors stepped into Tokyo's airport, bustling with people racing for their flights, they all kept a close eye on Kevin. They could see that he wasn't himself, sniffling, singing, muttering nonsensical phrases under his breath. They couldn't help but wonder if perhaps he was just stressed out from the competition and the looming overseas flight. Surely it would pass. He seemed harmless and almost childlike in his carelessness and wonder at things that were commonplace: the automatic sliding doors, the lines of people checking in to retrieve their tickets, the hive of cars ferrying passengers in and out of the arrivals hall.

Kevin smiled and handed his passport to the ticket agent—a good sign that whatever had gotten into him was shaking its way out, his teammates thought. Moments later, Kevin felt overwhelmed and that he needed to escape. He ran downstairs and fixed his eyes on the baggage carousel.

He darted off toward it, climbing up its metal beltway intended for displaying and moving baggage, and while dodging oncoming luggage, wrestled his way outside onto the tarmac on the other side. The asphalt expanse was abuzz with aircrafts slowly moving to and fro, small carts sputtering around, air traffic controllers waving their orange wands as Kevin ran toward the biggest plane he could find. He was underneath it when the police encircled him.

GORDON

IT WAS A strange feeling, Gordon thought, to be at work as an emergency room doctor and receive a call that there was an urgent crisis in his own family.

It was around midnight when the phone rang and on the other end came the voice of Kevin's sailing coach in Japan. Far away and across the Pacific Ocean, Kevin had been roaming the Tokyo streets at night and the police had surrounded him on the airport tarmac, the coach told him.

The rest of the team needed to head home to the States, but someone had to come to Japan and pick up Kevin.

Gordon needed no further explanation. Panicked and frustrated, he arranged for another doctor to cover his shifts and drove straight to Los Angeles International Airport to catch the first flight out to Tokyo that morning. Gordon had taken a post in Ridgecrest, California, a Navy town of twenty-seven thousand in south central California, where he was living with his second wife, Meimei. While the small size and quaintness usually made him happy to wake up there every day, now it just felt inconveniently far from where a crisis was brewing with his son.

Upon arriving in Japan, Gordon found Kevin wound up, manic, and talking fast, with ideas pulsing out like fireworks every which way. Again, somehow he had avoided any formal charges or legal fallout for storming the tarmac. Still, he seemed willing to travel back home with his father. Gordon booked two tickets, hoping that Kevin's agreeability would continue.

As they waited for their plane home to California, Kevin demanded a Coca-Cola, and Gordon was torn between what would be worse: the risk of giving Kevin caffeine which could further trigger his mania, or that denying Kevin what he wanted could make him erupt even more. Since Boston, Gordon had given up on trying to predict what was going on in Kevin's head. He met Kevin's demand and anxiously watched as his son balanced the red-and-white can on his head and muttered something about sponsorships.

They boarded and took their seats with the other passengers, Gordon's nerves even on edge now that he and Kevin were sealed in with strangers, leaving him with no viable exit options. As the engines roared and the wheels lifted for takeoff, Kevin seemed calm. He told his father he needed to go to the restroom, and Gordon let him go on his own. They were seated near the lavatory.

A few minutes passed. Kevin had not returned.

Then ten minutes passed, then fifteen. Gordon rose from his seat to investigate.

He found his son up front in the cockpit, mingling with the pilots, his eyes "wide and spaced out," he remembered later. Politely, he asked Kevin to come back to his seat, and he breathed a sigh of relief when Kevin complied.

Once they reached the airport, Gordon called around and was able to have Kevin admitted into Las Encinas, a well-regarded hospital in Pasadena. Shaded by a lush green canopy, surrounded by a blanket of green lawn, the facility could have been mistaken for a swanky resort. A mainstay in the community, it specializes in chemical dependency issues and psychiatric disorders. Despite the hospital's inviting façade, Kevin seemed irritated at the very notion of being there.

Gordon explained that whether his son liked it or not, he would have to stay at the hospital for several days. He remembered the debilitating depression that Kevin had suffered through after the Boston episode—his shuffling around the house, his complete lack of interest in everything—and knew that he would not be able to help him on his own.

KEVIN

THE FORLORNNESS THAT Kevin felt after coming down from The Show wasn't due just to the problems and guilt associated with the aftermath of his episodes—the credit card bills, the explanations and apologies to friends and family, the hospitalization, the guilt of knowing that he had a very privileged support system that many others with bipolar disorder did not. It was also due to grief over the loss of The Show itself and the bruising realization that he didn't have a mission to save the world after all. During The Show, he had felt so close to bringing about world peace, but after the episodes, he was not only thrust back into the harsh throes of reality, he felt more depressed than the people around him.

Some people with bipolar disorder have persecutory delusions, but Kevin's first visions were euphoric, sometimes even Jesus- or Buddha-themed, though he had never considered himself particularly spiritual or religious before. They also had overtones of dystopian science fiction, as in Kevin's mind, saving the world would require an army of powerful and well-connected individuals from a variety of backgrounds. According to the backstory being orchestrated by the Director, a small group of "old money" people who had survived the Great Depression and the Second World War and would join with Kevin to devote themselves to the prevention of another global conflict. Another group, the Council, which had already dictated some of his movements in Tokyo, would be a control center that governed key functions, such as funding, and mapped out experiments containing math puzzles and codes to be unlocked by the select few, including Kevin. The Director, of course, knew the solutions and was observing Kevin as he tried to unravel it all before an audience.

Delusions may be a way for the rational brain to try to come to terms with strange events, the psychologist Brandon Maher wrote in 1974. They're a person's way of trying to sort through the chaos of the mind, he wrote, an explosive reaction to a crisis or trauma. Similarly, Kevin's delusions may have been serving to help him sort through life's complexities. For the delusions to seem real, Maher also theorized, they had to be grandiose, so that no one could refute them easily. Yet to serve its psycho-logical function, a delusion had to feel tangible to the person having it.

In his journals, Kevin had compared some elements of The Show with lyrics from the band Styx. The song "Grand Illusion" spoke of getting tickets to "The Show," a stage being set, a band playing, the secret desire to be a star. The lyrics also urged people not to be tricked by pop culture messaging that indicates how someone is supposed to be, that it merely represented someone else's fantasy, a farce. "Cause you never really win the game," Kevin repeated in his notebook. "DEEP INSIDE WE'RE ALL THE SAME."

Kevin couldn't pinpoint exactly how The Show and its backstory had come to him, or the why of his own grand illusion. Yet when he was in it, he was determined to hold on to it as if it were true, even if in his clearer moments it felt nuts.

When Kevin was in The Show, it couldn't have felt more real.

KRISTINA

THE ROLE REVERSAL felt strange. Her brother was capable of sailing a boat better than anyone else in the country, or the world, and yet her parents still felt that Kevin needed his little sister to accompany him as he drove home from Rhode Island to California, where he would be coaching Olympians. They didn't trust his ability to be by himself behind the wheel for long stretches of time, a notion that Kristina couldn't help but think was an overreaction. Still, she didn't have anything better to do, so the two met up at a Motel 6 in Texas, a halfway point between California and the Northeast, hopped into his car, and headed west.

Amanda had traveled with Kevin from Rhode Island to Texas and then flown back east to finish her studies. Kevin had been sullen on that first half of the trip, and for the first time he began to see and understand the sadness Amanda felt when he was down. It pained him to know that his hurt, in its own way, was contagious, particularly to someone he cared so much about, and that only served to make him feel worse.

As Kevin and Kristina took off for California, beige, sienna, and blue skies fanning out before them on all sides, interrupted only by the occasional McDonald's or gas station, Kevin began to tell his sister in detail about what had happened in Tokyo. He also told her about what it had been like to be institutionalized, the details of which her parents had hidden from her. Kevin's descriptions of mania fascinated Kristina, as they didn't seem that different from her own hallucinogenic, drug-induced experiences. All this time she had been focusing on being the opposite of her brother, yet now it seemed that they might have more in common than she thought, even if they arrived there by completely different paths.

In conversation with his open-minded sister, Kevin still had a hard time explaining what it felt like to be on The Show. He couldn't even really describe it to himself. The only portrayal that came close was to compare the Director to a character out of a science fiction book or movie set in the near future. He also told Kristina that sometimes The Show wasn't 100 percent on, that there were flickers or small moments when he questioned which parts of life in The Show were being set up and which were not.

In The Show, Kevin went on, he felt the need to give the people, the audience, what they wanted—i.e., entertainment. So why not ham things up a little bit? The walks in Boston and Tokyo had been almost like breakdances, a rethinking of the mundane act of getting from Point

A to Point B. Everything he did in episodes felt laced with a grander meaning.

As Kevin kept talking, Kristina marveled at one particular inverse connection. She took drugs to feel as if she were in a different reality. Kevin took drugs *not* to.

KEVIN

IN ORDER FOR Kevin to remain in California and train for the Olympics, he needed to find a steady source of income. A job as a sailing coach would provide some money, but what he really wanted was to land a well-paying gig as a professional sailor—a fantasy, it seemed. At the time, even those fortunate enough to get paying jobs on the America's Cup boats earned very little money; sometimes they even packed their own lunches.

With Amanda still studying at Brown, Kevin moved back to his mother's house in Ventura and worked a prestigious job as a downwind specialist coaching Julia Trotman, a sailor who had qualified for the 1992 Games in Barcelona. She was based, along with many other sailors, at the Alamitos Bay Yacht Club, a fertile networking ground for an athlete like Kevin trying to get exposure to the Olympic training regime.

Around the same time, Kevin's own performance on the water was garnering attention. At age twenty-one, he sailed one of the best races of his entire career in August 1991 when he won the North American Laser Championship by a staggering 50-point margin in a fleet of 200, putting him squarely in contention for making the U.S. Olympic team, although the Laser was not an Olympic class at the time. The Laser is a smaller boat, a single-handed dinghy that is a delight to watch in action. Sailing can pose challenges for spectators, who are usually at a distance from the action, but Laser sailing still offers a dynamic dance for the eye. The sailors must carve their boats across the waves, finding a route that is fast and just on the edge, without capsizing. At times, their bodies can careen far over the edges of the small boats, as they try to maneuver the vessels, a strange and nerve-wracking sight as they look on the verge of falling over into the water.

SUSANNE

SUSANNE HEARD THE whoosh of the toilet as Kevin flushed his pills away.

Years of medical school, years of working with patients, and it all seemed to be failing her now. There were pills to help her son, but they were of little use if he wasn't interested in taking them. She wondered at how and when Kevin had become so difficult, and at how helpless she felt. She also worried about external events possibly triggering his mania: a loss on the water—anything, really.

Kevin went on The Show again, this time, again, at the Alamitos Bay Yacht Club. Susanne was less aware that Kevin had his thesis on Marguerite Duras in hand and a penchant for writing with fountain pens. At one point, he spread the ink and several pages out on the table. When he lifted up one page, Kevin saw the word *l'amour*, French for "love," glowing like burning coal, which was not only the last word of his thesis, but part of the world-saving mission of The Show. The impression stuck with him, and it felt completely strange. He struggled to brush it off. Susanne had agreed to drive him there for his coaching gig, but soon realized Kevin was not safe to head out on the water. Covering his face in zinc ointment, he climbed up and down a mast and into the back of a boat, quoting Herman Melville. He found a cooler full of lukewarm cans of Coca-Cola and began chugging one after another because Coca-Cola was a regular sponsor of The Show. The cameras were rolling and product placement made sense, especially since Coca-Cola was a longtime Olympic sponsor, too.

The episode had come about in part because of the constant push and pull Kevin felt between wanting to please his family by taking his medication and not wanting to feel dead, like a robot, away from being in his own body or feeling like a human being with real emotions. What did his Western-medicine-trained doctors with all their pills really know, anyway? The world's knowledge of psychiatric medicine was still in its infancy, and much was still unknown about using drugs to treat mental illness. The idea that popping a pill alone could "cure" Kevin seemed overly simplistic. As the author Andrew Solomon has noted,

> If you improved on Depakote, you must have had bipolar illness. If Zyprexa made you all better, you were probably schizophrenic. Useful though these agents are, however, work on them is still inconsistent, tangled on unproven theories, preoccupied with neurotransmitters that play an opaque role in illness. Reductive thinking about the nature of mental illness—the suggestion that it can be fully described by chemistry—satisfies those who fund research, and that research may help sufferers. It is also dishonest.

Kevin also refused the recommendation that he should see a therapist, not sure what the benefit could possibly be. The schism between believers in psychotherapy and adherents of pharmacology, the author William Styron wrote, "resembles the medical quarrels of the eighteenth century (to bleed or not to bleed) and almost defines in itself the inexplicable nature of depression and the difficulty of its treatment."

Susanne didn't know what was going on in Kevin's mind, only what was happening on the outside, the swirl of the toilet and the face of a man who seemed to be someone other than her son. Unsure of what to do, she called Kevin's father.

KEVIN

In April 1992, at the U.S. trials for the Finn class, Kevin finished in eighth place, missing an Olympic berth. That result was disappointing for him, but at age twenty-three, he knew that he still had time. Sailing is the rare sport that rewards longevity and experience, at least to a point. The Fijian sailors Colin Philp Sr. and his son Tony Philp competed at the 1984 and 1988 Olympics and qualified for Barcelona in 1992, and it wasn't unheard of for sailors to compete into their thirties or even forties. Additionally, racing in the trials gave Kevin some experience in competing in an Olympic environment, a process that would hopefully demystify the Games for him and increase his confidence in his ability to compete with peers there.

"I feel a part of it again," Kevin wrote in a letter to Amanda that September. He told her of watching the sunrise, writing, "I can imagine myself flying into it and going home. This week out east was very good for me. I go home feeling loved, respected, liked, and needed—as well as confident with myself and excited about the future."

Following the Olympic trials, Amanda wrote him a thoughtful card.

"This should be a great time in my life," Kevin wrote back. "It's up to me."

AMANDA

HE WAS IN California, she was still living in the Northeast and still at school, but they wrote to each other and spoke on the phone all the time. Kevin wrote to her about the Grape Nuts with peaches that he ate for breakfast. He asked about her schoolwork and he told her about the dreams he had of becoming a skipper in the America's Cup, of winning an Olympic gold medal, and of their life together. While a long-distance relationship was not ideal, the romance they cultivated at Brown translated to their letters and phone calls, Amanda feeling more connected to Kevin than ever.

Following the 1992 Olympic trials, Kevin embarked on a strong winning streak, a sure sign that he might be finally securing a good rhythm with elite racing beyond Brown, going undefeated in the Laser for nearly two years. Considering the differences in skills and techniques between collegiate and professional sailing, which still lacked a viable professional circuit, Kevin's accomplishment was significant. He was recruited to represent the United States at the upcoming January 1993 World Championships in Auckland. Even better news for Kevin: the Laser, his best and favorite sailing class, had been added to the Olympic roster, starting with the 1996 Atlanta Games.

"I am finding a self I haven't known for a long time here at home," Kevin wrote to Amanda. "I know the weather is really good for me, the exercise, but I think it has to do with being able to hope and dream. When I'm out alone on the ocean, no other boats to be seen—just the birds and seals and sun and me, life gets so simple and free. I don't have to be anywhere, buy anything, prove anything, or think too much. I think part of my recent difficulties have had something to do with thinking too much."

He also wrote to Amanda about a "false alarm" with The Show that had really disturbed him. "I feel like God's dog, and his son keeps teasing me with a piece of juicy, red carefree confidence. Just as I think he will finally let me have it, he pulls it away again, laughing. It's an eerie, piercing laugh that sounds as old as time."

"I guess the key," Amanda wrote back, "is learning to differentiate between dreams and expectations."

Amanda was one of the few people Kevin could talk to about his dilemma over whether to take his medications. A common cycle that befalls many who have bipolar disorder is that they will stop taking, or reduce the dosage of, their medication when they feel better, as they see their improvement as a sign that they no longer need it. What's more, they may do so suddenly, and without professional guidance, which can give their system a dramatic jolt. (In some cases, people on medications who intended to curb their symptoms of mania or depression reported feeling worse.)

In most arenas, Kevin had always followed the rules, and soared under disciplined structures, but taking the medications had dulled him and disconnected him from his body in a way that felt nothing short of oppressive, on and off the water. At times, the pills made him feel as if he was trying to keep on a diet while surrounded by doughnuts, cookies, and cake. Not only that, it felt as thought everyone else could eat the sweets but him. It was hard not to feel mad at the world and mad at his body.

"I'm not really making myself very clear," Kevin wrote to Amanda three weeks before Christmas. "Please hear: I Love You."

GORDON

INITIALLY, AFTER GETTING Susanne's call and arriving at the Yacht Club, Gordon considered getting Kevin into the car a significant victory. Once he was behind the wheel and on the road, though, one concern begat another and Gordon began to worry about his son bolting. Kevin had already made a point of throwing one of his journals out of the window as the car was in motion, and Gordon was nervous that Kevin's body might be the next thing to go.

As they drove, Kevin argued with his father about going to the hospital once again and cited the reasons why he didn't think he needed to be admitted. His pleas were impassioned in tone and Gordon kept quiet, fearful that even the slightest thing out of his mouth could be misconstrued. There was no way to reason with Kevin when he was like this. The cliché of walking on eggshells came to mind, an expression that Gordon had often heard but not really internalized until he experienced parenting his son when he was manic. Gordon knew he just had to get Kevin under professional psychiatric care as soon as possible.

KRISTINA

WHEN KRISTINA THOUGHT of psychiatric wards, the images of white walls, smocks, and austere nurses à la *One Flew Over the Cuckoo's Nest* came to mind. She knew with some certainty that lobotomies had fallen out of favor, but she couldn't be sure whether she would see anyone, including her brother, in a straitjacket or other restraints, surrounded by attendants in bleach-white scrubs.

So when her parents told her that Kevin was once again in a mental institution of some sort, she didn't know what to make of it. Once was a freak occurrence, twice strange, but three or more times made for a pattern. As a holiday gift and a gesture hinting at wanting to spend quality time together, her father had purchased passes for her and her brother at the California Speedway, but now the likelihood that the three of them would be bonding over driving race cars seemed unlikely. Her father had already mentioned to her his disappointment at Kevin possibly not being able to go racing because of the hospitalization, a reaction that struck Kristina as shortsighted. He seemed to be saying that he had spent money to do something special with his children but once again Kevin had screwed it up, which wasn't the takeaway Kristina had from hearing her brother was in trouble.

Kristina didn't want to go to the hospital empty-handed, so she brought a burrito and cigarettes, critical currencies in the hospital confines. In keeping with her rebellion against her doctor parents and Olympic-contender brother, she had taken up smoking casually years before, but it felt strange to now be sharing the habit with her athlete brother. What's more, the only time she could remember Kevin ever mentioning even wanting a cigarette was when he was in the hospital. In a place of healing, her cancer survivor sibling, for whatever reason, was drawn to lethal tobacco.

When Kristina arrived and asked for her brother at the nurse's station, they told her that he was in the lockdown ward. She didn't know precisely what that meant, but it seemed severe and strange. Her brother, the king of the overachievers, in lockdown? It seemed implausible, or at the very least overkill. The message it sent to Kristina was clear: these people were not messing around.

She was led farther through the halls of the hospital, and a big, heavy metal door clanked shut behind her, a not-so-subtle reminder that those inside were not allowed to leave without permission.

Then, she saw Kevin. Or at least a pale, exhausted, loopy version of him, bathed in harsh artificial light. The downers had rendered him sluggish, incoherent, a match for his fellow patients, who roamed around in similar stages of confusion. The siblings fumbled their way through a visit, Kevin accepting the burrito, cigarettes, and conversation, as Kristina felt awkward and the need to mask her sadness and discomfort. It was one thing to have intellectualized Kevin's mental illness, as she had during the past couple of years, but it was another to see it in front of her like this.

As she and her brother parted ways, she realized that she was wrong. Not only did Kevin belong in the institution, he belonged in lockdown.

What was even more befuddling was that her brother would talk in loops about the Olympics and the America's Cup and his need to train for and compete in both. Many of the nurses and fellow patients brushed off his comments as manic jitter—they had heard it all many times before. Grandeur. Lofty goals. Worldwide media coverage. But Kristina knew that for Kevin, such visions were actually well within reality's purview, not crazy at all.

KEVIN

KEVIN PICKED UP the phone and called Amanda. A letter wasn't appropriate for what he needed to say and he needed to say it as soon as possible. It wasn't related to sailing or bipolar disorder, but to a recent medical test. What should have been routine blood results came back anything but.

It was one thing to get cancer once, particularly as a spry young college athlete. To get it again seemed beyond unfair—and is statistically extremely rare, well below one percent of those who had it one time. This second round of surgery would be, even under the best of circumstances, very invasive and would pull him out of competitive sailing for months. This operation also presented far more complexities than the first one had, as it required an incision of his lymph nodes that would cross his chest like a sash of railroad tracks.

At Christmastime 1992, while everyone else was getting ready for the holidays, Kevin lay down on the operating table and doctors cut him from the sternum to the groin. After the operation, he felt intense pain, inside and out, and spent a week in the hospital recovering after he had been cut open, examined inside, then stitched up again. At first, doctors found that all of the nodes were negative and cancer-free. They sewed Kevin up and sent him on his way, everyone scratching their heads about what could have happened. But soon thereafter, Kevin's second testicle hemorrhaged and he was diagnosed with a second primary tumor, exceedingly rare as it indicated that Kevin had essentially gotten cancer twice, not that his first one had spread from one place to another. With the second testicle gone, so too would go Kevin's ability to have biological children.

He felt betrayed by his body more deeply than ever before; a key physical manifestation of what many thought made a man a man had failed him. He wasn't prone to victim psychology, but a part of him did wonder whether he was being punished, and if so, for what.

Now, Kevin thought, *I'm a completely castrated, crazy man.*

And one who wouldn't be competing at the 1993 World Championships in any capacity, just as his performance on the water was peaking.

The forced sailing hiatus was particularly devastating given his recent winning streak, and he and his family were worried that all of the external tumult would lead him into another bipolar descent.

"It is still very difficult for me to disassociate this pain from the doctors and the hospital," Kevin said to his father. "Unfortunately, this includes you." In the pages of his journal, he chronicled his feelings, writing a string of words and "FEAR" in all caps and drawing a doodle of a monster reaching out from the depths of the sea.

To everyone's surprise, though, Kevin's physical recovery from the extensive surgery was quick. The doctors monitoring his progress described it as nothing short of "miraculous." He even played some tennis. But he had dropped a significant amount of weight, an inevitability the doctors had said would come, from a lack of appetite, and landed at 150 pounds in January 1993, a skeletal shadow of his former champion self.

Some well-intentioned people tried to comfort Kevin by telling him to look on "the bright side," a term he got sick of hearing. He failed to see what bright side there could possibly be when he had lost one testicle, then another, and missed some of the biggest sailing opportunities of his life. People also told him that he should feel lucky to be alive, but he didn't feel lucky about much at all. His diagnosis had come long before Livestrong and other groups tried to change the image of cancer patients from one of pale faces in white hospital gowns to that of strong survivors who moved forward with robust lives. People aiming at the Olympics simply weren't supposed to get cancer.

This surgery also meant that Kevin would need to have biweekly injections of testosterone to replicate the testosterone levels he would have had if his second testicle had not been removed. Men who lose one testicle typically do not need injections, as the other testicle usually compensates for the loss, but men who lose two generally do. In the long term, low testosterone levels could lead to a decrease of bone marrow, putting Kevin at risk for anemia, osteoporosis, decreased sex drive, and loss of muscle mass.

Testosterone levels also can dramatically impact a person's mood and energy levels, and from his first injection, Kevin could feel the flow of the chemical as it coursed through his body. Typically, he felt high shortly after the injection, and low by the time he reached the last four or five days of a cycle. Through trial and error, he found that he liked taking his shots on Wednesdays, so that he could feel his best the first Thursday through Saturday of the cycle, although the notion was depressing. Ideally, Kevin would have liked to feel consistently good on most days, nor was there much research or advice on the intersection of testosterone injections and psychiatric drugs.

Even on Kevin's good days, there would be moments when he was reminded that he was fundamentally different from the vast majority of other men, inside and out. "I feel like an empty, metal skeleton, a phony person," Kevin wrote to Amanda in a letter. "I now have a life-long chemical dependence—Testosterone—just to keep my voice and beard. Sex? Well, yes, now that comes in a bottle, too, just like my thoughts and feelings."

Kevin had made it clear to Amanda that now, he could not be a biological father. By the time they had discovered the cancer in his second testicle, he had chosen not to bank sperm, despite impassioned pleas. She had visited him in California where he was recovering and helped him lace up his girdle that helped prevent his fifty staples from popping and walked him down the driveway and past the neighbor's house, and eventually, after a few days, down to the end of the block, a journey which had left Kevin winded and deflated. The two of them didn't speak for a couple of weeks after that, Amanda joining her family on vacation in San Juan. They each needed some air after the gravity of it all. When they did reconnect, Kevin's anguish and grief still weighed on both of them.

"I don't want to be a bitter, cynical, grudge-holding man," he wrote to her. "I want to be free, to love and be loved, but I feel like the prison walls just got a lot closer. While I'm not exactly macho, it's a rather enormous assault on my psyche to know that my 'manhood' (what's left of it anyway) comes from a needle. Every two weeks. Just so I can get it up. Harsh."

After the surgery, Kevin retreated to Aspen, Colorado. The fresh air and snow powder there had a calming effect, and he tried not to think of the staples that marked him, the weight he had lost, the regattas unsailed, the children unborn. The idea of sailing the Laser, a class that placed incredible demands on the abdominal muscles, was torturous. Even when Kevin was in good health, sailing that class felt like doing sit-ups for twenty excruciating minutes.

Increasingly, Kevin was being offered a greater array of antipsychotic drugs. A few months earlier, his doctors had changed his medication from lithium to Prozac, then to Depakote, Kevin being one of the countless patients for whom there is no one perfect drug, nor mix of them. In Aspen, he mostly took Depakote, and for the most part he found it effective in stabilizing his moods. Sometimes he would smoke some pot, relax in front of the fire, and imagine himself sailing, surrounded by birds and islands, sun and waves.

And after years of resistance, Kevin was starting to see a therapist regularly. As part of his treatment, he began reading the works of Carl Jung and became fascinated by Jung's interest in the unconscious aspects of people, and of Jung's focus on spirituality and creativity. The rethinking of his bipolar disorder through a Jungian framework proved helpful for Kevin, as it helped him probe further into his dreams and delusions, analyzing the content of them for what they could mean rather than merely dismissing them. This felt like a welcome contrast to what Kevin had perceived was the message that doctors had given him before: "Here's a sick bipolar person who needs to be kept on the rails."

Kevin's quest to understand his brain through books lead him to reading James Joyce's *Ulysses*, which instantly became one of Kevin's defining works as a reader. A famously dense read, *Ulysses* (the title drawn from the Latinized name of the hero of Homer's epic poem the *Odyssey*) tells the tale of Leopold Bloom, a man in Dublin on an ordinary day—June 16, 1904—over the span of eighteen episodes and roughly 265,000 words. Joyce captured the stream of consciousness that Kevin felt when he was in The Show and thus served as a sort of familiar spirit from another moment in time, a hand from the past reaching out to Kevin in the 1990s. In some ways, the book frightened him in its remarkable accuracy and understanding of his own story; he had never seen someone else's mind spinning just like his on a page, such vivid access into another person's inner world. What's more, Joyce, like Kevin, believed deeply in the power of coincidences.

For years, scholars have debated Joyce's mental state when he wrote the book, as well as questioning how he could have come to understand his daughter Lucia's schizophrenia so well. Jung himself had analyzed Joyce, his daughter, and his epic writing and concluded that Joyce and his daughter were two souls going to the bottom of a river, "one falling and the other diving." Over the years, Kevin had read the work of other artists later deemed to have bipolar tendencies, including Ernest Hemingway and Virginia Woolf, but they hadn't resonated with him the same way that

Joyce did. Kevin could read Joyce with the ease of most people tearing through a summer beach read, the author's words vibrating in his head like a good piece of music, his feeling for the text transcending his need to explain it.

Meanwhile, he kept writing to Amanda.

"I'm fighting a war with my body. Please don't take the stray bullets personally."

AMANDA

ONE DAY, KEVIN showed up at Amanda's dorm room at Brown and announced that the two of them were going to Boston, just an hour or so away on Interstate 95.

Sure, Amanda told him.

He seemed wound up as his sentences sputtered out with rapid speed and he briskly paced around her dorm room with alacrity. He told her he wanted to fly to Bermuda, that they deserved a vacation and a chance to get away from it all. They would drive to Boston's Logan International Airport and buy a couple of plane tickets at the counter for the next flight out.

By now, Amanda could quickly spot the difference between "normal" Kevin and "not normal" Kevin. This was the latter, but the thought of calling 911 didn't occur to her. She thought maybe a short drive, not necessarily one to the airport in Boston, might help him wind down.

For the last few days, Amanda had noticed a difference in Kevin's routine. He had moved back to Providence to coach after leaving Aspen, and had seemed to handle the change well in some respects, but he had been talking more and sleeping less. He stayed up late writing and skateboarding, and told Amanda that he was using "alternative" treatment methods, but he didn't specify what that meant.

The two of them hopped into Kevin's white Toyota truck with Kevin behind the wheel and began their journey to Boston. Along the way, they stopped at a Dunkin Donuts where Kevin walked ahead of Amanda and plunged a $100 bill into the tip jar.

Amanda wondered what she should do. If she went back in to retrieve the money, she risked leaving Kevin alone with the car keys. She also worried about his doing something irrational, like trying to physically hurt himself or, God forbid, take his own life. But somehow, she was able to dart back inside and snag the cash, though not without embarrassment.

They got back into the car and Kevin brushed off Amanda's offers to drive, leaving two tons of machinery navigated by a man who was rambling about a show of some sort. The Director wanted them to go to Bermuda and he would put them up somewhere that was really, really nice and secluded, a fantasy that was as pastoral as this moment wasn't.

Kevin and Amanda arrived at the airport and walked to a ticket counter. Kevin asked what it would take to get to Bermuda as soon as possible. From the other side of the counter, the agent politely told them that there were no more flights to Bermuda that night, but she could book them on the first one out in the morning.

That's great, Amanda thought. The flight delay provided her with a window in which she could lure Kevin to an airport hotel room and hopefully get him to relax. Maybe if he fell asleep, he would wake up with the mania having spun out of him somehow overnight. Then, the two of them could drive back to Providence and deal with the expense of the tickets once safely back home.

That's not what happened.

Amanda and Kevin did find an airport hotel where Amanda tried to soothe him, but as the hours lumbered on, he only seemed to be getting more anxious, pacing, rambling, and fiddling around more mercilessly than he had in her dorm room. He indicated no interest in sleeping at all that night and spent some time lying in the bathtub, reading the hotel Bible, flipping through its tissue-paper pages with deep interest. He asked Amanda whether she was "with him" or not, a mixture of confusion and anxiety in his voice. She assured him that she was, but still remained confused by the ask.

Soon it was time to head back to the airport to catch their flight to Bermuda.

With Amanda in the passenger seat once again, Kevin got behind the wheel and began to drive fast and recklessly, with no regard for curbs or medians. The truck, roaring, jolted back and forth and forward through space in a crooked, jerking motion, Kevin and Amanda with it. Amanda pleaded for him to slow down or let her drive, to no avail.

Kevin told her to grab the "oh shit" handle on the truck—the grip located just above the window—to steady herself, a feeble maneuver in the face of the truck's movement.

"If you don't stop bringing me down," he said, "I'm going to hurt you."

He careened the car toward Boston Harbor as Amanda's scream pierced the air.

KEVIN

POLICE OFFICERS PICKED up Kevin after he drove his car onto the curb at arrivals at Logan. That was after he had hit a fence, the fence that had kept him and Amanda from plunging into New England waters, a haunting possibility that law enforcement and doctors would learn about in the hours that followed.

The police handed him off to medical personnel, and just before three o'clock that afternoon, an ambulance pulled in to the rolling grounds of McLean Hospital with Kevin inside. An affiliate of Harvard Medical School, McLean was founded in 1811 and some of its grounds were landscaped by the famed Central Park landscape architect Frederick Law Olmsted (who would later be treated at McLean and die there in 1903), and it had a regal yet friendly feel. Legend has it that it was Mary Sawyer, a McLean attendant who joined the staff in the 1830s, who inspired the nursery rhyme "Mary Had a Little Lamb." Unlike many other institutions, McLean modeled its treatment of patients after restorative Quaker models rather than punitive ones. Over the years it had housed many famous patients, including the Nobel Prize–winning mathematician John Nash, the musicians Ray Charles and Steven Tyler, the poets Sylvia Plath and Robert Lowell, the writer Susanna Kaysen, and, not long before the time that Kevin walked through its doors, the author David Foster Wallace. With such an illustrious reputation, McLean seemed to Kevin like the perfect place for the star of The Show to recover from his latest episode.

The doctors there found Kevin wildly manic, talking in spurts of peace, beauty. "Distractible," one wrote in his chart. "Grandiose with flight of ideas." The doctors also confirmed his bipolar disorder diagnosis, adding that Kevin was "likely to be in denial of his reported disorder and his need for continued treatment."

At first, Kevin refused medication. Subsequently, he was found naked on the side of his gurney, trying to walk with restraints and at "serious risk" of having the gurney fold on him. The doctors told Kevin that he either had to have four-point restraints or take medication. He chose the latter and soon was heavily sedated.

Later, a tone of joy still in his voice, Kevin told the doctors all about the plot of The Show and about preparing to compete in the Olympics. All of that sounded like delusional thinking, but upon examining his records more closely, the doctors realized that at least part of Kevin's conversation wasn't as deranged as it had seemed. Kevin also told the doctors that he'd started experimenting with his medication, though he knew he shouldn't have, but he wouldn't tell them why.

At McLean, Kevin returned to his habit of ceremonial cigarette breaks. These became a focus of his day, a central goal for him to work toward; he relished having the small fire between his hands, having control over something, even if it was small and only for a few minutes. Smoking gave him a chance to socialize, making him feel as though he was leaving the hospital for a short time and fantasizing about who he thought he might be or might want to be once he was really out. He also ate a fair amount, even though the food was bland. Taking one bite after another made him feel comfortable, and eating was another thing over which he had agency in a landscape where otherwise there was none.

Hospital life gave him plenty of time to contemplate the consequences of his actions, and the guilt sank in. There had been too many near misses in the last episode of The Show for comfort. What if he and Amanda had really crashed into the harbor? What if his car had hit innocent pedestrians? The Show had created annoyances like lost wallets and such in the past, but this was the first time his mania had put not only his own life in danger but the lives of others, including one of someone he loved deeply. It felt nothing short of miraculous that no one had gotten hurt. How could he possibly begin to explain or apologize for what had happened?

The questions floated around his still-clouded mind as he roamed McLean's halls. Group therapy can irritate many patients, particularly if they are coming down from a manic episode, but Kevin enjoyed it most of the time, feeling a sense of connection with his fellow patients. He also quickly understood that good behavior served as the currency that could buy him out of McLean and back to his life outside, to sailing. They weren't about to let him out if he couldn't manage hanging out with a few people, crazy or otherwise. He enjoyed the music room, the kind doctors, and the thoughtful staff. His sense of spiritual crisis began to lift.

What especially bothered Kevin about his latest episode was that in The Show, for the first time, he had felt more persecuted rather than euphoric. There were people who were out to get him, and as he had gripped the steering wheel of his truck, he had thought that even Amanda was against him. How had the thoughts in his mind become so scrambled, so tossed and turned? Kevin could navigate a boat with the best in the world, graduate from an Ivy League school, hold his own in a conversation with his doctor parents and their peers. But for a few moments in the wee morning hours near Logan Airport, he hadn't been able to trust his own girlfriend, or himself, for reasons that he was the first to admit made no sense.

He found himself perturbed over what to do about his relationship with Amanda. She was young, beautiful, and intelligent, and she had her whole future ahead of her. Kevin couldn't help but wonder if he was standing in the way of that. He felt that she should be able to live her life, make her own choices, and see other people, places, and things without having to worry about him. His bipolar disorder and cancer were bad enough, but he also brought the complications of hoping to be a traveling professional sailor to the relationship.

Kevin finally told the McLean nurses and doctors why he had gone off his medication. He felt great without them, he said, which was a nice break from feeling terrible. Like the other times he'd gone off his meds, he hadn't told anyone his intentions beforehand—he saw no good in that. Now, though, he could tell that he had been playing some sort of game, both with himself and with others. Would anyone notice that he wasn't taking the pills? There was such a fine line between being off his meds and feeling better, and being off his meds and spiraling out of control. At McLean, Kevin received Haldol, a drug that typically takes only thirty to sixty seconds to take effect, and it is most potent in stemming psychotic bouts, be they from bipolar disorder, schizophrenia, or a bad LSD trip.

Because of the heavy downers, Kevin had a hard time reading or writing, a torturous experience, as he was a man in need of a creative outlet. When the tools for processing words did come back to him, he sat and wrote letters to friends and family. Checkered with crossed-out words, they lacked the eloquence that usually came to him so easily. His typically clear penmanship became a series of scribbles, diagrams, and drawings, though he also realized that he was now more willing to be disorganized. Poetry flowed, which emboldened him, and he felt a sense of peace when writing it, as it was just him and his thoughts. He wasn't trying to please his professors, Amanda, his friends, his family, his sailing teammates, or even the audience of The Show. Sailing rewarded creativity in some ways, but Kevin felt as though most sailing decisions were binary. One either tacked, maneuvering the bow of a boat into the wind, or didn't. Decisions were based on yes-or-no questions, whereas poetry felt like the opposite, a free form in which the more creative side of Kevin's brain could be looser.

Still, sailing continued to make its voice heard. When Kevin's parents learned about his second Boston episode, their reaction was to help get their son back on the water. It was there that he seemed most at peace and most focused, working toward a tangible goal. It was there he should return.

AMANDA

AMANDA AND KEVIN had talked about his mania at length in person, on the phone, and in their letters. But the near plunge into the harbor immediately showed her that the consequences of those lows could be far greater than she had realized. They could even put her life in jeopardy. Being close to Kevin was what she longed for, but it was also what could kill her.

She remembered Kevin calling her more than a year before and telling her all about what had happened in Japan. She had stood there in her dorm room holding the phone and tried to understand, among other things, why he had wandered out into the streets of Tokyo with his eyes closed. And as she tried to stretch her brain around his twisted logic, she remembered thinking, *This guy seems a little nuts. Maybe I shouldn't be with him.*

Yet she stayed. The time it would have taken for the truck to plunge down the ledge a few feet toward the harbor couldn't have been more than a few seconds, but it replayed slowly in her mind. The moment that the truck landed on four wheels on the ground, she was instantly shocked not to be drowning, not to be fighting in the water for her final breaths. As she took in the miracle of her nonaquatic surroundings—some kind of freight yard—Kevin kept his eyes fixed ahead and kept driving along as if they hadn't just nearly missed death. That, perhaps more than the plunge itself, had made her realize that this wasn't the version of Kevin she had fallen in love with in physics class, the Kevin of *Peter and the Wolf* and of love notes, but, was, rather, some distortion of him.

When the cops approached them moments later, the car clumsily perched on the curb, Amanda had struggled to explain to them that Kevin wasn't a criminal. Whatever his intentions, the case that he posed no danger to himself or others was hard to make.

Kevin had volleyed from being giddy about the prospect of a tropical vacation to being dark and paranoid, suspicious of what Amanda's "role" was. It was almost as if there were some sort of lever in his mind that could flip on or off, positive or negative, and Amanda had no clue which direction things could go, or who was in charge of the switch. She was angry at the manic Kevin because he had put her through hell, but she also didn't know if she could ask the familiar, nonmanic Kevin to apologize for the manic Kevin. She felt angry but had no idea where to place that fury and frustration; at times it seemed as though the man who had wronged her had left the room and had left a different version of Kevin standing before her.

Her parents back home in New York, coming from a place of love, wanted her to partner and partner well. Amanda didn't know how she could defend Kevin to her mother, and even less to her father, to whom she was so close, when Kevin had nearly killed her. She knew her friends back in Providence would support her when she tried to explain Kevin's episodes, but she wouldn't be able to admit as easily that part of her thrived on being Kevin's caregiver, his strength, his spine. She was as stable as he was unstable, a quick emergency responder, deriving huge pleasure from being a rock. Yes, he had nearly killed her in a fit of mania, but she would be lying if she said that the adrenaline rush leading up to that moment in the truck hadn't been precisely that—a rush.

As she spent time in and around hospitals with Kevin, listening to hospital chatter, Amanda shifted away from her earlier interest in physics to an interest in her father's field, health care. At first she fought the impulse, but the more she thought about it, the more she realized that she would find the challenge and rigor of medicine fulfilling.

Amanda was still madly in love with Kevin in spite of the trauma. After several days, Kevin was ready to come home to Providence. Amanda spoke with the physicians at McLean about what was best for him, and she vowed to help him recover and stay consistent with his health, his medication. To Kevin, who didn't know how to begin to apologize to Amanda, it seemed nothing short of miraculous that she didn't dump him.

GORDON

IT WASN'T THAT Gordon didn't have the money to pay for Kevin's medical expenses, it was that spending it felt so pointless, wasteful even. How was his son ever going to learn if his father kept financially supporting his illness? They were four years into this madness and nothing seemed to be improving. In fact, it only seemed to be getting worse. To Gordon, it was unfathomable that Kevin had gone off his meds even when he knew the consequences of doing so.

Over the phone, Gordon told Kevin that he would no longer pay his medical bills, including the insurance that covered his psychiatric care and hospitalizations. Kevin reeled at the news, wondering how he was going to cope with the bills and all the insurance forms on his own.

Kevin and his family had already spent countless hours arguing with insurance companies about what was covered and what wasn't, one hoop after another. His father and mother were both medical professionals and they still struggled to deal with it all. There were moments when they all wondered, What hope did he or anyone else have in navigating the system?

KEVIN

THERE WAS SOMETHING about seeing his mother's wedding that triggered Kevin's fears about his own marital future. For weeks leading up to the gathering, he had looked forward to bringing Amanda as his date, but something about the environment sent him into a tailspin about their relationship. The thought that he had had at McLean, that Amanda had so much ahead of her and he was such a mess, deepened in his mind, a conversation of doubt in which Amanda was not engaged. How could they possibly stay together?

Susanne and her new love, Ted Lammot, were married in North Hatley, Canada, in May 1993, not far from where Susanne had grown up in Eastern Townships, with Kevin, Kristina, and Amanda in attendance. All these years later, there Susanne was in a wedding dress, older, but not far from where she had spent endless hours on the water with her late father. Ted and Susanne had met at a party not long after her divorce, and she was charmed from the moment he offered to drive her home. Kevin welcomed Ted into the family. He was smart and kind, and he had a warm and compassionate attitude toward Kevin's mental health, never judging him. And he actually listened, which was refreshing.

Ted had seven children from his marriages. Susanne got along with all of them and dated Ted for six years before deciding to get married, both feeling no need to rush and wanting the dust to settle from their respective divorces. The large, combined family mostly got along and all enjoyed each other's company. Kevin and Susanne had different political beliefs from Ted, who leaned to the right, but no one minded much.

Kevin, like his mother, had refocused. He had taken a job at a Coffee Bean to help pay for some of his medical expenses now that his dad had opted out. He also did some coaching, which he enjoyed, but it wasn't particularly lucrative, and worked a few stints at a car wash. At age twenty-three, he still had time to figure out the feasibility of a bid for the 1996 Games.

Milling about at the reception following the ceremony, looking at his family, Kevin worried about how he and Amanda could ever build a family together, particularly after the removal of his second testicle. What was she doing here? Did she really understand the implications of what the rest of her life would look like with him? Amanda was intelligent, part of what had drawn him to her in the first place, yet at this juncture, she seemed naive, and unaware.

He broke up with her.

AMANDA

KEVIN HAD INVITED her to Canada to be his wedding date, to spend time with his family—and then to dump her?

It didn't make any sense. She hadn't "done" anything, nor had he. Kevin kept explaining to her that she was only twenty-one and he was nearly twenty-four, that it was unfair for her to spend the rest of her life tethered not only to him, but also to his bipolar disorder. Although he said he understood her heartbreak, she still couldn't see the years ahead and the wide array of options that she would have.

Amanda couldn't tell whether he was speaking from his heart or was on the edge of another episode. But she did know how she felt—devastated, and unsure how to handle the sudden rejection. Everything on Brown's campus seemed to remind her of him, and during some moments, the place that had been her haven started to feel like a cage. She was trapped in memories involving Kevin that she was more than ready to forget, but she had barely known life there without him.

Yet she was also at a juncture of her own. She would graduate from Brown the following year and had decided to go take some summer courses and perhaps pursue medicine, a track that would likely put her geography at odds with Kevin's. Once she would have considered that a hardship, but she now wondered if it would be for the best.

There it was between the two of them: complicated. They were no longer together but still felt immensely attracted to each other. It wasn't really clear to Amanda why they couldn't just date, be boyfriend and girlfriend, as they had been before.

She had no choice but to move ahead with her life, painful though it was to be doing so without Kevin.

KEVIN

AS HE STOOD outside New York's Grand Central Terminal, all Kevin could think about was Amanda. He felt completely deflated. By his own choice, he felt as though he had lost the love of his life.

It was the summer after his mother's wedding and Kevin was living near Long Island Sound, where he had taken a coaching job. Before dawn one morning, feeling that he needed some stimulation, he had driven into the city via its snakes of surrounding highways, just on the cusp of the workday morning, when garbage trucks clang and coffee carts open their windows. He parked his white Toyota truck, still bearing California plates, on a curb in Midtown and walked toward the opulent Grand Central Terminal. Much like Tokyo's Imperial Palace, Grand Central was the city's central temple, a Beaux-Arts train hub, constantly aflutter with the sharp elbows of commuters and the curiosity of tourists, a practical traffic hub with an aura of religious grandeur.

He stood outside Grand Central, thinking of love and of Michael Jordan. The NBA player had just finished his first three-part finals win with the Chicago Bulls, and his star, fueled by Nike's massive Air Jordan campaign, had taken his name and profile to a level never seen before for an athlete. A new way of thinking about sports marketing had arrived; Jordan was a modern global icon. One could travel anywhere in the world and find a red Chicago Bulls jersey with Jordan's "23" on it, or people talking about Jordan's coveted shoes, which had caused controversy, religious fervor, and even violence and death.

Shoes as a means to battle poverty would be part of a great way of saving the world, Kevin thought. He looked down at his own Birkenstocks, then found a pay phone nearby. He "called" Birkenstock headquarters, hoping to secure permission to use footage of him in an advertisement for their "Air Jesus" campaign. He quickly "negotiated the deal," then took his Birkenstocks off and left them behind, both to punctuate the phone call and to give the cameras a good shot of the product. A benevolent passerby noticed that Kevin had left his sandals behind and tried to hand them back to him, but Kevin wasn't interested.

The passerby confused him. Couldn't the man, possibly an extra on The Show, see that the Birkenstocks were a living sculpture, meant to be dropped there and left for all time? Kevin told the man that a museum might want the sandals and that he trusted him to look after them.

It was still early morning, well before the nine o'clock rush hour but well after sunrise, when Kevin retrieved his white Toyota truck and drove to Long Island in search of Amanda. He knew that she was taking some summer courses there and would understand. The weather was humid and thick, but maybe they could have a picnic and talk things through.

Kevin knew that Amanda was taking classes, but he wasn't sure where the medical school campus was located. He found another college campus, figured that it must be right, parked, strolled around, sat in on a math class, and carried a picnic basket that he had purchased a short time earlier. As he roamed the grounds outside, someone asked him what he was doing there and Kevin became upset, hurling the contents of the basket onto the lawn, thinking that he was distributing the wealth. He didn't understand why more people couldn't see the virtues of sharing.

Next he climbed to the top of a building, arousing the suspicions of a professor, who then called the police. Kevin had shed his shirt and shoes and appeared "disoriented," according to the professor, who asked him what he was doing there.

I'm here to see Amanda, Kevin said. *In the health department.*

The professor and a supervisor began a search for Kevin's vehicle. They found his white pickup parked in a walkway behind a building with its radio blaring and engine running.

As the responders tried to assess the situation, they found a medical bracelet in the back of Kevin's truck indicating that he had bipolar disorder. His family had persuaded him to get the bracelet at some point, but he hadn't worn it for long. It felt like a heavy weight and was a conversation starter for a talk he never wanted to have.

The responders transported him to a nearby psychiatric facility for evaluation.

This episode of The Show had concluded. At the hospital in Long Island, Kevin returned to drawing, one of the few things that made sense to him, as the meds kicked in. He drew a man and labeled one of his legs "crotch," a reference to his relationship and desire for Amanda, one of the pillars of his life, sailing being the other. He wondered what he was without sailing and without Amanda.

Although most people would find commanding a complex vessel in front of a worldwide crowd to be incredibly stressful, Kevin was starting to realize that in some ways, sailing was a meditative act for him, something that brought him back to who he thought he was and kept him

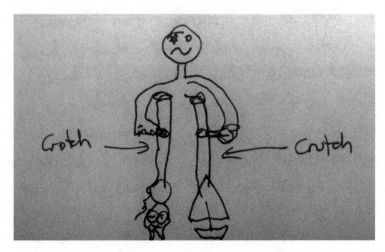

Crotch/Crutch

happily planted there. His stability on the waves was what he was known for, what had earned him attention from the time he was a child. Kevin tried to tell himself that he was not the sum of his sailing results, but the notion was so woven into his psyche that he still struggled to come to terms with it.

•

Even after Kevin dumped Amanda, the two had tried, briefly, to live together in Providence. Yet as they tried to reconcile, Kevin had learned that Amanda was dating some other guy that summer, someone she'd met when leading bike tours. She begged him to move back anyway and to give things another shot in spite of all of the drama, in spite of her having had a relationship with someone else at a time when Kevin thought she was with him.

"Feels like a lot of pressure to swallow it all and be the Dali [sic] Lama," Kevin wrote in his journal. "Especially what with the way it all went down and all, for the Relationship to essentially ride on the way I handle the pressure."

The idea of dating seemed too overwhelming to think about. Kevin sat at coffee shops in Providence, staring at the array of ads, notices, and proposals stapled over one another on bulletin boards, and thought about how it was the perfect visual of the inside of his brain, a scattered tapestry of conflicting messages, missives being fired out into the world with no knowledge of their outcome. He ate cheap English muffins and let the food in his refrigerator spoil without throwing it out. For now, he was going to sulk, write poetry, and plan a trip across the Atlantic, far away from Amanda and the whole mess of it all.

"I've 'given up' on the Future," Kevin wrote, "(wife, the whole kids, Volvo, etc.)." He was on edge. Maybe he needed a "real job"? Sail in the afternoons and write at night?

If life was a choice, Kevin felt less and less able to opt in. With his mind surrounded by pain and darkness so vast, so untouchable by comfort, suicide started to seem like the only way out. He detested himself as a person and wondered how he could ever be worthy of the love of his friends and family. If he ended it all and was not around, they could get on with their lives, he thought, even though this sentiment was quite literally the opposite of the regular string of encouragements and "I love yous" they sent his way. Yet suicide sometimes also felt like yet another thing that he could fail at.

Leo Tolstoy, writing about his own thoughts of ending his own life said that even though he was a "fortunate man," he walked from room to room of his home with a rope, contemplating hanging himself from a ceiling beam, and stopped hunting with a gun to rid himself of suicide's lure. "I myself did not know what I wanted," Tolstoy wrote. "I was afraid of life, I struggled to get rid of it, and yet I hoped for something from it."

In addition to such thoughts of dissatisfaction like Tolstoy's, Kevin thought about destiny, coincidence, synchronicity, and how there may be no final answer. He felt as though he had seen things no one else on the planet had, but didn't know what to do with the knowledge. What's worse, his attempts at trying to exist back on earth weren't going too well. He wrote:

> Now we are faced with a difficult situation for a man who is
> displeased with his life—was it supposed to happen at all, like
> this, some other way, to someone else?. . . Am I responsible then or
> not? Can I ever be sure I have greater significance than a

*conglomeration of molecules which affect others, sometimes predict-
ably, sometimes unpredictably, but most often violently?*

Someday, Kevin realized, everyone he knew would be dead, everyone
would be forgotten. It all felt wildly pointless.

One afternoon when Kevin was violently depressed, he went sailing,
but he didn't feel the water or hear the wind the way he normally did.
All he could feel was how absent he was and he returned to the shore
even more disappointed by the water's failure to heal. In other, calmer
moments, Kevin thought back to his episodes on The Show and reex-
amined their plots, themes, and possible hidden messages in the same
way that a museumgoer stares at paintings, trying to find significance
in the swirls, the use of paint and other materials, and the placement of
colors and forms on a canvas. Like works of art, his delusions, however
destructive, had motifs: saving the world, grandiosity, liberation. In
his journal, he wrote about television, "how the cable comes into your
room like a tarantula who lost his bus fare and begs you to plug him
back into the bathtub because that's where all the cool short-circuits
happen, and that means Post-Revolutionary leaps of paint and coffee
onto different varieties of bruised apples." What did it all mean?

Kevin recognized that he could embark on a new beginning. "But I
don't know where the start line is," he wrote. "I haven't the foggiest idea
what it looks like. I don't know if I want to race/play/go anywhere."

He booked a flight to France, and shortly before getting on the plane,
he wrote:

*Real life heroes live 24 hours a day, not just 2 hours in a football
game*

Big Daddy *Cat on a Hot Tin Roof*

And:

I want to live like a hero, present, peaceful, graceful, and kind. I wish to spend time in a Buddhist monastery. I want to compose music, to understand and know and feel tone and rhythm. I wish to be loved.

•

Nestled along the French Riviera, Saint-Tropez is a jewel box of cottages and resort homes, a longtime mecca for the most elite of jetsetters. The beaches are postcard-perfect, with neatly arranged umbrellas shading tanned bodies on rows of lawn chairs. For most visitors, stress doesn't get packed in their bags along with sunscreen and swimsuits, and if it does, the beach air whisks it away.

But Kevin had followed Kevin to his destination. Despite his presence in a bright, exotic locale, he still felt low. As he watched white luxury vessels pass to and fro along the lapis water, he examined the scars from his surgeries and began to process that they were permanent, that he was mourning the biological children he knew he wouldn't have. He ate stale croissants and went for swims in the fresh, open water. He wrote and spoke in French, swallowed his pills and tried to smile, all while grieving for the loss of his fertility and future with Amanda. "I feel a tremendous burden knowing I cannot live for my biological purpose on this earth, and so must serve some other purpose, or live for myself," he wrote. "It should make me free, but I feel obligated to make a future that cannot rely on convention."

Kevin still hoped to find work on a boat, and he made his way to Antibes, another Riviera resort town, tucked between Cannes and Nice, with a skyline that resembled a castle of a bygone era. Kevin found the waters of Antibes and the constant twinkle of the fountains that lined its streets soothing. The entire city seemed like a museum piece, offering some sprinkles of optimism. "The awesome thing about water is that it is never exactly the same as it once was," Kevin wrote in his journal. "And never will be . . . [Water] allows parts and whole to dance an ever reinvented, ever beautiful dance."

He wondered if Amanda knew that two men were in love with her at once. He didn't think it was by chance that he had met her—or that he had gotten cancer, or that he was on the beaches of France at that particular moment. He believed in destiny and still saw Amanda as part of his, even if the specifics weren't making sense at present.

Onward to Monterosso, Italy, where Kevin watched old fishermen, sat in an ice cream shop and wrote a letter to Amanda. When Sinéad O'Connor's "Nothing Compares 2 U" came over the speakers, he cried. Then to Genoa, where the sight of children and infants made him weep, too. Deep in the net of melancholia, even the slightest thing could shoot Kevin further down a negativity spiral. The knowledge of that nonsensicalness to his triggers made his mind shoot down even more.

His sailing job hunt was proving fruitless. One place after another said he was too qualified.

Great, he thought. Another thing he had failed at.

•

Kevin flew home to the United States and upon landing in New York, he dreamed about meeting Amanda there and making up. In his fantasy, somehow they would reconcile, be stronger than ever. He loved her. In spite of his dumping her at his mother's wedding, they were meant to be together. Being in her hometown made it painfully apparent that time and distance hadn't healed his heartbreak; it had only festered.

Kevin roamed around the city for a couple of days, writing poetry and watching people, before making his way to Providence. It didn't go well there, as Amanda officially dumped Kevin. She told him that she had struggled with it all and needed some time to grow into her own person without him. She had agonized over it. But she was clear: it was over.

Carrying his heartbreak from France with him back stateside, Kevin reconsidered his career and decided that he wanted to change the world and wondered if law school was the way to do it. It seemed like a relatively straight, sensible path, and he had a couple of friends from Brown who were on the legal track and seemingly doing well. For Kevin, law school still felt like a form of personal defeat. Lawyers weren't the stars of big sneaker contracts or TV commercials, nor did they win gold medals.

Kevin took the LSAT even as sailing still beckoned. He wondered if there was a way to train for the 1996 Olympic trials without investing all of his life's meaning in it; "just be peaceful and steady about it," he wrote. Slowly but surely, full-time careers in sailing were becoming possible, as races that paid athletes to participate were becoming more and more common. If that trend continued, Kevin thought, he might not only be able to use the money that he earned racing to subsidize his Olympic goals, but get some extra time on the water to boot.

He had a plan. One that didn't include Amanda.

AMANDA

SHE HAD MADE up her mind. She was going to call Kevin and tell him that she wanted to give it another try. She loved him and wanted to spend her life with him, build a family. It had been two years since they had officially been together, and she felt every one of them. Several exams and admissions applications later, Amanda had been admitted to Stony Brook Medical School on Long Island not far from where she had grown up. A prestigious research institution, it was housed in a sprawling complex of buildings, nestled near the calming waters and beaches of the Hamptons. She had heard some occasional buzz from mutual friends about what he was up to, but for the most part, his whereabouts (and relationship status) were a guess on her end.

She picked up the phone and dialed his number in California, recalling that he had moved back there after leaving Providence a few years before. He picked up. It was good to hear his voice. They exchanged some small talk, which she hoped would escalate into medium and bigger talk.

Then Kevin said that the timing of her call was funny because he had been about to reach out to her. He had big news.

He was getting married.

Amanda felt stunned. She had no idea who this woman was, what her relationship with Kevin was like, or even how Kevin felt about it.

All she knew was that he wasn't marrying her.

KEVIN

ANNE SHARED KEVIN'S passion for fitness, so it was no surprise that the two had met at the gym in California where Kevin worked out and where she was employed as a personal trainer. When she and Kevin were together, from the outside they looked like the quintessential California couple: tan, fit, youthful.

Kevin didn't have the same kind of deep, intellectual connection with Anne that he had with Amanda, but they enjoyed each other's company. Anne had been one of the first women he had met when he moved back to the West Coast, and it seemed perfectly fine to march ahead into matrimony.

In December 1995, the two were married. Later, Kevin couldn't remember whether he had even discussed his bipolar disorder diagnosis with Anne before the wedding, but if he had, it certainly hadn't been at length—a far cry from the long, deep conversations he had had with Amanda about it and how it related to his views on being human. His wedding, too, was a blur in his mind. In hindsight, he felt oddly passive about it, as if he was just going through the motions.

It had been three years since his last manic episode on The Show, and earlier that spring he had staged a remarkable comeback on the water. He had beaten forty-three other sailors to win the Laser title at the Alamitos Bay Yacht Club Olympic Classes Regatta. Then, on the heels of that win, he had won the Laser North Americans, besting eighty-eight other boats. The timing was perfect—the Olympic trials were months away and he was ascending just in time to earn a berth to compete in Atlanta. Then, the U.S. Olympic festival.

Sailing is, by nature, an escapist sport. For centuries, its practitioners have spoken of leaving their troubles on shore as they cast off, the bliss of the isolation of nature wrapped around them, the vastness of the sea. Kevin's bipolar disorder now seemed to be under control, but he was becoming increasingly concerned about something else he wanted to escape, something that could directly affect his sailing future—his testosterone injections.

In the 1990s, the World Anti-Doping Agency, the governing body that today oversees drug testing for the Olympics, had not yet been formally established. Nonetheless, testosterone had already been banned in Olympic sports because of its performance-enhancing qualities.

In March 1995, Kevin reached out to the officials with the United States Olympic Committee and explained that he needed to inject himself with testosterone on a regular basis—not to give himself a competitive advantage, but to keep his testosterone levels normal, as his two testicles were gone. In the testicular cancer survivor community, the treatment was commonplace, but no athlete had ever challenged the IOC on its testosterone injection policy.

Long before therapeutic use exemption waivers became a common practice (which gave some athletes permission to take drugs that were deemed medically necessary to their health but may otherwise have been on a banned substance list) Kevin wanted to get some sort of written agreement to ensure that should he make the Olympic team, he wouldn't be rejected for using what for him was a lifesaving drug. If anything, in his position, he was at a disadvantage. Kevin pointed out to officials that even if he showed up at the opening ceremonies on the day he took a testosterone injection, most of the men around him would still have more of it in their blood than he would. (If he showed up at the end of his testosterone cycle, some of the women could, too.)

Four months later, the director of drug control administration for the United States Olympic team wrote back to say that the "consensus opinion" was that a "waiver could not be granted for such treatment with this banned substance." Dismayed, Kevin appealed to the International Olympic Committee (IOC) in Lausanne, Switzerland. Famously opaque, the organization was then controlled by President Juan Antonio Samaranch, who since 1988 continues a multi-generational culture of corruption and secrecy in international sports. During his reign, the financial fortunes of the Games had ballooned, and Samaranch insisted on traveling via limousine, lodging at luxury hotels, and being addressed as His Excellency. Clear and logical governance, particularly concerning anti-doping matters, was not one of the group's priorities.

Backing Kevin's case was the United States Sailing Association, the governing body for the sport in the United States, and the American Civil Liberties Union, which had agreed to legally represent him. As part of the process, the medical records of Kevin's cancer history, including the opinions and diagnoses of various doctors, were made public, but the details of his bipolar disorder were not discussed, nor known to the IOC.

Kevin's conflict was a classic David-versus-Goliath tale, and the press was eager to cover the battle of a single person up against one of sport's most complex, corrupt, and intimidating institutions. Kevin told reporters about how his Olympic quest had put him more than $25,000 in debt— the cost of his training, equipment, and nutritional requirements climbing way up over his highest budget estimates. There was also a certain irony in drug testing officials being so concerned with Kevin's testosterone shots when many athletes in other sports were quite conspicuously using performance-enhancing drugs and easily evading what little drug testing existed at the time.

For years, people had been telling Kevin that he was crazy for thinking he was on The Show, a person of interest to the mass media. But by the winter of 1995, Kevin's war with the IOC was being chronicled by the *New York Times*, the *Washington Post*, and *Good Morning America*, among others, with many journalists putting actual cameras and recorders in front of him. What's more, his persona in the news was as a cause-driven, American hero, one out to change the world for the better, akin to what he experienced in The Show. In the *Times* national section on February 15, 1996, his case garnered even more print real estate than President Bill Clinton's trip to the Pacific Northwest to assess recent flood damage.

"Many in the field consider Mr. Hall to be the best American hope for a medal in the Laser class," the *Times* wrote. "That hope now appears to be on the verge of collapse."

It had been three years since the removal of Kevin's second testicle, and yet he was forced to relive it all, on a public stage, no less. This wasn't how he had pictured his Olympic dream.

"If the Olympics is not for Kevin Hall, then who is it for?" Mark Rosenbaum, Kevin's ACLU attorney, told the *Times*. "He is the embodiment of the Olympic credo. Instead of keeping him from the starting line, they ought to have him carrying the Olympic torch."

Reports emerged that the IOC was reconsidering its stance and was likely to approve Kevin's right to compete at the Olympics and the U.S. trials. Yet the rumors remained just that—rumors. By mid-April, less than a month before the trials for the Laser class in Savannah, Georgia, were scheduled to begin, Kevin was tirelessly training every day, but still didn't know where things stood. The IOC had said that it wanted to gather more blood samples to measure his testosterone levels.

Finally, at the last minute, Kevin was cleared for the U.S. trials, but not yet the Olympics. Now all he had to do was beat forty-seven other boats to earn his spot.

AMANDA

WHEN AMANDA HAD accepted a summer job to lead mountain bike tours in Europe, she had thought that it would be the perfect escape from the pressures of medical school, from the heartbreak of no longer being with Kevin. All she wanted to do was forget about him.

It didn't work. The news of Kevin's battle with the IOC was plastered all over newspapers, particularly in Olympics-hungry Europe. She read that he was sailing the best he ever had and was a contender for the 1996 Atlanta Games. She even saw him on television, which felt very bizarre because of what he had told her about The Show and their experience together in Boston. In real life, as the cameras rolled, Kevin was on his way to achieving his Olympic dream.

Part of her was happy for him, knowing how much achievement in the sport meant to him. But as she watched the media storm, the strangeness of a real-life Kevin Show manifesting, she couldn't help but think that it should have been her, not Anne, at Kevin's side.

KEVIN

KEVIN HEADED INTO the Atlanta Olympic trials as the man to beat in the Laser class. But unlike the other sailors in Savannah, Georgia, Kevin hadn't spent a season sailing on the international circuit. It was difficult to know whether that would make him fresh and rested at the trials or naive and devoid of experience.

Dozens of boats had gathered at the brand-new Savannah sailing center, a gleaming addition to a Southern city already heavy on charm and buttery cuisine. The Olympic torch would soon make its way through town, en route to Atlanta 250 miles away, where most of the Games would be held, but the sailing events were to be staged at Savannah. Those hoping to watch the races, including Kevin's parents and Anne, boarded viewing boats that positioned them closer to the courses, far from shore. "I'm in much better shape than most of these guys," he told reporters. "I enjoy the gym. My wife is a personal trainer, so it works out for us."

However, Kevin's first four races that weekend "were not pretty," the *Washington Post* reported. Perceived as one of the top Laser sailors going into the competition, by the end of Sunday he was not near the front of the pack, thirteenth of forty-eight boats. The following Monday, with moderate to strong breezes, he made a second- and a third-place finish. That brought him to fourth place in the standings, with ten races to go. Kevin told reporters that he wasn't worried, that he was trying to be patient. If the conditions continued to be strong and rough, it could work to his advantage, as those were the elements in which he thrived. But he was missing his downwind rhythm and he knew it. Although his mind was fully in the present and the Director seemed at rest, his sailing was having a full breakdown. At one point, his boat even capsized.

At age twenty-six, Kevin wondered if he was already sailing like a has-been. He could understand that the 1992 trials may have been too soon for him, but this Olympic cycle was supposed to be his. Most of his competitors appeared sympathetic to his struggle with testicular cancer and the still unresolved matter with the IOC, but some didn't hesitate to take swings. "Kevin is definitely disadvantaged because of his illness," said Andy Lovell, a sailor who had sailed past Kevin to take the lead on Monday of the trials. "He used to be faster downwind, but not anymore."

The trials became hard to watch as Kevin lost control on and off the water. One of his Brown teammates found him curled up in a ball on his boat, "unable to keep his mind together."

Ultimately, Kevin finished in fifth place, not earning a berth for the American team competing in Atlanta.

The testosterone controversy with the IOC was moot.

•

After the Olympics bust, Kevin went back to work crewing, including a stint sailing skiffs in Australia with Morgan Larson, an old friend and sailing partner from his days on the junior circuit. He also went back to his marriage with Anne, still somewhat feeling as if he was on suburban autopilot. Sailing: check. House in California: check. Marriage: check.

Years later, the author Olivia Laing would write about the gentrification of emotions underway in much of Western culture. "Amidst the glossiness of late capitalism," Laing said, "We are fed the notion that all difficult feelings—depression, anxiety, loneliness, rage—are simply a consequence of an unsettled chemistry, a problem to be fixed rather than a response to structural injustice or, on the other hand, to the native texture of embodiment, of doing time, as David Wojnarowicz put it, in a rented body, with all the attendant grief and frustration that entails."

Kevin's rented body had had cancer, twice. But his body was also his means for achieving professional success, his identity, part of what he considered to be his personal fabric. In his marriage and life, just like everyone else, he had to hold it all together. Kevin just wondered why his fight to do so felt so difficult.

From time to time, Amanda appeared in his mind, especially when he was asked to do some coaching work at a sailing event in New York. He wondered what she was doing, how she was faring in medical school, whether she was seeing anyone. He had heard the occasional nugget of news from their shared friends over the years, but he and she hadn't spoken much or exchanged many letters since he'd told her about his marriage to Anne. Kevin didn't feel any anger toward Amanda and still considered himself her friend. He still cared about her and couldn't help but wonder if she felt the same way about him, too. He shook his head. It didn't matter. They had both moved on.

On a whim one day while he was in New York, he gave Amanda a call. He didn't have much spare time while he was in the city, he said, but maybe they could grab a drink somewhere near the airport, just to catch up.

Kevin felt a thrill when he heard her answer. She told him that she was back in town and would love to see him.

AMANDA

MANY OF KEVIN'S episodes, including the near-death car chase in Boston, had happened in or around transit hubs, and as Amanda made her way to LaGuardia Airport to see him, she was starting to see why: there was an inherent manic energy to them, as people were constantly in motion, as if rushing to shake off versions of themselves. Travel, by nature, inspires personality changes, with some travelers returning home with tchotchkes, some with new thoughts, and some with a new wrapper, having shed the old skin behind somewhere. They're places of infinite possibilities: flights to Bombay, Buffalo, or Baghdad, each gate representing an entrance into another experience, or life. (His R.E.M. fandom also brought to mind the song "Airportman," in which great "opportunity" blinks.)

Yet LaGuardia Airport in New York City is a place where charm dare not tread. Originally dedicated in 1939, with little updating since, it is consistently ranked as one of the worst airports in the country, likened by several dignitaries to a product of the Third World rather than an entry into one of the globe's wealthiest cities. Pilots landing there jokingly dub it the USS *LaGuardia*, as it is surrounded by water and so resembles an aircraft carrier. Similarly, it has the dingy lighting of a warehouse, the odors of a locker room, along with the neon-accented signage of the 1970s and fragile, cardboard-like walls that burst at the seams with grumbling travelers. Like much of New York City, LaGuardia seemed to be in a constant state of construction, but unlike the rest of New York City, it didn't seem to show any signs of improvement.

Three years had passed since Amanda and Kevin had broken up, and since their parting, she had had no problem finding boyfriends, her current one being a nice man named David, but they all, in spite of their merits, seemed to exist in her eyes as shadows of Kevin.

As Kevin approached her at the airport, he looked the same as she remembered him and how he had looked on television, tan, athletic, smiling. They sat at one of LaGuardia's questionable bars, ordered beers, and began chatting, the chaos of the airport bustling around them on all sides.

In an effort intended to be polite more than nosy, Amanda asked Kevin how Anne, his wife, was doing. The two had never met, but it just seemed like a nice thing to ask.

"She's not you," Kevin said.

The air left her body. What could he possibly have meant? Was he joking?

He went on to say that he had married the wrong woman. He had been wrong all along. He had been in love with Amanda the whole time. He wanted to get a divorce and spend the rest of his life with her.

They exchanged a kiss. Amanda's knees collapsed.

KEVIN

IT SEEMED INCREDIBLE to Kevin that Amanda, the woman he loved, didn't care about his sailing results, his mental illness, or the fact that he couldn't provide her with biological children. She loved him. It was finally time for the two of them to start the rest of their lives together, even if he had dumped her. They exchanged powerful letters saying as much, and agreed that Kevin needed to sort things out with Anne on his own.

Even as Kevin rejoiced in being reunited with Amanda, sadness loomed, a miasma that seemed to creep into his mind as effortlessly as it left, often with no reason. While some people take comfort in chronicling the things that they're grateful for, Kevin sat down to his journal and made a list of his failures, sorted by the year in which they occurred. He had failed at his relationship, failed to make an Olympic team, and failed to pursue a "real" career outside of sailing, and that was just for a start.

'89 my mind fails me—hospital, medication, no answers just pain.

'90 my body, indeed half my hormone factory, not only fails but threatens to corrupt the rest of me.

SO WHAT, I CAN DO IT, ETC .—2nd at Singlehandeds and feel like a failure.

'91 my mind fails me again, just as I am completing my thesis and preparing to return healthy and accomplished to California.

'92 my mind fails again, fail to coach Julia, make a fool of myself in front of the US Sailing Team, white face, "Amour" hallucination.

'92 my body fails me—we think it's in the blood. Abdomen open, no trip to the Worlds, etc.

'93 just when I thought I could begin trying to recover again, I lose the other testicle.

'93 my mind can't deal and revolts, searching for meaning and fails again {Boston Harbor, trying to get to Bermuda}

'93 again, even with all the medication, but this time I feel my friends are failing me too. {I have pushed them away/made it impossible for them to stay.} My world is collapsing.

'94 removed from all of it, I am essentially carefree & at peace. My responsibilities are few and easily managed, but I can't "afford" it.

'94 just to make sure I had to think of it again, a new prosthesis, still the wrong size, is put in.

'94 even Amanda gives up on me

'94 flee the country, fail even to get a stupid job scrubbing rich peoples boats {"overqualified"!}

'94/5 fail to get accepted to law school

'95/6 fail to resolve IOC issue

'96 fail to win Trials

'96/7 *fail to* do *something with my life, be a great and amazing doctor, lawyer, businessman, whatever*

'97 *fail to grab the mainsheet out of the gybe in the Finals* . . .

The list went on and on.

Kevin also made a list of his accomplishments—his junior sailing title, early admission to Brown, finishing school and nearly winning a national title after being diagnosed with cancer—and wondered why he couldn't celebrate those things. He had two lists, wins and losses, but the dark list screamed louder. In fact, he couldn't shut the failure up.

Kevin thought about his first couple of years at Brown before The Show, and while they seemed simple in a way, he also couldn't help but wonder if he had been overly arrogant. "My world was about 'Accomplishment,' about 'goals,'" he wrote. "About jumping through the hoops to please dad, to validate myself. I could hang out with adults—'so mature,' I could hang out with girls—'so nice, sensitive'—but I couldn't hang out with peers. Even blamed it on them!"

Unbeknownst to many of those who knew him best, Kevin was in a spiral, this time heading down.

KRISTINA

A LONG BEACH Dub Allstars ska show near Ventura seemed like as good a reason as any for Kristina to visit her brother. And it was nice to have something other than his mania bringing them together.

The two siblings went for a drive and then parked outside their mother's home where they had grown up, a spot that had changed surprisingly little since they were kids. Kevin had something he wanted to talk to Kristina about. He told her that he was still in love with Amanda. He wanted a divorce from Anne and he needed Kristina's help.

The news of the split with Anne surprised Kristina just as much as the news of his marriage to her had in the first place. When Kevin had called her back then to let her know about his engagement, she hadn't even known that he had a girlfriend. The idea of a divorce was unsettling, but she could see why Kevin wouldn't want to stay in a marriage that he felt was wrong, a marriage that made him miserable.

Kristina went back to Bend, Oregon, the small ski town where she was living at the time. But she knew that she should move to Santa Barbara, about forty minutes from Ventura, to be near her brother while he was going through his divorce yet far enough away to have her own space. He would need her to talk to, to be with, to help through the difficult process. Once again, this was not the time for her to be focused primarily on her own career or her own relationship status. Her parents needed her to be there for Kevin. Kevin needed her to be there for Kevin. And Kristina needed to be there for Kevin, a kind of sibling support he thanked her for and didn't take for granted.

KEVIN

NOT LONG AFTER the Olympic trials in Atlanta, Kevin began planning his bid for the 2000 Sydney Games. Maybe this time, he thought, instead of sailing in the Laser, he could pair up and go for the 49er, where his likelihood of making the team could be greater.

Due to make its Olympic debut in Sydney, the 49er was like a two-person cousin to the Laser. A lighter, faster dinghy that was remarkably small, it was named for its hull length, 4.99 meters. Foils, which place the boat just over the water, almost like a seaplane, helped the 49er carry large loads but also turn and twist quickly with both people on board having the ability to control their boat's power. The 49er had quickly captured the imagination of sailors, some of them dubbing it the Batmobile.

As for finding a partner, Kevin immediately thought of his friend Morgan Larson. Morgan was the kind of guy who was good at everything, Kevin thought—sailing, being a solid friend, even surfing at an elite level. Whenever Kevin had been in a two-man boat, he had never sailed as successfully as he had with Morgan. Like Kevin, Morgan loved how the wide wings and hull of the 49er allowed it to plane, or soar, over the water quickly—"a wild machine."

Highly unusual for any top sailor, Kevin had switched classes so often by now that he felt as if he had sailing attention-deficit/hyperactivity disorder. Once again he would have to rebuild his body and learn how to use it differently. The light, intimate 49er had an ideal combined crew weight limit that ranged from 320 to 360 pounds, meaning that Kevin would have to lose as many pounds as he could. Although Kevin would have to drop some weight, the benefits of teaming up with Morgan and their odds in succeeding in the class far outweighed that.

The pair quickly found that they and the 49er were a well-suited combination. They won a bronze medal at the first-ever 49er Open World Championships in 1997 in Perth, one of the strongest finishes in either of their respective careers. They reclaimed the bronze the following year in

Bandol and again in Melbourne in 1999. They patched together their existence from a stipend from the U.S. Olympic Committee, patrons, sponsors, and their personal savings, a typically scrappy personal financial setup for striving Olympians. The investment paid dividends, as they were awarded the title of Team of the Year by U.S. Sailing.

Kevin's sense of security in sailing may have been somewhat misplaced, as the sport had entered a more dangerous era. During the 1998 Sydney to Hobart race, which is one of the three jewels in the crown of elite ocean sailing, winds reached 90 miles per hour and waves soared to more than eighty feet. Only a third of the 115 boats made it to the end of the race, and some fifty-five sailors were airlifted by rescue helicopter from their yachts in what was Australia's largest-ever peacetime rescue operation at the time. All told, the event saw the loss of six lives and five yachts, the most catastrophic outcome in the history of the storied event. The billionaire Oracle founder Larry Ellison, sailing on board the 80-foot *Sayonara*, won the race.

Kevin Hall and Morgan Larson (courtesy Kevin Hall)

"We certainly thought it was possible we wouldn't make it," Ellison told *BusinessWeek*. "It was like being dropped off a four-story building onto asphalt every 45 seconds. That happened for three hours. It was very bad."

Ellison also said that while he would continue to sail, that race would be his last around-the-world event. He would "not do another Hobart if he lived to be 1,000."

•

Kevin and Morgan's great success on the water brought with it great expectations of winning a medal at the Sydney Olympics. And Kevin's dreams began to mimic the big media stories that he was ingesting at the time: Michael Jordan, America Online, satellites. He thought about coincidence and saving the universe constantly.

One evening while sitting at home in Ventura, Kevin became fascinated by what he was watching on his VCR—a 1995 made-for-cable movie called *Harrison Bergeron*, a loose adaptation of Kurt Vonnegut's short story of the same title. The story was one of a dystopian suburban future in which the government requires everyone to wear a crown of electronic bands that slow their minds to a crawl so they can only ingest banal television programs. In the story, the devices are the government's reaction to a war and a significant economic depression that grew out of both technological developments and a growing gap between the rich and the poor.

The VCR wasn't working properly and the television screen began to flicker. Kevin examined the back of the machines and traced the knot of cables back to the TV and the wall. He wondered where the cables led, if there was a camera or some kind of feed in there? He reached his hand into the snarl, wiggled some of the cables around, and ripped them away from the wall.

After some more fiddling, he managed to fix whatever it was that was wrong onscreen, but part of him felt freaked out. Of all of the things that could have been on the screen, why did it have to be *that* film that caused static? Was the Director sending him a sign?

Kevin's lows started to resemble dark hangovers, complete with a deep desire not to leave his bed, a sense of defeat and exhaustion before the day had even begun. When he was in such a state, taking medication felt like a cop-out, an easy way to escape his deeper problems as well as his looming concerns about the side effects. To think that he could just take a pill and make everything feel better seemed too simplistic to him, an outward solution rather than an inward one.

Meanwhile, in pop culture, reality television began to bloom, most notably with MTV's *The Real World*, which followed a set of strangers living together in a shared home while the cameras rolled. Kevin understood that people watching the shows could see themselves on the sets with "real" people, and he, too, could see himself on a reality TV show more clearly than on, say, something anachronistic like *Gone with the Wind* or an Alfred Hitchcock film.

Also, in 1998, the film *The Truman Show* was released. A satirical comedy, it centers on Truman Burbank, played by Jim Carrey, a seeming everyman who lives his life inside a simulated reality TV show. His friends, family, and wife are all actors on the show, which includes product placements and elaborate set pieces. He tries to leave "The Truman Show," but his attempts are thwarted, including when a throng of cars pulls in front of him, stopping his exit. "You never had a camera in my head!" an angered, frustrated Truman exclaims.

Kevin watched the film on his VHS, using the same player that had spooked him when watching the Vonnegut film. He felt that finally, *finally*, someone understood what he had been trying to explain for years. The film's scenes with the boats, in particular, seemed prophetic to Kevin. At the end of the film Truman sails out on a boat and hits a blue wall. What he had thought was the horizon, the infinity of water, was just the edge of a stage. He asks the unseen director, Christof, played by Ed Harris, who Truman is.

"You're the star," Christof tells Truman.

"Was nothing real?" Truman asks.

"You were real," Christof tells him. "That's what made you so good to watch."

As Kevin watched, he thought about all the times that he, too, had been out on the water sailing alone. He thought of never being sure that he wasn't going to be blown out to sea. He tried to be vigilant about not getting on a boat by himself when he was spinning up toward an episode, lest he try, like Truman, to keep sailing farther and farther from shore. And just as in the film, Kevin couldn't help wondering what would happen if he were to do that, if all along the sky, the horizon, had actually just been a wall.

As Kevin turned his eyes to the screen, it was hard not to imagine being on the boat with Truman, together.

KRISTINA

KRISTINA WASN'T A doctor, affording her a distance from Kevin's diagnoses that her parents didn't have. She began to question the entire premise of Western medicine, and wondered what had triggered Kevin's bipolar disorder and given him cancer in the first place, especially since no one in their family tree had a history of either. And, aside from insurance purposes, what the reason for labeling someone in that way? At times, it felt like the DSM was just a handy excuse not to listen.

One of Kristina's aunts approached her with a theory that connected the mind and the body: Kevin's cancer had to have been related to his bipolar disorder somehow, but she couldn't put her finger on how or why. Or, maybe it was the other way around. The timing and circumstances of both seemed too uncanny for her.

Kristina thought the same thing. What had created such a strong backlash against Kevin's brain and his body? Was it some kind of hormonal imbalance? A physical manifestation of his psychological issues? A general discomfort with societal pressures surrounding masculinity? She started reading the works of Malidoma Patrice Somé, a teacher and author from Burkina Faso. In *The Healing Wisdom of Africa*, Somé explores human-kind's connection with nature and individual destiny, writing that "everyone is born with a purpose, and that this purpose must be known in order to ensure an integrated way of living. People ignorant of their purpose are like ships adrift in a hostile sea. They are circling around."

Obvious ship metaphors aside, Kristina wondered if Kevin's sense of purpose was off in his adult years. "If something in the physical world is experiencing instability, it is because its energetic correspondent has been experiencing instability," Somé wrote.

Reading Somé, Kristina didn't understand why in some cultures, people with visions of grandeur, who spoke of having portals to higher planes of thinking, were seen as respected shamans, while in modern Western cultures they were strapped to beds, medicated, and stigma-tized. Ancient Greeks, in particular Plato, had also viewed madness as a potential gift and centuries later in the 1960s and 1970s, Thomas Szasz and other critics had argued that mental illness itself was a construct, a "myth."

Maybe the truth was somewhere in between, but at the very least, it felt like a conversation worth having. Kristina presented her more holistic and spiritualistic ideas to her parents, but they appeared uninterested and were quick to dismiss. Much to her frustration, they seemed entrenched in their Western medical perspective. Kristina tried to press them by asking what they thought it was that Kevin was working through in each of his episodes. Did his mania somehow provide him comfort or a defense against something? And, if that was the case, a defense against what?

What if, Kristina asked her mother, the family just put Kevin out in the woods and let him roam in the wilderness, so that he could fully live within his episodes in a space where he felt safe and free?

It was a lovely thought, her mother told her, but not really within the realm of possibility.

KEVIN

KEVIN STROLLED DOWN Wakefield Street, a wide thoroughfare near the University of Auckland's campus with the Sky Tower, a futuristic white spire. As he made his way down the street, which sloped downward toward the water, he took comfort in the orderly arrangement of office buildings, parking garages, restaurants and bars. He could feel the cameras rolling and the presence of The Director again as he observed one large gray building with an awning over the street, adorned with a red sign letting drivers know that parking spaces were available. The first few floors of the building were devoted to a parking garage, while above were offices. He craned his neck to look up several stories to see a sign with some letters at the top of the building: ORACLE.

Oracle! Of course! That *had* to be a sign.

Kevin walked toward a silver door—an elevator—that faced the street. No key or parking ticket was necessary for opening it, a fact he marveled at. The Director was once again doing a great job of ensuring that everything had been set up properly. He stepped in, pushed the Up button, and took satisfaction in the whish of the metal doors sliding to a close.

When they opened again, Kevin was all the way up on the roof, where he belonged, cloaked in the night.

The Director told him that he was supposed to jump off the top, just like in the 1997 David Fincher thriller *The Game*. Like the protagonist in that film, a wealthy investment banker played by Michael Douglas, Kevin had opted into a game that promised to change his life and the lives of others. And the *Oracle* tower, of course, made the most sense for such a scene, given its cofounder, Larry Ellison's, passion for sailing. Kevin stood above the hum of the street noise thinking that it would make a really good scene and that the audience would be sure to applaud.

He looked over the edge of the building and prepared for flight.

•

In some stories, people standing on the edge of a building or bridge, determined to end their lives, finally come to their senses. They realize that life *is* worth living. Or a voice of reason, sometimes a friend or onlooker, shrieks and pulls the potential jumper off the ledge to safety.

In Kevin's case, he just got distracted. As he stood on the roof, a seagull flew by, drawing his attention away from the Director's commands. He became fixated on trying to look the bird in the eye, and stepped away from the ledge. The bird, quite unintentionally, had saved his life.

Shaking off his potentially fatal flirtation with falling off the building, Kevin took the elevator back down to the street. As an American, he became engrossed with the sight of pedestrians crossing the street diagonally in an X-like pattern (known as a "pedestrian scramble"). Rather than taking turns and going in one direction at a time in a square formation like in the United States, this seemed symphonic somehow, a coordinated composition of strangers all moving forward yet not hitting each other. Much of New Zealand felt that way to Kevin, comfortable and Western but still quirky.

He joined the sidewalk dwellers with the impending conclusion of his marriage to Anne now weighing on his thoughts. As Kevin walked by a fountain, he examined the wedding band on his left ring finger, his divorce with Anne not yet officially finalized. Removing the ring, Kevin held it in his hand nervously, its circular shape that was supposed to symbolize the eternity of his union with her. Then, feeling the cameras rolling, he took it off and chucked it into the fountain, and with it, his thoughts about his marriage.

Later, a festival was taking place on the outskirts of town, and Kevin hitched a ride, skateboard under his arm, and danced through the night and into the morning. Why sleep, Kevin thought, when there was partying and the world to see? Resting was for the dead. He was alive.

Part of Kevin knew that it wasn't right for him to feel this good, even if now he was surrounded by other like-minded revelers. Something was wrong, but he wasn't interested in sorting it out. At least not now. He felt amazing.

As the music blared, Kevin decided to climb up one of the thick poles of a large tent. The sun was rising and the crowd was thumping, the perfect scene. He scooted his way up. The audience took notice and cheered him on.

Kevin was nearing the top of the tent when he heard a police officer braying at him from below, which confused him. Why didn't the police understand that what he was doing was a scene in The Show? And a really cool scene, if he could say so himself. Each episode of The Show was wildly different and each offered a unique window into humanity, this one clearly the next great installment of a wonderful series.

The cops coaxed Kevin down. When he reached ground level, they asked him outright: Was he on drugs?

No, Kevin enthusiastically replied. He wasn't on drugs.

That was the whole point.

And it felt completely awesome.

•

In the aftermath of the episode, Kevin's good fortune with law enforcement appeared to have come to an end and he was summoned to appear in court before a judge in Auckland. By the time of his hearing, he was medicated, calm, and polite, the opposite of what police had described when they had picked him up. He watched the judge up on her bench as she examined several pages of doctors' notes he had provided which described his bipolar disorder in detail.

It must be terrible to live like this, she said.

Kevin was surprised and comforted to be met with such sympathy. He knew that given the circumstances, he had gotten lucky. The judge said that what Kevin had done had jeopardized his own safety and that of others but told him that it wasn't his fault; it was a manifestation of mental illness. She dismissed the charges and allowed him to go, wishing him a positive and healthy recovery.

Kevin would later become even more aware of the privilege that his race and class had brought him in the courtroom and in other interactions with law enforcement. The Auckland judge could easily have changed the entire direction of his life, but instead he had been allowed to go, and into a robust support system, no less. Incarceration rates for mentally ill people of color were significantly higher than that for their white counterparts by any metric, and particularly so in the United States during the 1990s, as many in local, state, and federal law enforcement took a "tough on crime" stance. The result, built up over many years, was that many U.S. prisons were teeming not with serial killers, but with addicts and people with undiagnosed or untreated mental ailments. In many cases, the trauma of being incarcerated only made existing psychological problems worse.

Yet for Kevin, life after police apprehension would go on. After the Auckland episode, Kevin's divorce was finalized. Amanda's long wait was finally over and she and Kevin could go forward with their lives together. She explained to Kevin that she had tried to date other people and found that none of them had compared to the guy she met as her lab partner all those years earlier. Kevin told Amanda of his own heartbreak when she had dumped him, how the more he thought about it, his marriage to Anne was in the shadow of that rejection. Yet both of them admitted that maybe each of their own respective romantic paths made them less likely to take each other for granted. Some couples grow together and some may, in their own peculiar ways, grow while apart.

She flew to California to meet him and they officially reunited. His words at LaGuardia had not been empty.

•

Kevin knew Long Beach, California, well enough to know that it wasn't a place of colorful, wavy, wonderful whirlpools, yet there they were, right before his eyes. When the wind blew, the colors of the whirlpools shifted back and forth in an experience that transcended Kevin's words.

He and Morgan were there that day to race in an important regatta that wouldn't directly impact their ranking to get on an Olympic team but could help them secure funding. Kevin had begun seeing the whirlpools the day before, when they were on the boat, but he hadn't said anything to Morgan at the time, worried that he might have been in The Show and was perhaps untrustworthy. It was hard for him to discern whether he was witnessing an illusion, hallucination, or just misperceiving something that really was present before him. As fantastical and surprising as the images may have been, they came with an aura of anxiety, and had Kevin wondering if others could see them or if they lived merely in his head. He hadn't stopped taking his medication, but he had been drinking a fair amount of alcohol and missing sleep.

Figuring that it must be time for the racing part of The Show to begin, Kevin headed toward the competition's start, his perspective still a swirling panorama.

MORGAN

WHEN KEVIN WAS late for race prep, Morgan knew immediately that something was amiss. When Kevin was on, he was punctual, organized, and completely ready for competition. His reliability and consistency were part of what had made them the team to beat heading into Sydney and as Morgan rigged up the boat, he recognized how out of character this was for Kevin.

Ready to hit the water, but waiting, Morgan remembered Kevin, and maybe his parents, too, mentioning at some point that he had had some form of bipolar disorder. They had given him advice on how to help if anything should happen, but Morgan hadn't really thought that it would ever come up.

Finally, Kevin strolled up to Morgan and the boat, dressed in street, not sailing, clothes, save for a life jacket. He was smoking a cigarette, talking in nonsensical loops between puffs.

The minute Morgan saw Kevin, he knew that the two of them were not going to race that day. "He was totally dysfunctional," he said.

Morgan tried to broach the subject of Kevin's getting some help, but Kevin immediately flipped out, and within seconds he was off. Morgan sprinted after him for a while, but then gave up. The race was a bust, and Morgan's teammate and best shot at making it to the Olympics was manic and missing.

GORDON

IT TOOK SOME time for Gordon to piece it together, but eventually, he learned that after leaving Morgan, Kevin climbed behind the wheel of his grandfather's canary yellow Cadillac and had driven it onto the grass median of a road. The move had felt perfect, he later told his father. He had done some kind of power slide, causing the car to land sideways and completely on the median, perpendicular to the road.

Kevin opened the driver's side door and exited, miraculously uninjured. He wandered away and was about four blocks from the site of the abandoned car when the cops saw him. Kevin explained to them that the car's position was intended to straddle the "doorway" to the other side.

The cops pinned Kevin to the ground. This was far from the first time that law enforcement had made an appearance on The Show, but this was the first time they had physically pushed him down. It pulled him out of The Show somewhat and back to Long Beach. But by then, it was clearly too little too late.

Kevin again found himself in police custody and then transferred to a hospital. It was a handoff with which he and his family were becoming familiar, but to which they were still not accustomed.

Gordon wasn't one to nag Kevin about his appearance, but as he once again received the news about his son being taken into police custody, then handed over to mental health experts, he felt that it must have helped his son that he had kept his hair cut short and his clothes clean, that he had no tattoos or scars and didn't reek of alcohol or marijuana or any other illegal substance.

Gordon renewed his ongoing argument with Kevin about his medication. Kevin tried to explain to him that the downers *really* brought him down, not just from the mania, but to the darkest corners of his mind. This aroused little sympathy from Gordon, as he reasoned that at least depressed people didn't usually come to the attention of the cops, and that even if Kevin was depressed, at least he was less likely to cause the kind of trouble that he did when manic. It was the lesser of two evils in Gordon's eyes, but to Kevin, that still meant there was an unbearable evil.

For his father, Kevin's track record of going off his meds spoke for itself. Sure, he might feel better for a while, but it was only a matter of time before his mania mushroomed again, requiring hospitalization and causing trauma for himself and those around him. Gordon's own life had flourished in routine and he observed that Kevin's seemed to also be at its best when he was stable. He won titles, landed good grades, and he wasn't a burden for those around him.

It was simple, Gordon thought. *Take the pills.*

MORGAN

MORGAN FORGAVE KEVIN for what happened, knowing that it was the illness doing its work, not any intentional attempt on Kevin's part to sabotage their sailing goals. Kevin seemed surprised by his kindness, but Morgan was on Kevin's team—literally—and felt it was best to move forward. Kevin was the best sailing partner he had ever worked with, the left brain to Morgan's right, and that balance was more than worth the risk. (Although, once Kevin crossed over to The Show, the opposite dynamic took hold.)

They still had time to make it to the Olympic trials for the 2000 Sydney Games.

•

To prepare for the November 1999 trials, Kevin and Morgan based themselves in St. Petersburg, Florida, and partnered with Zachary Leonard, Kevin's friend who had helped coach him at Brown, who would help prepare them for trials. Aside from being a friend, Zach, only four years older than Kevin, had gained experience working with several Olympians.

Zach deeply understood the complexities of, and sharp differences between, collegiate sailing and Olympic sailing: in Olympic sailing, a single race could last for hours instead of a few minutes, athleticism and speed were premiums over tactics, because sailors could be out in the open ocean. Strangely, youth sailing was more like its Olympic counterpart than collegiate sailing because of its rules, classifications, and structure, and Zach knew that some people were good at one and not the other. Kevin had been the best youth sailor in the world, as well as part of an NCAA championship team, making him a serious threat on the water at trials and beyond.

Knowing that drinking alcohol could interfere with his bipolar disorder and testosterone levels, Kevin completely abstained. Preparing for the trials gave him a perfect excuse without having to go into the details of his medical history or medication regime. Surprisingly, many would-be Olympians say that the trials to make the American team can feel more stressful than the Olympics themselves. If you don't make the team, you can't even call yourself an Olympian, and what's worse, if you fail to make the team you have to sit through weeks of relentless media coverage of the event that has been the sole focus of all your energy and work for four years. A competitor who overestimates how prepared he or she is for the trials risks not being ready for an unexpected new entrant who can cause an upset. If a competitor overprepares, there's a risk of burnout, physical and psychological.

The lead went back and forth between Kevin and Morgan and their opponents, but ultimately, they finished in second place. For a third time, Kevin had failed to make an Olympic team, this time just barely.

•

As far as consolation prizes for not qualifying for the Olympics go, making an America's Cup team sounded like a pretty good deal to Kevin and Morgan. They accepted an invitation to join the AmericaOne team and headed to Auckland.

In becoming part of an America's Cup team, Kevin became part of one of sport's deepest lineages. From its genesis, the America's Cup was fueled by those with wealth, power, and ego, starting in the summer of 1851, when the industrialist John Cox Stevens built a yacht called *America* and successfully raced it against British counterparts. Stevens and his co-owners received a silver cup for their victory. Fueled by nationalistic zeal, Stevens returned to the United States a hero and presented his silver cup to the New York Yacht Club with the proviso that it represent a challenge for a recurring international competition.

A top professional sailor competing in the America's Cup could earn an annual income of upper five to mid-six figures, plus bonuses for Cups won. Additionally, some had side gigs as professional sailors for hire, as many wealthy amateurs enjoyed the bragging rights and experience that came from being taught by an America's Cup athlete.

The dynamics of America's Cup sailing are vastly different from those of Olympic-level or collegiate sailing, almost to the degree that marathon running and sprinting have little in common beyond the intensive use of the legs. In Olympic sailing, the technology element is minimized as much as possible, with sailors competing in boats that are virtually identical. In the America's Cup, the course, the boat, and the rules of play are subject to change every cycle, which would be like the winner of the Super Bowl getting to redraw the lines and dimensions of the football field and redesigning the pigskin each year to better suit their own team's strengths. Engineering is of foremost importance, and among the teams there is a perpetual arms race of dollars and design to create the fastest boat. Additionally, the boats must be designed according to certain rules; as one sailing tome put it, they must be similar enough to create the feeling of a level, competitive playing field, but different enough to make the races interesting and suspenseful.

For the competition, AmericaOne constructed two boats, their designs based on the latest technology and research, in partnership with companies such as Hewlett-Packard and Ford. Everything and everyone was excited about August 2001, when the 150th anniversary of the Cup would take place in Cowes, a small English seaport town of nine thousand that more than doubles in population during significant sailing events.

Everyone's task on the AmericaOne boats was clear: The bowmen at the front, strong and acrobatic, were responsible for changing sails. The midbowmen worked with the pit crew during sail changes, and the pitman coordinated the front part of the boat. Trimmers worked with the skipper to determine if the boat was generating as much speed as it needed, and the skipper was in charge of making tactical decisions. Many of the guys onboard had suggested that Kevin take on the role of navigator, the person in charge of the onboard computers and data, and of communicating that information to the skipper, strategist, and helmsman. The navigator's task was to decipher not only complex computations but also the feel of the wind, and know how much of which to believe in a given moment. It was the perfect marriage of Kevin's left and right brain. But such a role for a rookie in the event would have been a big call for the top brass with AmericaOne, so Kevin was assigned a coaching and spy role.

Spying is as old, and accepted, in the event as the America's Cup itself, a race ripe with gossip. Information, and dis-information, about the construction of America's Cup boats, in particular, was prized. (The word "scuttlebutt" is nautical in its origin, "scuttle" referring to a water cask for drinking and "butt" meaning barrel. Sailors gathered around the "scuttlebutt" to exchange information, a precursor to the modern workplace water cooler.) The America's Cup had rules for the boats' design, including the size of the "envelope," or the maximum dimensions of the boat. But how one's opponents were working within or around those confines was of paramount interest, with millions of dollars and international titles at stake.

Because sailors switched between being competitors and being allies so often, it wasn't uncommon for an athlete to know a lot about his enemy, or to seek out information about who could be making what kind of move to a different team. No one was more aware of this than Kevin. He was a quick study when it came to scouting out the enemy boats, lurking near docks, snapping photographs, and then reporting back to the AmericaOne designers, all in the name of having a competitive edge.

KEVIN

IN SOME REGARDS, the rigid structure of life with AmericaOne, like many America's Cup teams, felt paternal. The team had a logistics operator who handled everything but sailing: where the team ate, lodged, spent its time, dressed, traveled, and so on, in effect managing the entire team's schedule from five in the morning to eight at night. AmericaOne's coordinator was Sarah O'Kane, a youthful British woman who became something of a den mother to the sailors, a liaison between the insularity of the military-like sport and the life some of them tried to lead outside of it.

As in Olympic sailing, weight mattered in the America's Cup; however, the body image issues in elite sailing are seldom, if ever, discussed. The America's Cup boats had individual and group weight targets depending on what role the sailors had on the boat. Grinders, the sailors who were the human engines of the boat, were expected to weigh more than people who had less physical roles. All of the sailors carefully watched what they and the others were eating, and there were playful photos of teammates caught eating ice cream, as every pound, as well as where it sat, was part of the team strategy. Yet unlike, say, cheerleading, where everyone is trying to be thin, group weight targets made for a sort of strange prisoner's dilemma among the athletes. One sailor being heavier necessarily meant another person would have to be just that much lighter, as the object was having a perfectly balanced combined weight.

When Kevin first joined the team, Sarah O'Kane, the go-to for all internal team crises, knew nothing of his mental health history. As for Morgan, the memory of the Long Beach episode had stuck with him, but he observed that Kevin seemed to be adjusting to his new surroundings well, both on and off the water. It seemed to no one's advantage to bring it up, particularly when Kevin, by outward appearances, had moved on.

A new era in sailing was beginning, one in which the boats were being backed by more corporate sponsorship money than ever before. While some traditionalists may have decried the shift, it was good news for sailors like Kevin and Morgan, who could now actually earn a living by being on a boat. The growing influence of technology and math in sailing played to Kevin's strengths, too, as he forged out a path in the niche of navigation. A natural longtime lover of math and tinkering, Kevin joked that he had landed the technical duties because he was "one of the few guys on the team who didn't mind restarting Windows twice."

MORGAN

ONE DAY, WHEN Morgan returned home to the apartment he shared with Kevin in Auckland, he could see that Kevin had made some odd, artistic decorating decisions, including rearranging the furniture in an unconventional pattern. Over the last couple of days, Kevin had also been coming and going at odd hours, inconsistent with the team's rigid schedule. Then, there was the morning when Morgan had woken up to find Kevin frying eggs on the stove with sugar, then leaving the concoction on the hot burner and going to sleep.

Morgan went to Sarah and said that they had a problem. He told her what he knew of Kevin's history with bipolar disorder and described what he had seen in the last twenty-four hours, and what he hadn't seen—Kevin.

Sarah, the daughter of a doctor and by now a veteran of handling the mechanics and inherent drama percolating underneath an America's Cup team, was not particularly alarmed by the news, having been exposed to some psychiatric disorders over the years. In fact, she had wondered privately whether there was some kind of connection between mental illness and sailing; many of the men she worked with were extremely technically adept but struggled with basic social skills, anxiety, and general mood management. Then again, the high-pressure lifestyle wasn't exactly always conducive to mental well-being, either. She appreciated Morgan's concern, and she also knew, from what he had told her, that Kevin was not himself.

She and Morgan hopped into a van. They had to find Kevin.

•

At first Morgan couldn't believe it was his friend and teammate. But then he knew it *had* to be. Kevin was dancing along the streets of Auckland and seemed enraptured, a smile beaming off his face, his body swaying with the effortlessness of Fred Astaire. Morgan and Sarah approached him in the van with extra-friendly smiles. They played dumb, chatting Kevin up, and eventually succeeded in getting him into the van under the pretext that they were going to go grab a drink together.

Instead, Sarah and Morgan brought him back to the AmericaOne residence, and Sarah quickly called her father to ask him what she should do. This was her first experience with someone having a full-blown manic episode, and while Kevin seemed to be calming down a bit, she wasn't sure how long the lull would last. Morgan called in a couple of teammates to hang out with them, not wanting Kevin to suspect that they were waiting for a doctor to arrive to give a psychiatric evaluation. Sitting on the eighth floor, Morgan was worried that Kevin might try to jump out the window. With their other teammates standing in his way, Morgan thought, he might reconsider.

•

The doctor arrived soon after they called, but it had felt like a century, time having its way of stretching out when the mind feels anxious or stressed. As Sarah and Morgan had predicted, he deemed Kevin to be in a deep manic state and best handled at a psychiatric ward.

To their surprise, Kevin agreed to be taken out of the room and into the doctor's care. Sarah went with him.

At the doctor's office, Kevin asked Sarah, with complete sincerity, whether she was having fun yet or not. He clearly had no handle on how his episode could have cost him his career on the boat; it would be Sarah's lobbying that would allow him to keep his spot, though he would spend most of his time on shore as a spy.

AMANDA

THE PLAN HAD been for Amanda to get a break from school and for her and Kevin to meet up and go to Vermont and hike—a romantic New England date, somewhat evocative of their first few months together as students in Providence. The weather, however, had different plans. Rain poured down, rendering many of the trails muddy slip 'n slides.

Kevin and Amanda watched the canvas of gray skies from the window of a Motel 6 not far from the hiking trail. The ill weather gave rise to a conversation about deeper things, including marriage, fueled by champagne sipped out of Styrofoam cups. They talked about their mutual desire to spend the rest of their lives together and create a family.

Amanda, tipsy, asked if Kevin would marry her.

Then, she passed out.

Kevin looked around the room, realizing that they were indeed the only two people there, so she was asking him, not someone else. He was dumbfounded and secretly glad for the mental break to try and process it all.

When she came to, they discussed it and, with a Styrofoam toast, considered their engagement official.

Their respective families welcomed the news. That included Kevin's father, but his reasons for being in favor of the marriage were not what Kevin had hoped for. Gordon was happy that Amanda was taking over the responsibility of making sure that Kevin remained stable. She was well aware that Kevin had bipolar disorder but was opting into the relationship nonetheless.

"I'm glad you two are getting married," Gordon said. "Now Kevin is off my desk and on Amanda's."

The coldness of that statement, whether intended or not, would reverberate in Kevin's and Amanda's heads for years.

KEVIN

AMANDA AND KEVIN were married on the lush and meticulously manicured grounds of the Brooklyn Botanic Garden on April 29, 2001, a decade after their first meeting in physics class at Brown. Amanda's mother had spearheaded most of the planning, as Kevin was absorbed with sailing, Amanda with medicine, and neither one had much interest in an elaborate ceremony. Kevin insisted on wearing red shoes; Amanda, a classic strapless white dress.

Kevin and Amanda's wedding, 2001 (courtesy Kevin Hall)

After the ceremony, the couple made their way to the reception. For their first dance, Kevin and Amanda chose Alanis Morissette's "That I Would Be Good." With a circle of people in suits and dresses around them, smiling and watching, Kevin heard the Director again.

Kevin looked into Amanda's eyes. He was desperately trying to talk himself out of The Show. He could see everything spiraling into something like the Boston Harbor fiasco, with him bursting out in front of their family and closest friends and accusing Amanda of being a spy. The moment fired off a new level of intensity for Kevin, and a feeling hit him, as if a light switch had been flipped on.

Where were the cameras?

that I would be good even if I lost sanity

The Director went away after what felt to Kevin like several minutes, though it was probably more like forty-five seconds. But he still came too close.

•

Five months after Kevin and Amanda danced in the Botanic Garden, al-Qaeda terrorists hijacked planes and crashed them into the North and South Towers of the World Trade Center, killing 2,996 people. For Amanda, the disaster had literally hit close to home, her birthplace just uptown from where the towers had fallen.

It also raised questions about the Olympics—typically a global, feel-good gathering—in a new age of terror. Still, Kevin had set his entire being on making the American team bound for the 2004 Athens Games. He began to put together donations to finance his campaign and was pleased when both his mother and father agreed to chip in. Making their lives somewhat easier financially was the money that Kevin had earned from the 2003 America's Cup cycle, further benefitted by a strong New Zealand-to-U.S.-dollar exchange rate. It wouldn't be long before that had evaporated, however, and according to their most optimistic estimates, Kevin and Amanda would be looking at atleast $20,000 of debt for him to compete at the Olympics, plus what Amanda owed from medical school.

For the Athens Games, Kevin decided to return to the Finn class, the same one he had tried heading into the 1992 Olympics. Once again, he worried about being something of a chronic event switcher in sailing, but the challenge of it was irresistible, the steep end of the learning curve being where Kevin felt most at home.

In the spring of 2003, he scraped together what funds he and Amanda had saved up and had a 16-foot Olympic Finn dinghy shipped to them in the United States from Holland. He sailed one event, performed horribly, and almost quit altogether. With his body feeling out of shape and his pocketbook anemic, Kevin's first few weeks of Finn sailing was brutal. Although he had gone to such great lengths to make that first week of Olympic training happen, he seriously considered returning the dinghy to its owner, but knew that he couldn't. When he had sailed as a child, long before The Show, he had acted like he belonged in the front of the pack, and his sailing had matched that attitude. Somewhere along the way, though, he had lost his confidence and was struggling to get it back. But Kevin had been dreaming of the Olympics since childhood. He *really* wanted the medal.

This time, things felt different. This Olympics felt like his.

PART III

THE LOWS

. . . yet from those flames,
No light, but rather darkness visible.
　　　—JOHN MILTON, *Paradise Lost*

It's terrible, Bob, to think that all I've suffered, and all
the suffering I've caused, might have arisen from
the lack of a little salt in my brain.
—ROBERT LOWELL, writing to his publisher, Robert Giroux

The biggest lie told in professional sports is "We're
just going out there to have fun."
　　　—LARRY ELLISON

AMANDA

AMANDA AND KEVIN shared a one-room home in Bowie, Maryland, both of their days long but rewarding, with Kevin on the water and Amanda on her emergency room shifts. She was living in a world balanced on the edge of the area's most harrowing poverty, he in a world balanced on the cusp of extreme wealth. Yet both were finally living and working together.

The University of Maryland Medical Center unit was one of the more grueling places to spend time in as a medical resident, or as a human of any sort. One of the top programs in the world for emergency doctor residents, it was located in an area that had a harrowing history of homicides and street violence, part of the city that would one day serve as the inspiration for David Simon's gritty television series *The Wire*. Through it passed a stream of gunshot and knife wound victims, bodies worn out with the long-term effects of drug addiction, and patients who lacked regular medical treatment. The first shock trauma unit in the country when it had opened fifty years earlier, it was initially known as the "death lab"—until more patients began to survive.

Kevin didn't stay in Maryland long, though. To make it to Athens, he would need to be based in Fort Lauderdale, Florida, where the U.S. trials for the Olympics were scheduled to take place. He had attempted the U.S. trials enough to know that the more time he practiced in the actual competition waters, the more relaxed and prepared he would be for the actual competition. He and Amanda made a schedule of flights and visiting times, and with his boat in tow, Kevin left for Fort Lauderdale with a kiss.

KEVIN

FOR THE SIX months leading up to the Finn trials, Kevin had to both try to completely focus on preparing for a single series of moments, and create a sense of muscle memory to kick in during big moments. Imposter syndrome crept in from time to time, and he wondered if Amanda might wake up one day and think she had made a mistake in marrying him, or if making his fourth bid for the Olympics was an even more insane notion than anything he experienced in The Show.

There were new tactics to learn, as Kevin had to retrain on how to tack with the Finn's low, square boom (putting the bow of the boat into the eye of the wind) and gybe (putting the stern of the boat into the eye of the wind), and had to remember that downwind, not upwind, was where the bold maneuvering lay with the Finn. The harder one pushed, the faster the boat could go, but the greater the likelihood of crashing.

Kevin spent his weeks in Fort Lauderdale completely consumed by preparing for the competition. He lived in a tiny apartment across the street from where the trials race would take place. If he wasn't at the gym, he was on the water or asleep. It helped that some of his former teammates were also in the area, providing a built-in social and support network, helping him find everything from a coach boat to an apartment to a gym.

Kevin knew that his weakness in previous competitions hadn't been to start on the upwind, uphill climb (that was mostly about strength and risk management), but sailing downwind in the second half of the race. Then he had lost confidence and tightened up, his finishes weak compared to his forceful starts. The other boats had torn by him and beat him to the finish line as his hopes sank to the bottom of the water like an anvil.

Now, to practice his downwind technique, Kevin sailed the thirty-mile stretch between Miami and Fort Lauderdale nearly a dozen times, his route chosen by the direction of the wind over impossibly blue waters bordering the cities' playful skylines and shores. In his lower moments, which he didn't share with anyone at the time, he thought of himself alone on a 16-foot boat, and if he were to crash, he would be swept to the sea by the Gulfstream current and never seen again.

When the trials began in Fort Lauderdale in February, roughly six months before the Athens Games, Kevin's entire family, including his divorced parents, assembled to watch his fourth attempt for a spot on the U.S. team.

All of them were unaware that he had gone off his bipolar medications. He had been so steady and methodically committed to training, they hadn't even thought to ask him about it. Kevin was doing some of the best sailing of his life and nobody wanted to risk throwing him off when, by all outward indications, he was hitting a rhythm on land and sea.

Kevin, who often maintained that his meds dulled his sailing abilities, had decided to go off them four months before, in spite of knowing the risks involved. Everything from his balance to his reflexes to his vision (literal and metaphorical) was thrown off when he was on them, he said. He once described sailing while medicated like "trying to use a mouse that's turned sideways on your desk. You can do it, you can learn, but you will never, ever get your high score on Missile Command unless you were born with a sideways mouse in the first place." He knew that this could be his last shot for the Olympics that his friends and family would support him in, as, understandably, their patience was wearing thin after they had already demonstrated incredible generosity and support. The way Kevin saw it, he couldn't risk *taking* his medication, even though he was well aware of the potential for tumult that loomed whenever he saw the plastic bottle collecting dust in his medicine cabinet.

GORDON

IT WAS STRANGE to think that his son was getting too old for anything, let alone sailing. Because, of course, admitting that Kevin was getting old was tacit admission that he, too, as his father, was aging. Kevin was now thirty-four, old by most Olympic standards, yet Gordon was still supportive, albeit a bit skeptical, of his son's ability to make the team in the Finn class.

During the trials, Gordon stood with Amanda and Susanne on board the boat of a local yacht club member and watched in awe as Kevin ran away with the regatta. It was some of the most inspired sailing Gordon had ever seen from anyone, not just his son. Kevin was so far ahead in the trials by the last day that he didn't even need to compete, having already secured his berth by a wide margin, though he decided to go out anyway, as big of a show of the love of the sport as he had ever seen in his son.

Gordon was the first to tell his son that his win was a huge accomplishment. After all those years spent driving him around the junior circuit and helping him deal with cancer treatments, all the times he had bailed Kevin out of the aftermath of being on The Show, Gordon felt an immense sense of pride in his son. Kevin had set a goal and he had reached it. He was an Olympian.

The next stop was the podium in Athens.

AMANDA

As Kevin and Amanda sat in the sperm clinic flipping through profiles of donors, they couldn't help but chuckle. One donor described how he wanted to make a "pungent" difference in the world. Another, when asked if he liked animals, responded simply, "Yes, ducks."

Amanda and Kevin had talked about wanting a family early in their reconciliation, Kevin's testicular cancer having brought the conversation to the forefront, but they were unclear on how exactly to start one. They had already applied to and been accepted by an adoption organization and paid a significant sum to an expectant mother they had met with through the group. But the mother took the money and did not follow through with the adoption, a painful setback to Kevin and Amanda in their first attempt at trying to build a family. They still loved the idea of adoption, and hadn't ruled it out, but Amanda was also curious about the experience of being pregnant.

They saw no harm in trying to get both processes going simultaneously, knowing that both, even under the best of circumstances, would take some time.

Amanda saw one profile that didn't actually look too bad.

What did Kevin think?

KEVIN

KEVIN LATER DESCRIBED sitting in the sperm bank clinic browsing through the profiles of potential biological fathers for his children as "one of the most unsettling spiritual experiences I have ever had."

He was torn between the joyful idea of finally starting a family and the peculiar feeling that some other man would be impregnating his wife. He worried that a sperm donor child would feel more like Amanda's than his, that a bond would form between them and that he wouldn't or couldn't ever catch up. He also understood why Amanda wanted the experience of pregnancy and wanted to be a fair partner.

Here he was, an Olympian (finally) and professional athlete, filling out paperwork saying that for him, biological procreation was impossible. "It seems so primal, and human, and part of the cycle of life and yadda yadda in a reverent way," Kevin later wrote. "It seemed like it would be very easy to end up with regrets or resentment, if we didn't try to get pregnant."

Kevin also thought about his "old, reptilian part of the brain" and what he called his "Me Tarzan, you Jane" male instincts. He knew those impulses were evolutionary throwbacks, but that recognition didn't necessarily mean that it was easy to shake them in the moment.

He and Amanda selected vial #3606, a number that would remain printed in his brain permanently.

They waited.

•

Another sperm-related issue loomed, this one far more public: Kevin's dispute over his testosterone shots with the International Olympic Committee. Since he had failed to make the Atlanta 1996 or Sydney 2000 Games, the matter of his taking the injections had never been resolved. Five weeks before the opening ceremonies in Athens, he found himself in the same position he'd been in years earlier, trying to get what anti-doping experts now officially called a Therapeutic Use Exemption waiver, the whole frustrating fracas revived. He dusted off a thick file folder he had labeled THE HASSLE.

The waiver process was designed in a sometimes haphazard fashion for athletes who had illnesses or medical conditions that required them to take a medication that was on the World Anti-Doping Agency (WADA) banned substance list. WADA had just recently been formed; what little drug testing had been done earlier was conducted by the IOC. Some common cases that had come up so far involved asthma, cardio-vascular issues, and transgender athletes who said they had to take hormones. To apply for the waiver, an athlete, in consultation with a doctor, had to fill out an application describing the relevant condition and necessary medications, then submit the application to the anti-doping authorities, who then reviewed the case.

Kevin had a hard time believing that after all he had been through—two bouts with cancer, three failed attempts at qualifying for the Olympics, a divorce, and several manic episodes and depressive aftermaths—the fine print scribed by the international sports bureaucracy was going to stop him.

Several years into his testosterone shots, Kevin had become accustomed to needles and blood work. Still, he resented being required by anti-doping officials to head to a laboratory to give even more blood—at precisely the same time he was scheduled to be in Athens for workouts ahead of the Games.

Not only that, Kevin, like all Olympic athletes, had to report his minute-by-minute whereabouts to anti-doping officials. The idea was to make drug testing more effective by making it spontaneous, because if an athlete knew that a drug test was looming, it would be easy for him or her to dilute urine of a banned substance in plenty of time beforehand. While randomness increased accuracy, it also made for some odd moments, as drug testers could knock on doors at any hour and interrupt practices, family gatherings, or dates. For Kevin, the anti-doping protocol blurred the boundary between The Show and reality; now, as cameras and newspapers followed his saga, he actually was being watched by a large, bureaucratic organization that was global in scope and ambition. And they had permission to show up in his life at any time.

Immediately following his triumph at the trials, Kevin had gone back on his medication for his bipolar disorder and stayed on it. He had flirted with the idea of going off it in Athens, but had fought against that desire. What everyone around him seemed not to understand was that with his meds, he felt like he was living his life inside parentheses.

AMANDA

IN EARLY JULY 2004, with just a little over a month before the Olympic opening ceremonies, Kevin had still received only part of his waiver to compete in the Games. Under the Therapeutic Use Exemption guidelines, Kevin and Amanda were told that Kevin now needed an "independent referee" to review his case. Considering that Kevin had first broached the subject of his testosterone shots nearly a decade prior to Olympic competition, it was agonizing to be so close to the Games without formal approval. Amanda and Kevin had also heard that an adjudicator who had been tasked with reviewing his case had accidentally seen Kevin's name on one of the documents, meaning that a second one had to be chosen and the review started all over again. U.S. Sailing, the national governing body that had backed Kevin, declined to speak publicly about his case, citing confidentiality rules.

That was it for Amanda. She wrote a letter and blasted it out to members of the media: "Kevin has endured logistically challenging mandated blood tests, tedious and repetitive paperwork demands, inconsistent and contradictory stipulations on his time, his energy and his patience," she wrote, "all the while keeping a smile on for the press, keeping his optimism alive, and with little moral support and advocacy from the very organizations established for those purposes."

She added that in nine years of testing, Kevin had not once shown an elevated testosterone level and had "not *once* asked for anything more than fair and equal treatment. As far as I am concerned this is the last straw in a long line of stalling techniques that amount to a spit in his face."

What some of the members of various governing bodies in sports saw merely as a job was "a lifelong dream to the man I love," Amanda wrote. "What may be a simple bureaucratic hurdle to them is a constant reminder to Kevin that cancer took away his ability to procreate and threatened his life at a young age. His courage and his determination are a shining example of making it against the odds.

"Medal or no medal, Kevin's success in Olympic sailing is already a testament to the power and triumph of a childhood dream."

Amanda also had other news that wasn't ready for prime time.

She was pregnant.

KEVIN

ALTHOUGH THE OLYMPICS is an experience that most competitors prepare for all of their lives, there is still a surreal nature to it all when it actually happens. There are things that can't be explained or prepared for: the worldwide press, fans, sponsors, cameras on at all times, the increasingly whirlwind pace of online news, and psychological pressure tied to competing on the world's biggest stage. For fifteen years, people had been telling Kevin that he was crazy for thinking he was on television and having his story beamed out around the world. Now it was actually happening.

Among the topics in pre-game advice addressed by the U.S. Olympic Committee was how much, if at all, athletes should see friends or family before a competition. Generally, the advice was that seeing loved ones can be a distraction, unless a particular family member is established as part of a pre-competition routine. In theory that made sense, but in practice it was difficult to adhere to. Family members, even with the best of intentions, want to load up their Olympian with well wishes (and, unintentionally, the weight of their expectations). Kevin loved his mother, but couldn't have been more angry with her when she approached him at the team hotel, as it unintentionally rattled his focus.

Tension ahead of the Athens Olympics was exceptionally high, as the Games would be the first ones staged since the terrorist attacks of September 11. As a representative of the United States, Kevin was both a symbol of patriotism and a target, something the news media was reminding Athens-bound athletes of on a daily basis. Knowing this, and hoping to keep the pressures of being an Olympian at bay, he not only stayed on his medication, but increased his dosage.

Amanda was scheduled to arrive in Greece earlier than the rest of Kevin's family. Two weeks before her flight, she called him with the news that she had just returned from the doctor's office. They were pregnant.

Kevin felt a wave of joy mixed with an unexpected hit of sadness and grief over the biological children he couldn't have swelling up in him again. "When it was hypothetical that we were making a baby with the help of someone we'd never met," Kevin later wrote, "it all sounded pretty great. When it was staring me in the face, the thing I couldn't do, it felt completely different. Combined with the trip to the lab to again give blood—so that some bureaucracy could maybe, but maybe not, tell me once and for all that I was 'okay enough to join the rest of the Olympians, despite my differences'—Amanda's news was ten parts happy and exciting, ten million parts rubbing my face in the fact that I wasn't a man."

Right, wrong, or somewhere in between, Kevin couldn't deny how he felt. The timing of it all—just weeks before the Olympics, should he be allowed to compete—couldn't have been worse.

•

The Athens opening ceremonies were anticipated to be the grandest ever. Held in the brand-new Olympic stadium in Maroussi, a suburb of Athens, the event would be broadcast worldwide in high definition for the first time and would attract more than seventy thousand spectators in person, including myriad heads of state, members of royal families, and former U.S. president George H. W. Bush. The ceremony would weave in artistry and references to the ancient Olympic Games, as the competition was being held on the very soil where they had started centuries earlier. Never mind that the small Mediterranean country wasn't entirely sure how it would pay for such a spectacle; beneath the welcoming smiles, confetti, and Olympic rings, the budget was swelling.

The countries were to march, one by one, and as was typical, the United States would have one of the largest delegations. Owing to Greek opposition to the recent American-led invasion of Iraq, there was some concern that the American athletes would be met with boos when they entered the stadium.

In spite of such concerns, excitement still permeated the American athletes and there was much buzz among them that Kevin Hall—the man who had beaten cancer—would be the Games' flag bearer for their country. It's tradition for the athletes to vote and decide the position on their own and when the votes were cast, Kevin found himself in the position of runner-up, as his teammate Dawn Staley, a basketball player who had previously won two gold medals at the Atlanta and Sydney Games, received the most votes. Kevin had a hard time letting go of this loss. His feelings had nothing to do with Dawn Staley; rather, he simply bought into what the media had suggested about how he deserved the title. But "runner-up flag bearer" was what he would have to live with.

As the night fell and loud music blared, he stood behind the stadium with his fellow athletes, getting ready for the march. The jitters and joy of the parade were infectious. Examining the words written on the jacket that the U.S. Olympic Committee had issued him, he read a reminder of Olympic icon Pierre de Coubertin's credo: "The most important thing in the Olympic Games is not to win but to take part. Just as the most important thing in life is not the triumph, but the struggle."

Fuck that, Kevin thought. He wanted a medal.

KRISTINA

KRISTINA BOARDED HER flight to Europe with her fiancé, Bud. The two had met when both were living in Kneeland, California, a small town in Humboldt County when Bud was enjoying a post-cycling drink at a bar with a friend and spotted a woman at the end of the bar doing a crossword puzzle. He reasoned that a woman who spent her time doing word games must be smart, and so, with some nudging, he made his move. They compared notes and realized that they were both Grateful Dead fans and that they might even have attended at least one of the same shows, ages ago in Oakland. Kristina wondered if he had been the guy who had passed her a joint and said his name was Bud. At the time, she had shaken it off as a joke, but later, she couldn't help but think that might have been the first thing her future husband had ever said to her.

Even by West Coast hippie standards, Bud had an astonishingly tranquil and peaceful demeanor. He had spent twenty years working at the cooperative grocery store and remained unflappable when dealing with even the most unruly of customers. It served him well in dealing with any form of volatility, including the bustle of international travel to an Olympic Games with future in-laws.

As they entered the tube of the airplane for the long journey to Europe, Kristina noticed a copy of *USA Today* sitting on each seat. She examined it. A photograph on the front page showed a pack of smiling Americans in red shirts, navy pants and matching berets, marching proudly behind the Stars and Stripes. She looked closer. She was never great with faces.

Is that my brother next to the flag? she asked Bud.

It was. Kristina couldn't help but think that this whole Show thing was quickly becoming very meta.

KEVIN

KEVIN HAD AGREED to meet anti-doping officials at nine o'clock on the morning of his first Olympic race for yet another round of blood testing. The plan was for the sample to be tested while Kevin was on the water, and it was a drill that was to be repeated daily.

So he was surprised when his team cell phone rang at 5:45 a.m. An official told him that there had been a change of plans. He would have to come through more than thirteen miles of Athens traffic to the Main Stadium for his blood testing no later than seven. This last-minute hiccup was precisely the kind of unexpected kerfuffle that can test the fragile, game-day psyche of an athlete.

This wasn't the plan. This wasn't the plan at all. Even up until the day of the race itself, there had been one hurdle after another, one person, place, or thing telling him that Olympic racing wasn't for him.

Kevin threw the cell phone across the room, smashing it into chunky plastic fragments. It had to be The Show. They were messing with him on the first day of the Olympics. It seemed perfectly clear. There was no other explanation that made any sense.

Observing his outburst, Amanda calmed Kevin down and persuaded him to take his meds. This was not the moment for pharmaceutical experimentation.

•

Kevin arrived at the Agios Kosmas Olympic Sailing Centre just in time. Located in southwest Athens along the coast, it was a hangar-like complex that could accommodate more than three hundred boats, and more than four hundred athletes across all the sailing classes were present. The venue was brand-new, having been built specifically for the Olympics, and there were still stickers on some of the furniture and spots of wet paint. The hope among Olympics organizers was that the facility would help revitalize the waterfront district after all the medals had been handed out and the anthems played.

Sailing took place during almost the entire three-week span of the Olympic Games. Eleven events, each involving a number of races, were scheduled over seventeen days: four for men, four for women, and three that were "open" to both men and women, the rare coed Olympic sport. The marina was located about nine miles from Athens city center, with a long port that had an extensive security system, including cameras, to ensure that the millions of dollars in equipment remained safe.

Kevin was to compete in grueling marathon of eleven races spread over ten days. The athlete who had compiled the best score at the end of his or her races would win. The races encompassed a variety of conditions; shifting breezes made for a mix of light, medium, and heavy sailing. At the first turn of the first race, he was well positioned, asserting himself early against his competitors. Soon, however, he dropped back a few places, which crumpled him emotionally for the rest of the day.

In a later event, as he was leading a race, he received a yellow flag for "pumping"—meaning that a judge believed he had fanned the sail too much. It was a first for Kevin in his career, and it meant that he was on notice: another yellow flag risked disqualifying him from the race altogether. The flag hung in his mind as he sailed tight downwind for the rest of the event.

The start of the last race was one of Kevin's most brilliant moments on the water. His boat soared with an effortlessness typically reserved for sailing in paintings. But his performance zigzagged after leading the first turn, he bounded for the finish line, his friends and family watching, and it was unclear how he would finally fare.

AMANDA

ALL OF THE sailboats at the Olympics were virtually identical, only flags distinguishing them from afar, making it hard for Amanda to tell how her husband was holding his own against the competition from her perch on the family spectator boat. The flag on Kevin's was a navy blue with USA at the top, but Amanda could barely make out her husband, dressed like many of his fellow competitors: a hat to keep the sun off his shaved head, sunglasses, a long-sleeved white, Lycra shirt, tight gloves, white vest, and gray wetsuit.

She wondered if it had been a mistake to tell him about the pregnancy so close to the Olympics, but she reasoned that it could have been far worse not to. She also knew that as husband and wife, and after all they had been through, she couldn't have kept the news a secret much longer. Doing so would likely have led to her acting differently and stressing out Kevin even more. It was exciting news, something they had hoped for and gone to great lengths to make happen. What's more, she had endured weeks of in vitro treatments that had left her feeling bloated, hormonal, and exhausted during her rotations at the hospital. Perhaps she had underestimated what Kevin's reaction to the news would be.

Amanda and the others watched as Olympic gold medalist Ben Ainslie of Great Britain started the event poorly but made it to the finish line and the final race in first place, nabbing the second gold medal of his career and the second gold medal for the 2004 British Olympic sailing team. Spain's Rafael Trujillo Villar was behind him with the silver, and Poland's Mateusz Kusznierwicz came in with the bronze.

From there, the boats just seemed to whir by, one after another.

Kevin finished eleventh overall.

GORDON

It would have been tremendous for Kevin to make the Olympic podium, of course, Gordon thought, but he was still proud of his son for having made it to the Games at all, especially after what he had been through. Kevin didn't need a round piece of metal on a ribbon to show his grit as an athlete and Gordon wondered if expressing this feeling to Kevin was too little too late after all the years he had spent impressing on his son the importance of achievement. He thought back to the mantel at their home in Ventura, crammed with the trophies that Kevin had brought home from his run on the junior sailing circuit. Gordon now realized that what he had thought was encouragement and positive reinforcement might instead have been unintentionally harmful in establishing such a narrow definition of success.

The results were in.

Gordon didn't know what to say.

KEVIN

AHEAD OF THE medal ceremony, Kevin roamed with his family, crest-fallen as they tried to find seats. The whole moment was starting to stress him out, even though the competition had concluded. Kevin spotted one of the American coaches and bolted away from his family, watching the ceremony with him instead.

Television cameras rolled, capturing the action. A green olive wreath was carefully placed on the head of each medal winner, a nod to the ancient Olympic tradition of crowning the victors with laurels. A gold medal hanging from a multicolored ribbon was placed around the neck of Ben Ainslie, who smiled and waved in his white and navy Team GB track jacket to fans and cameras. Over loudspeakers, the British national anthem "God Save the Queen" blared as the Union Jack was hoisted up the flag-pole, with the flags for Spain and Poland on either side. The ceremony reminded Kevin of the many times he'd stood on the podium after sailing in the junior regattas that had so consumed him in his younger years. This time, however, he had lost.

Kevin also wondered if, as a child, he had been so immersed in the life of a junior sailor that he'd never had a real childhood at all—and whether that was by his own doing or his parents'. But it was futile to ruminate over all that at this point, he thought. And intellectualizing what had happened at the Games seemed a worthless pursuit as well.

•

Kevin's memory for races was usually sharp, but he was quick to block out much of what happened in Athens. It was as if he had boarded the

plane to Greece, then suddenly found himself at the medal ceremony, sitting next to Team USA's coach. He knew he had raced, and
he knew he wasn't pleased with the outcome, but the details existed in a
haze.

Looking at his family, seated far away, he felt a profound sense of
shame. He interpreted his father's face, which seemed to be set in a mix
of confusion, disgust, and disrespect. The thought of watching some of
his friends win Olympic medals, being the stars on camera after all of his
work, was complicated. On the one hand, he was really happy for Rafa
and felt moved by Mateusz's joy in winning, a long gap since he had won
a gold medal in the Finn eight years before in Atlanta. Yet Kevin felt he
had shamed his family and himself, his perfectionistic tendencies slam-
ming him harder than ever before.

He had thought during his last race that he could bounce back in the
second half, but his strength and stamina had failed him.

"There wasn't an evil conspiracy designed to keep Kevin Hall from
having a nice week at the Olympics, not at all," Kevin had told a reporter
with the Baltimore *Sun.* He had been reluctant to talk to the press during
the competition and only agreed to talk once his final race was over. "Not
at all. Even with team doctors here and the paperwork done, it turned
out to be a big deal to get an injection."

One of the peculiarities of elite sports is the expectation of the press
and fans for an athlete not only to be articulate, but to be so within
seconds of a major life moment and the endorphin rush of a physical feat.
As Kevin spoke to the press, he found himself in that strange window of
processing what had happened, his thoughts still a jumble, his brain in
overdrive.

"I hate to even talk about it," he said of his results, "because it sounds
like sour grapes and I'm blaming everything on that. It's not that. It's just

that my goal was to sail well here, personally, even if that meant that I was last.

"I think I would have been somewhat pleased and realized I don't have the skill, but at least I tried and gave it my all," he said. But, he said, he didn't feel as though that was the case in Athens; he felt that he could have pushed harder. Even U.S. Sailing's Olympic director acknowledged that Kevin getting his testing and shots taken prior to the races "didn't go as smoothly as it should have."

Kevin tried to tell himself that he hadn't done so badly; he'd placed mid- to top-of-fleet among the best sailors in the world. He had finished ahead of some competitors who had been far better prepared than he was, especially considering that he had been sailing the Finn for less than a year. Sailing insiders and lay fans alike talked of their admiration for Kevin's perseverance in the wake of cancer, with many news outlets comparing his saga to that of Lance Armstrong, the cycling champion. (It would be eight years before Armstrong would be banned from his sport when his role in an elaborate doping ring came to light.) In those simpler times, the comparison with Armstrong was considered a compliment: both men had rebounded from diseases that tried to take over their bodies, only to return to their athletic endeavors stronger than ever.

None of that was processing with Kevin. Eleventh wasn't what his childhood self had been gunning for. Eleventh wasn't what he wanted stitched into his Olympic jacket. Eleventh wasn't the text he wanted to see following his name in the record books, a documentation of his immortality in a sport that would endure long after he would. Eleventh, to Kevin, meant failure. What would he tell his soon-to-be-arriving child?

The last night they were together in Athens, Kevin and his family went out for a farewell dinner. As a child, Kevin and his father had always engaged in post-race dissections, breaking down the details of how Kevin had handled each turn, each shift of the wind, each decision, but the idea of a recap, even if it was constructive in intention and academic in tone, now, the ritual was too painful. Honestly, Kevin thought, he wasn't even sure his father had watched his race, and Kevin didn't want to ask, let alone get tedious notes about what he had done right or wrong on the world's biggest stage.

If there was an upside to the post-Olympic funk, it was that Kevin had a good job waiting for him and little time in which to sulk. He would be joining Team New Zealand in its America's Cup bid. Before going home, though, he and Amanda would take a vacation in Italy, during which he drank heavily and she, expecting a child, abstained. They slept late, lounged by the pool, and read mediocre celebrity magazines, a welcome decompression.

AMANDA

THEY HAD BEEN away from home for only a few weeks, but it had felt like years. The Olympics were over, and now she and Kevin were in Maryland with a $20,000 debt to show for it. Fortunately, with Team New Zealand putting Kevin on a retainer for its next America's Cup bid, that debt could soon be erased.

Amanda was impressed that Kevin had been able to pull off life as a well-paid professional sailor during all of the years they'd been married, especially since the opportunity hadn't really existed even a decade ago. At least on that front, Kevin had been, and still was, in the right place at the right time, as there was a niche demand for the incredibly specific skill set that he offered.

Shortly after their return home, Amanda and Kevin waited in the doctor's office for a baby checkup, which would include an ultrasound.

Within seconds of the test starting, Amanda knew.

They had lost the baby.

KRISTINA

A FEW WEEKS after Kristina and Bud were engaged, she was pregnant. She loved the idea of being a mother, but not long after she gave birth, the panic attacks came and came swiftly. She and Bud had started a postal supply and shipping business, which was causing stress for both of them, and she felt devastated by the sudden death of her stepfather, Ted. Kristina thought that somehow, strangely, between the timing of his death and her pregnancy, it felt as if Ted's spirit had been transferred into that of her new son.

One perk of having a doctor for a sister-in-law was being a phone call away from any diagnosis. She called Amanda and described her symptoms: the shortness of breath, the stress, the overwhelmed feeling in her head. *They're probably panic attacks*, Amanda told her.

Kristina's mind raced back to her bad mushroom trip and near-death experience at Disneyland more than a decade prior, and had similar thoughts to what she had had then. She couldn't go nuts, she couldn't fall apart. She was the family moderator. They needed her.

AMANDA

ON PAPER, KEVIN and Amanda looked like perfect candidates for adoption. A few years into marriage and more than a decade into knowing each other, they had a six-figure household income, a robust network of friends and family, and a compelling backstory as to why they couldn't conceive children on their own. Both she and Kevin hailed from "square" families of two parents and two kids, and early on they had decided that they wanted the bustle and energy of having a family of their own, perhaps with as many as three children. Although they often had to move with the sailing season, they had the resources to accommodate a family wherever Kevin's boat assignment took them. It was an unorthodox lifestyle, but one that most of the adoption agencies they spoke to seemed willing to accommodate.

Amanda and Kevin weighed whether or not to disclose Kevin's bipolar disorder to adoption agencies. If they did, they risked not getting the child they so desperately wanted, but they feared that if they withheld the information and the agency found out about it later through other means, their credibility would be lost.

After some discussion, they decided to disclose Kevin's diagnosis. At the same time, they also pointed out that he was in excellent care, healthy, and committed to staying mentally sound. What's more, it had been a while since his most recent episode. They waited.

In late 2004, they received word that they had been approved to adopt a little boy. The news was thrilling, particularly after their first attempt at adoption resulted in financial loss and emotional pain, but like many adoptive parents, Kevin and Amanda began to worry that their application could be discarded, a birth parent might change his or her mind, or something else would go wrong in the process. Nothing felt certain until they met with the six-month pregnant mother, who lived in Long Island, New York, and agreed to an open adoption, meaning that biological and adoptive families have some contact. On New Year's Eve 2004, Amanda and Kevin welcomed Rainer, named after one of their favorite poets, Austrian-Bohemian Rainer Maria Rilke, into their family. Now they had an adorable, cooing little person to remind them of the poet whose words had sprinkled so many of their love letters in earlier years.

The following year, Kevin and Amanda bought a home in Auckland, a city they had been in and out of for five years, eager to finally be planted somewhere for a while. Their home in the Ponsonby neighborhood had enough bedrooms to accommodate the large family they wanted to build and also ensured that Kevin would always be near the best sailing facilities in the world. Amanda found work in an emergency room in the area and had less hassle with malpractice insurance than she would have had in the United States. Auckland was beautiful, clean, warm, and one of the most livable places on earth.

The transition seemed to go smoothly for Kevin, who during his first year there had only one minor episode when some red wine had "unlocked" more of his brain than he had intended. It ended with Kevin visiting the psych ward to get some more medication and having to stay the night. He and Amanda both saw it as progress that they had been able to control and react to the early symptoms of The Show before total mayhem erupted.

A year later, a second boy, Leo, arrived in the Hall household, also an open adoption from a different mother in upstate New York, and named after Leo Robbins, one of Kevin's first sailing coaches. Kevin debated how or even whether he should make a bid for the 2008 Beijing Olympics, arriving at the Team New Zealand gym at 5:15 a.m., an hour earlier each morning, to do extra leg and abdominal workouts for the Finn class. But after much painful stewing, he realized that making a hard push for

Beijing, with his new duties in the America's Cup and as a father, would be extremely difficult. Tears came as he reconciled the two dimensions of what he saw as failure with the success of starting a family.

Having made an Olympic team, Kevin was faced with the awkward, though often well-intended, question from strangers and acquaintances, "How did you do?" The vast majority of Olympians, by definition, did not win, a harsh reality that is not seen on television but can fill the Olympic Park with a sense of malaise as the calendar of events rolls on. The grounds fill up with people who feel like they're losers and the test to one's psyche upon returning home in the shadow of one of the world's strictest achievement models, can be nothing short of taxing. All sense of context is completely lost on most athletes, as well as many friends and family members. Who is eleventh-best at anything in the world? Or even one of the fifty best people? How is it that so many of those who make it into such an elite pool to begin with end up leaving feeling like failures?

Kevin sometimes wondered whether if he had completely tanked in Athens, like finishing in last place or close to it, that would have made it easier. In that scenario, he would have been so far from the podium that his sense of entitlement in being there would have been nonexistent.

Years later, it felt bizarre to not be either a winner or an outright loser: the strange, overlooked psyche of a middle-of-the-pack Olympian.

SARAH

EVEN THOUGH IT had been nearly a decade since Sarah O'Kane had first met many of the sailors on the AmericaOne campaign, she still saw them as Peter Pans. They never seemed to grow up, boys trapped in the bodies of athletic men. But if they were Peter Pans, traversing the professional sailing circuit as though it was some sort of Neverland, Sarah knew that that must make her Wendy. As she continued to grow into her role as the head of the team's logistics, she was something of a mother-away-from-mother to all of them, a caretaker, a confidante, and a boss with a smile, long blonde hair, and a soft British accent.

Sardinia, with its turquoise waters, pink sand beaches and inviting temperatures, was chosen to be the site of a 2008 Audi MedCup regatta, the world's premiere Grand Prix sailing circuit. The event featured many of the same sailors as the Olympics and the America's Cup, and like the America's Cup, its team rosters were constantly being reshuffled each cycle, with new team combinations popping up at each event.

In professional sailing, as in Olympic sailing, all distractions that pulled the sailors away from the boat were supposed to be eliminated. As that dimension of the sport grew and more money entered the campaigns, the stakes for the athletes naturally became higher. The athletes were told where, when, and what to eat and what hotels to stay at. They were handed their boarding passes for planes, and their collective schedule was sliced like a loaf of bread into distinct, specific parts. Their sole focus was to figure out how to make their boat go as fast as possible.

Over the years, Sarah had gotten to know the spouses of sailors, too, and the dynamics of their relationships with their husbands. She had observed that in general, the men on the boat were good partners, but they often paired best with those who could take charge. The sailors were loving, caring, fun to be around, engineering mavens, and many boasted handsome salaries and an arsenal of medals and trophies. But when it came to laundry, cooking, cleaning, or talking feelings, they could be utterly hopeless.

The Mean Machine, headed up by Kiwi Ray Davies, had performed well in the Sardinia Regatta, helping move them up prestigious circuit standings.

A celebration was well earned. Wearing sleek sunglasses, matching gray T-shirts, and black shorts, Kevin, Ray, and the rest of the team popped open bottles of champagne and proceeded to spray each other. A victory party on a docked boat followed later that night, with Kevin among the most enthusiastic of those present, sipping rum and Cokes instead of his usual beer. Then, Sarah observed something that the other revelers probably shrugged off as merely drunken behavior. Yet Sarah, recalling her experience with Kevin back in New Zealand years earlier, knew better. Kevin had taken off his Olympic watch, pulled his wallet out of his pocket, and chucked both items overboard. He did keep his shoes on, though, unlike several earlier episodes in which he had taken them off to be closer to the earth.

Immediately, Sarah began circling around Kevin's teammates, telling them that she needed their help. The memory of seeing Kevin moon-walking down the street in Auckland with his Discman played in the back of her head. He had seemed fine earlier in the day, and during the stellar competition, but that was clearly not the case now.

•

Flanked by his teammates, Kevin walked back to the hotel. He kept asking if they could go out for another drink, if they could just keep celebrating, and he spouted off to anyone who would listen about the meaning of life, trying to save the universe, his place in it. His mood jolted back and forth from euphoric to desperate, and he was on the verge of tears in either direction, with a rickety bridge of sarcasm in between.

As his mind ricocheted, he thought he tripped over a couple of things on the sidewalk and could have sworn that he saw a bull roaming the streets. Then he spied a large cactus. The sight of it captivated him and become the focus of every ounce of his concentration, again lyrics from R.E.M. coming to mind ("I am a cactus/Trying to be a canoe"). He lunged for it, and before his teammates could pull him away, Kevin had already wrapped his arms around the cactus. It was necessary, he said, to give the prickly plant "a hug."

Kevin's teammates peeled him off the plant, his shirt now specked with dots of blood from where the needles had pricked his skin through the cotton of his T-shirt. Then they made their way up to his hotel room.

As the men searched for Kevin's downers and tried to occupy his wandering mind, Sarah walked out into the hallway of the hotel. She knew that she had to get in touch with Amanda as soon as possible. Making sure that Kevin couldn't hear her, she punched in Amanda's number and told her what had happened. Calmly, Amanda told her where the medications were stowed in Kevin's luggage.

If they were *really* lucky, Amanda said, they might be able to get Kevin to take a sleeping pill. It was unlikely, but if that was the case, he could get through the worst of it, the downers kicking in and pushing him to sleep until the next morning. Complicating matters was the fact that both the uppers and the downers Kevin had at the time were purple, meaning that he alone would have to help them figure out which were which.

The team was supposed to leave Sardinia the next day, and it was unclear to the sailors what the implications of Kevin's being hospitalized in Italy would be. How long would they keep him? What would the treatment be like? How would Amanda, with their two young sons far beyond Italy's borders, be able to retrieve him once he was out? They had to get him calm enough to fly back to Amanda in New York, where she was with family for the summer, a journey with a couple of major legs that Kevin would have to complete solo.

Meanwhile, in the hotel room, his teammate Ray talked to Kevin, who by now was sitting on his bed with his laptop splayed open and on top of his head, like the roof of an A-frame house, Pink Floyd's "Comfortably Numb" emanating from the speakers. The references in the lyrics to a distant ship, waves, and being without pain all seemed perfect for the moment.

Sarah approached Kevin, night now turning into morning, about taking a sleeping pill. To her surprise, he identified what he said were the proper downers, agreed to take them, and seemed amenable to the idea of one of Kevin's teammates, Tommy Dodson, agreeing to reroute and fly to Rome, where Kevin would get on a plane to New York alone and Tommy would head back to Auckland. The meds were in Kevin's system, but it was anyone's guess how long it would take, or how effective, the drugs would be.

Nor did it help that the Pink Floyd blaring in the room included a line about "going to The Show."

KEVIN

KEVIN COULDN'T REMEMBER what sentence it was or whose mouth it came out of, but he did remember feeling, within seconds, as if he had gone from partying on the boat to being on The Show. Thomas Pynchon's

The Crying of Lot 49 came to mind, coupled with the notion of being uncomfortable in one's skin. In the book, Oedipa Maas, the protagonist, discovers and begins to unravel a world conspiracy that may or may not be real. " 'I came,' she said, 'hoping you could talk me out of a fantasy.' 'Cherish it!' cried Hilarious, fiercely. 'What else do any of you have? Hold it tightly by its little tentacle, don't let the Freudians coax it away or the pharmacists poison it out of you. Whatever it is, hold it dear, for when you lose it you go over by that much to the others. You begin to cease to be.' "

To Kevin, the Sardinia episode had a similar feeling, as if it was some kind of practical joke. Sure, his teammates had tried to calm him down with arguments about the meaning of life. But that was part of The Show, as they were actors, too, and had been training their whole lives to know Kevin, his mission, and their role in it. "Shall I project a world?" Pynchon wrote.

Although the sailing press had been brimming with positive coverage about the Mean Machine performance, Kevin privately wasn't satisfied with his own personal performance. He felt that he had made a few bad calls, and he felt the pressure of a larger stress, too: he was uncertain of his place in the America's Cup circuit, and having put in what he had perceived as a mediocre individual contribution in Sardinia wouldn't help his case.

Still, it was time to head home and see which elements of the episode awaited him there. At the counter for customs with Tommy, Kevin listed his address as Auckland, Planet Earth, The Universe. During the layover in Rome, he purchased for Amanda what he believed to be the most expensive Gucci bag available as a gift. He had wanted to buy three more, just to make sure she had options that she liked, but Tommy persuaded him that just one would suffice. This was among Kevin's most expensive souvenirs from The Show, and it only made sense, he thought, that his wife, the leading lady, should be treated to the finest of brand-name possessions.

Often, during other episodes, Kevin had opted to save twigs, pages torn from magazines, bottle caps, and collages of nonsense that he perceived as works of art. At least once during an episode, too, he had filled his pockets with breadcrumbs, the way a child collects shells at a beach, mementos of euphoria. Usually, after Kevin came down, he studied the objects he had collected, wondering why he had thought they were once so laced with significance, confronted with tangible evidence of a version of him that he no longer recognized. Occasionally he made grandiose purchases that were just as inconsistent, then had to barter with store clerks and credit card companies about how to procure a refund.

Near a men's restroom in the airport, Kevin noticed a plastic plaque on the wall that appeared to be precisely the same size as his thirteen-inch MacBook laptop. That must be some kind of port of significance. He stopped and placed his laptop against the plaque. Tommy chuckled, then gently escorted him onto the plane.

Later, back home and well after Kevin had cooled down, he felt amazed that Tommy had been able to get him on the plane to New York and Kevin had kept himself entertained, but essentially in his seat, the entire flight back across the Atlantic. He wasn't sure how he had done it.

Amanda maintained that she actually liked the Gucci bag.

AMANDA

KEVIN AND AMANDA had traveled to Russia before for various sailing events, and Amanda considered herself a bit of a Russophile, as she had long been taken with the country's distinctive accent, layered history, and curious customs. Russia was also their best shot at the time for adopting a girl.

They made their way to Rostov-on-Don, a town of a million or so people located in the southern part of the massive country. The city prides itself on being the birthplace of the poet Alexander Pushkin and the heart of Cossack country. Many years after the fall of the Berlin Wall, statues of Vladimir Lenin still spotted the streets. The juxtaposition of economic realities was also odd: one street could be a beautiful paved boulevard that rivaled Europe's most cosmopolitan thoroughfares, but around the corner could be a dirt road with exposed manholes. Travelers to Russia often compared the country's psyche to that of the nesting dolls that are a popular tourist gift, one layer opening up onto another, another and yet another, a proverbial cultural onion of complexities.

In the summer of 2011, Amanda and Kevin visited the orphanage where their soon-to-be daughter lived and completed a dossier of paperwork similar to those they'd completed for their sons. Then, once again, they waited.

That November, a little girl, Nina Stevie, came home with them. They had given her the middle name after Amanda's father—the one who had given her the distinctive watch that she and Kevin had talked about on their first date all those years ago in Providence. Stevie eventually asked to go by that instead of Nina, a desire that was happily granted.

KEVIN

AFTER SARDINIA, KEVIN went three years without an episode. He sailed on a retainer with Team New Zealand in Auckland for a couple of seasons, then spent two seasons on a TP52, a large carbon fiber boat that could surf with stability in strong downwind breezes well over 20 knots, or 23 miles per hour.

Sardinia stayed with him, mostly because he had never had an episode of that magnitude on the water before, and the Sardinia one had hit just hours after he had sailed, and well, no less. Miraculously, too, he had returned home safely and avoided hospitalization, his downers having taken effect before the plane landed. The mystery of the triggers and their aftermaths still felt inconsistent, even after years of trying to figure out what sparked the episodes and how to deal with them once they came.

When Kevin was in The Show, he had a sense of "everything happening all at once in the span of an instant," a description similar to what he later read in David Foster Wallace's short story "Good Old Neon." Wallace, like James Joyce, seemed to be fluent in a secret language, but a language that Kevin connected with deeply. Wallace's story opens with a declaration of imposter syndrome, which still plagued Kevin in his career as a professional athlete, husband, and father even many successful years into all of it. "My whole life I've been a fraud," wrote Wallace. "I'm not exaggerating. Pretty much all I've ever done all the time is try to create a certain impression of me in other people. Mostly to be liked or admired." In shattering detail, too, Wallace wrote about what was real and what was a scene. The main character in his story realizes that at "an early age I'd somehow chosen to cast my lot with my life's drama's supposed audience instead of with the drama itself."

After reading "Good Old Neon," Kevin started devouring Wallace's work and also became fascinated with Wallace's own life, which ended on September 12, 2008, when Wallace died by suicide, a tragic last act after decades of battling depression.

The years without an episode of The Show created moments for Kevin when he felt as if his life was all finally coming together. He and Amanda were forming a family with children he loved. He felt engaged with his work on Team New Zealand. Auckland was enough like California to make him feel at home, but still a new enough adventure for there to be a learning curve as he and Amanda found a home and schools for their children and made friends.

When the phone rang one day with an offer for Kevin to compete in the upcoming 2013 America's Cup race with the *Artemis* team, founded by the Swedish businessman Torbjörn Törnqvist, Kevin was confident, calm, and thrilled. Although he had enjoyed his time with Team New Zealand, he was worried that he'd been pigeonholed to a certain extent and no longer had ample space in which to grow his skill sets. On the *Artemis*, his role would involve his running the instruments, load, and performance data department. He would be plugged straight into the boat's brain, and responsible for telling the other sailors what it was trying to say. It was an opportunity on a par with competing in the London Olympics—a chance at redemption and possibly an America's Cup title. Finally.

For the Halls, Kevin's new job meant moving back to the United States, to San Francisco, where all the America's Cup teams would be based. They rented out their home in Auckland and found a new one in Berkeley, and Amanda secured a post in the emergency room at San Francisco General Hospital. The sense of impermanence that comes with the sailing lifestyle—suitcases, storage units, paper coffee cups—was now something to which the family had grown accustomed.

The 2013 America's Cup was to be unlike any other. Team Oracle, per America's Cup tradition, would be staging the event, having won the previous title in 2010, and the new boats were called AC72s, a class of 72-foot-long, 46-foot-wide catamarans with 131-foot-tall hard wings instead of soft sails, and each boat weighed fifteen thousand pounds, or seven and a half tons, roughly the heft of three elephants. The *Artemis* looked like a skyscraper on the water—fragile, fierce, and futuristic—and like a skyscraper, too, it was elegant and inspiring in its ambition. But it and the other three boats lacked the foundation of a building. It gave viewers, perhaps unconsciously, a sense of anxiety about whether the boats would stay afloat, even in the most capable of hands, as they swayed against and away from the wind and waves. If they were to hit the water at those speeds, it would be like smashing into a wall.

Traditionalists deemed them monstrous, and they would require a level of athleticism and engineering unlike that of any previous regatta. The Oracle chief and impassioned sailor Larry Ellison wanted to transform the event from being one which had historically inspired relatively little spectator interest among Americans, into a popular international sporting brand, akin to Formula One auto racing. It was clear to Kevin and his teammates that no matter what happened, Oracle was going to be there to the end, having the will—and finances—to get there at any cost (and the defender was always in the final). Ellison's personal drive to push the boundaries of the sport was all the more fascinating considering that he had nearly been killed in the deadly 1998 Sydney to Hobart race.

"There are two aspects of speed," Ellison told the journalist G. Bruce Knecht. "One is the absolute notion of speed. Then there's the relative notion—trying to go faster than the next guy. I think it's the latter that's much more interesting. It's an expression of our primal being. Ever since we were living in villages as hunter gatherers, great rewards went to people who were stronger, faster."

What Kevin didn't know then was that his assignment with the team would pose the most difficult challenge in his life, in and out of The Show.

•

The exterior of the *Artemis* compound where Kevin worked in Alameda, California, showed no outward signs of the panic within its walls. However, on the first day of work there, one of the tasks was to peel all of the blackout paper off the walls, as Kevin had heard that parts of one of the Matrix movies had been filmed there in years prior, a Show-like coincidence he held off on remarking to his teammates about. One of many beige boxes in a row of buildings on the bay, it was on a street far from Alameda's main thoroughfares—one traversed only by dock and factory workers. The *Artemis* team was directly across the water from their competitors in a neighborhood that offered stunning views of the San Francisco skyline but maintained the blue-collar audio of buzzing machinery from nearby factories and the clanks and booms of cargo ships depositing and picking up their freight. The tidy layout of the symmetrical buildings and their wide concrete façades evoked the feel of an army base, framed with chain-link fencing and barbed wire.

For several months, it had been clear to Kevin and his teammates that this would be the most expensive America's Cup yet. Unlike Kevin's first campaign with AmericaOne, the four teams for the 2013 cycle were each made up of a mixture of nationalities, making it common for the sailors to be teammates with the same people they had competed against in the Olympics or previous America's Cup cycles. The rosters had been reshuffled, and the teams earned their spots through a series of selection races. The bill for the four teams would total more than $400 million for the

2013 cycle, which, adjusting for inflation, approached the entire amount that 123 teams had spent on the Cup from 1870 to 1980. Higher payrolls, larger and more sophisticated boats, and more time and money spent on research and development were among the reasons for the increased expense. Nor were the boats' costs remotely equal. Luna Rossa Challenge 2013 spent $65 million on its boat, compared with $156 million spent by Ellison's Oracle Team USA. Kevin's Team Artemis spent $115 million, not far above Emirates Team New Zealand's $105 million.

More teams with bigger budgets was good news for sailors like Kevin, as they provided more well-paying jobs and opportunities to keep careers active. Kevin continued to thrive under the strict schedule of an America's Cup cycle, and joining the team seemed like a win for everyone, especially with a third child under the Hall roof. Now seen as a veteran of the Cup, Kevin felt mentally strong and solid about his ability to handle the pressure of competition, excited about it, even. The athletes and team owners held press conferences and posted updates to Twitter and Facebook to build anticipation. But behind the scenes, the teams were continually spying, eager for even the slightest tidbit of information about the others, the cliché "loose lips sink ships" taking on a literal meaning.

The sailors had varying levels of understanding about the dimensions of risk in the old sport. Kevin and his teammates wore helmets and impact-resistant clothing more akin to that of motorcycle racing than yachting, and it made them look more like comic book heroes than sailors. With the ever-present danger of capsizing, now at a faster speed than ever, all the men on the boat carried oxygen canisters and knew how to employ them should the boat bend, break, flip, or succumb to some combination of all three. In the 2013 boats, the two hulls, or bodies, of the boat were separated by a platform that was about the size of a tennis court and made up of webbing similar to that of a trampoline. Because they had two hulls, the boats did not need heavy keels underwater to counteract the wind's resistance on the sails. Less weight and less resistance meant greater speed. With the increased girth of the new boats, communication between sailors on board was a greater challenge; even the speakers and headsets built into the sailors' helmets were often a futile match against the deafening roar of the wind. The conflict between speed and safety that had been under way for more than 150 years was amplified; the two-hulled bodies made for a faster regatta, but with an unknown risk to the men on board.

For the first time in recent history, the America's Cup would be visible to fans on the shoreline, part of Ellison's vision of "stadium sailing." Ellison and the event's organizers also felt that sailing had an unrealized potential for television (and hopefully the lucrative broadcast deals that come with it), especially since sports remained one of the few pockets of television where being live on-air still mattered.

As yet another nod to the highest-tech sailing bout ever, Kevin received a pair of Google Glass from a subcontractor he had done work with. A tool that at the time was lampooned by many in Silicon Valley and still not fully available to the public, the device could be used as a hands-free computer, able to capture video and photos and share the thrilling experience of what it was like to be on board. No one was aware of his experiences with The Show and the Director.

Even Kevin didn't think much about Google Glass being a potential trigger for his mania. He enjoyed the half day he spent learning how to use the device, fiddling and asking questions. He thought the mapping and texting functions were nifty, and he could see how the camera could be useful for taking videos and photos, both while sailing and when on family vacations. Google Glass married data and film, it was wearable, and its fit with professional sailing seemed natural to Kevin.

•

As soon as Kevin heard the term "The 'Truman Show' delusion," he plugged it into Google, where he learned that it was a term used to describe a type of bipolar disorder in which, during manic highs, one felt as if he or she was the star of a reality TV show. "The 'Truman Show' delusion" was a term coined by brothers Drs. Joel Gold and Ian Gold to describe what others were now discussing on online forums like Reddit. Dr. Joel Gold was a psychiatrist at Bellevue in New York City, and Dr. Ian Gold was a philosopher of psychiatry and neuroscience. More and more, Dr. Joel Gold had observed, patients were coming in for treatment with technology as the focus of their delusions. Many felt that their lives were being filmed, but in a city where the streets *were* being monitored by cameras, and everyone had access to live streaming via smartphones, Dr. Gold was finding it more and more challenging to convince his patients that they were delusional. From a factual standpoint, they made a compelling case. "How do you address someone who can point to the internet and say, 'They *did* write about me'?" Dr. Joel Gold said.

For years, Kevin had thought he was crazy in, well, a particularly eccentric way, but now he wondered if he wasn't alone after all. Strangely, the thought made him feel cheapened. It sounded absurd, but he had thought his experience with The Show was special. Now not even his mental illness was remarkable anymore.

The Gold brothers believed that biology alone didn't account for mental illness, including bipolar disorder; rather, there seemed to be environmental factors that helped push people over the edge, or at least informed how they got there. They had found, for example, that for some reason delusions of jealousy were more prevalent in Germany than in Japan, that a wealthy Pakistani man was more likely to have delusions of grandeur than his poor female cousin, who in turn was more likely to suffer from erotomania, a delusion in which one person believes that another person is in love with them. Delusions involving biblical or religious figures had waned over the last couple of centuries as the influence of organized religion had diminished. This backdrop posed challenging questions for the "Truman Show" delusion. What role was the typical American media diet playing in modern mental illness?

Having read up on the subject, Kevin learned that there were many different kinds, some more obscure than others. There was the Cotard delusion, in which a person believed that he or she was already dead, either figuratively or literally, or that he or she didn't really exist. There was Lesch-Nyhan syndrome, a self-mutilation disorder in which one may consume his or her own body parts—until, that is, one's teeth are removed, which is often seen as the "cure." There was Alice in Wonderland syndrome, in which people see objects in real life as being distorted compared to what they really are, as if they were viewing the world "through the wrong end of a telescope." Boanthropy referred to people who felt that they were a cow, ox, or other bovine creature—some falling on all fours and eating grass. Reports also surfaced of Foreign Accent syndrome, in which a British woman, after she woke up from surgery for a migraine, inexplicably found that she had a Chinese accent. Critics may decry some of these labels, like Truman Show Disorder, as boutique diagnoses, ways for doctors to garner attention or funding, but whatever the branding, their circumstances continue to befuddle and fascinate those in the field.

Underlying the doctors' descriptions was a deeper belief, one that resisted turning those suffering from mental illness into the "other." The Drs. Gold believed that all human beings had parts of their brain that could be manic, depressive, delusional, or psychotic. It was just a matter of keeping those potentially disruptive parts at peace.

Kevin sent an email to the Gold brothers inquiring about their research, partly because he thought he could be helpful to them as a case study, partly because he wanted to know more. The doctors' descriptions of the delusion seemed uncannily similar to Kevin's experience in The Show, and the way they had described it, the "Truman Show" delusion could exist in people with schizophrenia, bipolar disorder, or just about any psychotic illness.

Kevin's case posed a new dimension for the doctors: What were they to do when the patient actually *had* been on television, written about extensively, and competed at an international sporting event that many treat like the most important thing in the world? In fact, Kevin was the first case the doctors had ever encountered of a quasi-public figure with "Truman Show" delusion. Dr. Gold was not Kevin's official psychiatrist, but he and Kevin developed a friendship, mutually fascinated and informed by each other's experiences from opposing sides of the proverbial couch.

When emailing back and forth, Kevin and Dr. Joel Gold got on the topic of their educational backgrounds. It turned out that not only was Dr. Gold a fellow Brown University alum, but he had graduated in Kevin's year, and in revisiting the cartography of their dorm room assignments, the two realized that they had lived close to each other for years.

Kevin had to tell himself this couldn't be the work of the Director, but rather just an uncanny coincidence.

•

Across the Bay from Artemis headquarters, at Piers 30 and 32 in San Francisco, the sailors of Team New Zealand knew they had a weapon in hand that was going to forever alter America's Cup sailing: foils, or wing-like structures added to the bottom of a boat that make the entire vessel fly above the water. When the team first took its foiling catamaran out on a warm July day in 2012, spectators thought the sight looked Photoshopped, or involved some sort of visual trickery, everyone recognizing that in that moment, the sport had been forever changed. How could a boat that large seemingly fly above the water? And how could it move so fast? At the command of the sailors on board, the boat could suddenly lift its left or right side, or both, out of the water. It also created a different crash risk. Not only could a boat sink, but it could hit the wall of the water's surface at a speed of 50 miles per hour or more.

Foils, or hydrofoils, as some preferred to call them, weren't new to sailing, but they had never been used at this level, this speed, before. Smaller boats, such as Moths, had long foils. In a first, a hydrofoil Moth had won the Moth World Championship in 2001, and later, foiling became ubiquitous in the Moth class. Sailors debated whether adding foils to boats placed them a different class altogether, and whether foiling and nonfoiling boats should be competing against each other.

The vertical lift of the foils on the AC72s, developed by more than thirty engineers, designers and programmers, added speed, as they reduced the friction of the boats against the ocean surface. "But," Nick Holroyd, Team New Zealand's technical director, told *Sailing World*, "it does lead to serious control issues when you get it wrong."

Adding foils to the boats instantly magnified the tension between speed and safety, pushing the boats and sailors to the technical edge of risk. The design team had taken many of its cues from the science of flight. It was easy to "fall off the foils with a severe crash," he added. "You might

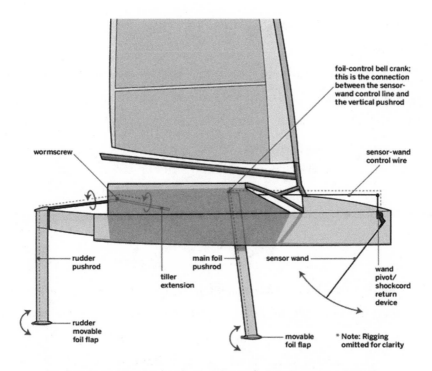

foil-control bell crank;
this is the connection
between the sensor-
wand control line and
the vertical pushrod

sensor-wand
control wire

wormscrew

rudder
pushrod

main foil
pushrod

tiller
extension

sensor wand

wand
pivot/
shockcord
return
device

rudder
movable
foil flap

movable
foil flap

* Note: Rigging
omitted for clarity

Moth diagram (David Schmidt. "Learning to fly," *Sail* magazine [2007].
https://www.sailmagazine.com/racing/learning-to-fly-2)

survive that crash, but the average speed won't be good. It's all about finding and maintaining a high average speed."

With echoes of how the NFL used to promote the most spectacular collisions between players (which are now known to lead to devastating brain damage)—America's Cup marketing and public relations experts began to upload and promote videos on YouTube of the large boats capsizing. While the videos garnered millions of views, the risks to the sailors on board were seldom, if ever, discussed or considered. In a capsize, most sailors didn't have time for emotions, instead focusing on the mechanics of securing whatever was left on board and getting themselves and teammates off the water safely. But the chasm between the experience of a fan watching the sport and a sailor on board only seemed to be widening, even though, ironically, there were more cameras on board than ever before.

With the introduction of the foiling *New Zealand*, the sport had been instantly redefined. Anyone hoping to have even the slightest chance of competing against the Kiwis was going to have to do a major overhaul of their catamarans to incorporate foils.

Kevin watched the flying boat and his thoughts were clear.

Oh, shit.

•

The *Oracle* team had the same problem as the *Artemis* sailors, which was that their boat was not designed to foil in the first place. Many years and millions of dollars into the competition, the team would have to turn their boat into an airplane—at a breakneck speed and without being able to compare notes with anyone else.

It wasn't going well. During a test run in October 2012, the *Oracle*, the best-financed of the America's Cup boats, to the tune of at least $8 million, capsized.

•

A few weeks later, those standing on the rim of San Francisco Bay saw a perplexing yet oddly majestic sight. It looked as if two giant red hot dogs were suspended in the air by an unseen thread. Only a few days after the *Oracle* crash, the *Artemis* was arriving. Dozens of onlookers watched under clear skies as a massive crane lifted and gently deposited the two bright red hulls into the water, the white letters ARTEMIS legible from far away.

She was late. The boat was supposed to have launched weeks earlier, but it had been damaged in tow-testing on the morning of the original launch, causing delays.

The news of the *Oracle* crash had jarred the *Artemis* team members. If that boat, with its brilliant engineers, hefty financial backing, and strong sailors, had capsized after adding foils, what did that mean for everyone else in the competition? Like the human body, so many things on a boat could go wrong, sometimes without a clear explanation, and it seemed miraculous when all of the pieces actually lined up. It looked as though New Zealand had done its sailing due diligence, but now the *Oracle*, *Artemis*, and *Luna Rossa* teams would have to play catch-up. Still, the *Artemis* sailors thought that their boat was as safe as it could be, considering the engineering challenge of adding foils under a tight deadline.

The sailors stood on board with their red, white, and black practice uniforms on, their hands on their hips, cradled by views of the Bay's bridges. During a structural test on the water, a beam of the large boat was damaged. The team hauled the boat out of the water so the design team could assess what had gone wrong. "Already broken?" a headline from the blog *Sailing Anarchy* read. "At least they haven't capsized . . . yet."

The skirmish also delayed the christening of the boat by a month, a slight embarrassment considering the pride that typically accompanies the event. Still, on November 13, Kevin and his *Artemis* teammates cautiously launched their boat onto the waters of San Francisco Bay. The effort was closely watched by many who questioned whether or not the boat should have been refashioned for foiling.

"Think about a car when you're driving down the road at sixty miles per hour," *Artemis* skipper Terry Hutchinson said, "and you stick your hand out the window, in essence, that will slow the car down. If you have a smaller car that's capable of the same type of speed, but doesn't have the arm sticking out the window, that car is inherently going to go faster. The boats will go faster, and they'll be more dangerous and on-edge. My personal opinion is that people leading the event aren't applying any logic or reason. They're just trying to make something that is perceived to be cool and have zero forethought into the actual consequences of what they're proposing."

By the end of November, Hutchinson had what he later called "a massive falling out with the owner of the team and CEO about the safety of our yacht," which he said was their cause for deciding to terminate him. Hutchinson said he wasn't tech-averse; rather, he was concerned with the possible consequences for his fellow men on board with the changes to the boat. He added: "It was a known thing that the boat was not safe."

Three months after that, with seven months until race day, a new fleet of sailors joined the *Artemis* team, a considerable investment in high-quality payroll. Among them was 2012 Olympic silver medalist Iain Percy and Andrew Simpson of Great Britain, who added their most recent Olympic performance to follow up the 2008 gold medal he had won in Beijing. Kevin was excited to have Simpson on the *Artemis*; through the tight social network of the international sailing circuit, the two had known each other for a decade. Those in and out of sailing liked and respected Simpson, including those he had sailed against. Kevin was seven years Simpson's senior, and the two had first met in 2003 when Kevin was sailing the Finn ahead of Athens and Simpson had been hired as a coach to help the United States sailing team. At the time, the Americans needed outside expertise from the established British sailing squad, and Simpson was a supportive voice, as well as a great guy to just hang out with. Simpson's nickname was Bart, a nod to the spiky-haired, devious, yellow-skinned cartoon character from *The Simpsons* who shared his last name. Kevin and Simpson both had Olympic and America's Cup experience and had risen through the sport during a similar era, making them familiar faces to each other in an otherwise chaotic tableau.

The same month as the announcement of Simpson's joining the team, representatives from the team said that they had sent the *Artemis* to the shed for modifications. Kevin and his teammates continued to go to work every day, certain that their engineers were improving their boat, but some were privately concerned like Hutchinson about safety.

When Amanda saw her husband leave the house each day, kissing her and their kids goodbye in his superhero-like plated protective wear, she couldn't help but wonder.

•

The conditions on May 9, 2013, appeared to be perfectly sound for sailing. On board with Kevin that day were ten of his teammates, including several Olympic champions like Simpson. There was nothing happening on the water that day that they hadn't all seen a million times in their respective careers.

To turn away from the wind in an ultra-high performance boat is one of sailing's trickiest feats, known as a "bear away." For Kevin and the men on the *Artemis*, however, it wasn't a new move, and it was standard fare for a practice run on the waters between Treasure Island and Alcatraz Island, home of the famous prison that has counted Al Capone and James "Whitey" Bulger among its inmates. The boat started its turn. The vessel seemingly moved in slow motion—Kevin had seen those kinds of angles and maneuvers on smaller boats over the years and knew when something was off.

Then came the sound of a crack that was as sickening as it was sharp. Most of the sailors on board didn't know until that moment that a professional sailboat was capable of making a noise like that, a series of snaps that curdled the blood.

The left side hull of the boat dug into the water, a structural failure that made the entire balance of the boat careen. The tall wing sail, black and white with horizontal lines like a Japanese shoji screen, the blue and yellow of the Swedish flag at the top, tilted away from the sky and toward the water. From the distance, the men on board looked like little black specks as they clung to the high side of the boat, one half of it going higher into the air as the other half plunged more deeply into the water. A violent crash of white waves fanned around the vessel, temporarily blinding anyone who was near it.

Some of the sailors saw it happening in slow motion, the boat that they had worked on for two years, that had cost millions, collapsing before their eyes and taking them down with it. They clung to the red of the hull with all of their strength, some suspended only by their arms, their legs dangling beneath them, kicking and searching for grounding of any kind and instead meeting air. The horizontal plane of the boat became a wall, then a ceiling, in just a few seconds. A support boat sat nearby, unsure what, if anything, could be done.

It became clear amid the chaos that Andrew Simpson was in trouble. And Kevin wasn't entirely sure whether the scene before him was really happening.

AMANDA

As Amanda sat with Rainer, now eight years old, at the orthodontist's office, her phone buzzed with a text message. It was from someone with the *Artemis* team who needed to speak with her right away. She immediately knew that something had gone wrong.

The last time she had seen Kevin was that morning as he left for work with a smile, as always. She knew he would have been on that boat and have left his cell phone ashore, as he and his teammates did on all their practice runs. Locking into emergency physician mode, she debated whether to call the *Artemis* office (too slow, too bureaucratic) or one of the other sailing spouses (not likely to have any more information than she did). She decided to dial her workplace, San Francisco General Hospital, reasoning that if anyone had been injured on a boat of the *Artemis*'s size and stature, they would likely have ended up in her hospital and if not, her colleagues would know where they were.

She dialed. She waited.

KEVIN

Shortly before one o'clock, the San Francisco Police Department's marine unit responded to the call and met the *Artemis*, or what was left of it, on the water. The red frame of the boat had "turtled"; no mighty sail was scraping the air. Instead, two white triangles of rudders lay flat on the water, a mess of tangled metal.

Andrew Simpson was trapped, wedged between a few tons of carbon fiber, fighting to break free. His teammates dived beneath the water, hoping to free him, and handed him an oxygen bottle to give him some air until rescue crews arrived.

By the time the police came, an *Artemis* chase boat had nosed up to the capsized catamaran, where numerous sailors were still on board, as the vessel had stopped moving. They had finally succeeded in pulling Simpson out of the water and onto a backboard and had begun CPR. The police and crewmembers quickly transferred him onto a more stable platform and carried him onto the chase boat to get him to an ambulance. They continued doing CPR on the way, trying in vain to dry off Simpson's chest and apply the defibrillator pads. They kept slipping off, and one responding officer lost a razor kit and the child set of defibrillator pads in the process.

When they landed at the San Francisco Yacht Harbor, the medics took over.

Andrew "Bart" Simpson was declared dead.

GORDON

THE HEADLINE FLASHED on Yahoo News when Gordon, now retired from medicine and living in Oregon, logged in to check his email. An America's Cup boat in San Francisco had capsized that afternoon. The report was live, only an hour or so after the accident had happened.

Preliminary reports indicated that the *Artemis* capsize, unlike the *Oracle* one before it, hadn't happened because the sailors had pushed too hard or had made a mistake. Rather, the boat had simply buckled under its new flying loads, then flipped over. The *Oracle* capsize had happened in rougher conditions, but what little was known of the *Artemis* capsize didn't make any sense.

Before Gordon could try calling Kevin and Amanda, his phone rang, Kevin's name flashing across the screen in a comforting display of pixels.

Gordon's blood pressure returned to normal when he heard his son's voice. Kevin said that he was safe. He told him that he had seen the crash and was one of the sailors who had pulled Simpson's body up from the water. He was devastated, and still very much in a state of shock.

The conversation lasted only a few minutes, and after hanging up, Gordon struggled to process what the accident might mean for Kevin and his mental health.

A couple of days later after the crash, Gordon and Kevin were on the phone again.

I want to understand things better, Gordon said to Kevin, trying to get more information about what had transpired on board.

Kevin's answer to his father was clear. He never wanted to talk about the accident with him ever again.

KEVIN

IMMEDIATELY AFTER THE crash, Kevin and his teammates threw themselves back into work. Some of that was necessary, as they tried to examine any kind of data that could point to what had gone wrong and help law enforcement understand the nuances of professional sailing. Kevin worked ten days straight, the time drain also affording him distance from people he knew who would want to talk about the more emotional aspects of the crash. All of the sailors were in a state of shock but went into analysis mode as professionals as much as they could. At least his teammates could relate to what he had gone through, sharing in the horrible experience and subsequent stress.

Kevin had met Amanda on shore shortly after the accident that afternoon, both relieved that he was okay. Grief took a robotic turn, and in a strange way, going back to work to try to understand what had gone wrong was the only thing that felt right to Kevin and some of his teammates.

More and more, research has shown that human beings may be more hardwired than they think to have a hard time accepting what science reveals about the universe: that it is inherently unstable. Kevin handled uncertainty nearly effortlessly on the water, steering a craft according to the contours of the wind, reading data with both scientific methods and his gut. But handling instability when not on the water was something else altogether. Somehow, the mental tools he could apply so well in one realm weren't fully translating into another one.

More and more, too, researchers were finding that personality isn't as fixed as had been previously thought—rather, it can be flexible and malleable, and changes both over time and in a variety of situations. Human beings rewrite their memories as they revisit them, so the memories themselves in a way seem to change, even though most think of memories as static photographs, solids that can be picked up whenever one wants to recall them. Really, a memory can be more like a photograph that looks different than it did before each time it is retrieved. The benefit of that is that one can use the brain's pliability to overcome mental maladies like post-traumatic stress by taking control of behavior, and become a functional, happy person. The negative is that those very same forces can distort or destroy. The aim for human beings, the psychology professor Walter Mischel of Columbia University says, is "to not be victims of their biographies."

Kevin picked up the ever-morphing photographs in his mind of the crash over and over again in the following weeks, splicing them together with moments from his past regattas, episodes of The Show, and time spent with friends and family.

In the wake of the crash, he continued to be a man full of questions.

KRISTINA

It was a song Kristina had heard a million times at countless different Grateful Dead shows, yet it felt almost unfair and a tad spooky for the band to be playing it now. From the first time since she had heard it in college, she couldn't help but think of Kevin. It was called "Lost Sailor."

The song tells the tale of chaos at sea, of not being able to find oneself in the vast void of stars and the moon. That even though the shore beckons, "there's a price" for the freedom of the ocean—broken dreams, not being able to belong properly on land, but of being a lost sailor who has "been away too long at sea."

Even the most mentally stable of people would struggle under the weight of the violent crash and the loss of a friend. She thought of the drive they had taken after her brother's Tokyo episode, and how he had described to her the world he lived in—the manic episodes, the depressions, the feeling of being on the edge of losing reality's grasp. How different it all was from her world. She thought of the psych wards, the victories on the water, and the photo of her brother on the front page of *USA Today* parading as an Olympian. She still couldn't really grasp how he had narrowly averted death at the America's Cup.

Bud stood at her side as the crowd gently swayed, and she wondered again, as she did every time she heard the song, whether she should send it to Kevin. She never had, because she was worried that the similarities in it to his own life could trigger something in his mind. She knew how he clung to coincidences, particularly when in a manic upswing and didn't want to encourage them, lest he spin out of control again.

Kristina could feel her eyes glaze with tears as the band played on.

KEVIN

A FRIEND WHO knew that Kevin had been on the *Artemis* told him that post-traumatic stress disorder was very real and that he should be on guard against it. What he had gone through on board with Simpson's death was beyond horrible and more than merited some time for healing and extra self-care.

Whatever, dude, Kevin replied.

He had nightmares about the crash, his relationship to the water inverted from one of trust to fear, the sound of the boat snapping in his ears at inopportune times. That summer, in a manner that was both quiet and unconscious, he suspended his belief in mental illness being a real thing rather than a construct, for him or anyone else. His meds didn't feel as though they were working right and when he mentioned this to his doctor,

Kevin was told that this was not a good time to change them. With less than ideal information and support, he stopped taking them on his own.

Kevin's lows were as unpredictable as his highs, but for different reasons. When he was manic, his life was one plot point after another, and there was no telling what he was going to do next as the star of The Show. During his lows, there was no telling how long he would stay curled up in a ball in bed. A few hours, a day, a week. Or, if he would act upon his threats about ending it all, feeling that life was without meaning.

After the crash, Kevin thought of the end of Philip K. Dick's *Exegesis*, a compendium based on thousands of typed and handwritten notes and journal entries by Dick, in which he describes how he spent eight years trying to understand a specific experience of the universe. Kevin had started reading Dick in high school and his themes—isolation, loneliness, the future—continued to strike him. He had particularly loved *The Man in the High Castle*, an alternative history novel that takes place in the years after the Axis powers claimed victory in World War II and *Time out of Joint*, about a man living in a false reality. Dick totally "got it," Kevin thought, particularly the feeling of living in two parallel worlds, and how when pushing away voices in his head, one could actually get more and more out of reality and less grounded. It was a strange paradox Kevin could relate to; the more he tried to resist the commands of the Director, the more he wondered if part of him was slipping away.

Kevin wondered if the world would have been more understanding of his disorder if he had won a Pulitzer or Nobel Peace Prize by his twenty-second birthday, or made the NBA draft, or composed like Beethoven. Deep down, Kevin knew that the romanticization of the mentally ill prodigy, be it an athlete or an artist, was dangerous, as it typecast creative people as crazy and then could make crazy people feel obliged to be brilliant. But somehow, those who were seen as geniuses received more latitude, he felt, when it came to assessments of their sanity. As a middle-of-the-pack overachiever, it was as though he was afforded less room to act abnormally than the indisputably brilliant.

Then there were the thoughts about his father, who still seemed to honor achievement above all else. That mindset had served Kevin well as a child in some ways, but he no longer knew how he felt about it as an adult. Gordon watched opera screenings at his local movie theater, he listened to music, he appeared to enjoy art, but the cynic in Kevin wondered whether his father was interested in art for the art's sake, or interested in watching the achievements of people who were perceived to be the best at something; they weren't just opera singers, they were singers for the Met, therefore successful in a traditional sense. Still, Kevin had played the game. He had made an Olympic team and taken part in several America's Cup bids. He was married to a kind, successful woman and had three beautiful children. Was it ever going to be enough?

For years, Kevin had felt that living the lifestyle of an athlete had allowed him to hide a bit. The training regimen gave his life a rigid, unquestioned consistency and sense of purpose. When he was at the gym, there wasn't time for asking questions—rather, the focus was on getting more and more weights on the bar and making sure that nothing got in the way of improving his physical prowess. With most of his time occupied by trying to become a world champion, there wasn't a lot of time for self-pity. Now, after the *Artemis* crash, all of that had changed. Kevin stopped going to the gym his usual six to ten times a week. It seemed utterly insignificant.

In writing about his own depression, author William Styron described it as a failure of self-esteem. "Depression," Styron wrote, "is a disorder of mood, so mysteriously painful and elusive in the way it becomes known to the self—to the mediating intellect—as to verge close to being beyond description. It thus remains nearly incomprehensible to those who have not experienced it in its extreme mode."

The external world didn't do Kevin any favors in providing logic or closure, either. Although the San Francisco Police Department issued a police report, neither the *Artemis* group nor the America's Cup publicly released the results of any further investigation into the cause (or causes) of the crash. In its eighty-three-page report, the San Francisco Police Department cited broad factors, like "excessive speed," "machinery failure," "equipment failure," and "racing" as causes of the accident. The police also conceded that the crash and its vessel were unconventional; "it should be noted that America's Cup Race Boats present cutting edge technology" and that the boats are "designed to operate with little margin for error." Therefore, the America's Cup boats "do not have many of the safety features that would normally be associated with recreational vessels or commercial vessels."

In a press conference following the crash, Iain Murray, the regatta director, sat before a gray backdrop and addressed a crowd of reporters and TV cameras assembled at the pier. He choked up several times and said that the organization took "the safety of this sport very seriously." Citing the then pending work of the San Francisco Police Department, Murray and America's Cup officials were quiet about the details. The event's website showed gray clouds above the Golden Gate Bridge, not far from where the capsize had taken place, and that their prayers are with Andrew Simpson's family.

"The entire Artemis racing team is devastated by what happened," Artemis CEO Paul Cayard said. "Our heartfelt condolences are with Andrew's wife and family."

By the third week of July, just over two months after the *Artemis* had capsized, three hundred or so *Artemis* team members, friends, and family gathered in private to launch another boat, *Big Blue*, out into the bay. Like its red counterpart, it was a foiling catamaran, but it had two blue hulls and a tall black sail. The sailors swapped their red-and-black suits for all-black ones, topped with bright yellow helmets, visible from far away.

While the rest of Kevin's teammates were able to get back on the water, he was not. He spent many hours staring out the window of his home in Berkeley, gazing at the water and listening to Coldplay's "Fix You" on repeat. When watching fictitious characters on television or film, he found himself moved to tears by scenes that ordinarily wouldn't have provoked such sensitivity. It all felt connected to Simpson's death, everything a reminder of life's fragility. He wondered: Was there anything more he could have done on the boat that day? In the weeks leading up to it? Every line drawing, every comment in a design meeting, every maneuver on the water kept replaying itself in his mind, through the distorted prism of grief and anxiety. The accident had made no sense when it was happening and made even less sense the more he chewed on it.

In the past, Kevin had been able to work through things by getting back on the water, but that didn't seem like an option now. He thought about his love of reading and writing and wondered if he could make a new career doing something literary, but it didn't seem particularly viable as a way of financially supporting his family. He had always taken pride in what he described as "the status of killing the deer and bringing it back" for his wife and children.

For years, Amanda had sacrificed her career to some extent for the sake of the family. She had repeatedly moved or compromised on hospital placements based on where Kevin needed to be for sailing or where the children would be better served by a consistent home life and schooling. Kevin wondered: Was he doing right by his family?

It seemed only natural that Kevin would mourn the loss of Simpson, and his time together with him on the *Artemis*, particularly given its violent end. Given Kevin's history, it was hard for him and others to tell what was a phase of grieving and what was a more lasting sign of a mental health crisis. Kevin knew that it was difficult for Amanda to go about her day as he drank more than usual, or woke up at 4 a.m. each morning. The guilt this generated only made him more depressed, creating a vicious cycle. At times, it even felt as though depression was just another thing that he was bad at.

Kevin wondered if the symptoms of his bipolar disorder were a coping mechanism, a way for him to make order out of the bedlam he felt surrounded him. When things were going right, the thought of going off the rails felt less compelling, The Show less intoxicating. Yet when he was on the threshold of an episode coming, it felt as if he had no choice but to dive in. Only afterward, when he thought about the implausible plot of The Show, did the notion that he was the center of the world, or that he by himself could save it, feel ridiculous.

For decades, Kevin had felt like a gerbil stuck on a wheel chasing achievement, but the *Artemis* crash had forced him to stop and look up and take a raw assessment, something he felt he had never done before, because he worried that it risked being counterproductive to moving forward. It felt like a cliché, but as he witnessed the life leaving Simpson's body in the Bay that spring day, a part of his life had actually flickered in front of him. Did he really want to spend the rest of his days trying to win a sailing race, especially when something as horrific as Simpson's death could be a by-product? Simpson had the one thing that Kevin had thought he wanted—an Olympic gold medal. But, in the end, what good had it done him?

Kevin joined his teammates in flying to Sherborne Abbey in the United Kingdom for Simpson's memorial service. They gathered in the historic church, surrounded by lush green lawns and cradled inside by sweeping ivory arcades, light streaming in through stained-glass windows high above.

A choir sang Coldplay's "Fix You" in perfect pitch, their solemn voices echoing through the cavernous nave. The narrow pews were packed with a gathering of Simpson's friends, family, and fellow sailors. People unable to fit in stood outside. No one left with dry eyes.

Kevin stood in the church, along with everyone else, in tears and still in a state of shock. Memorial services are, by definition, designed for the living, not the dead, but it was unclear to him how he or anyone really could begin to process the loss of Simpson.

AMANDA

KEVIN WAS STILL drinking too much, she knew that. Beer, vodka, sometimes while around people, sometimes probably while not. He could be spiraling down into depression, she thought, or he could still be mourning the loss of a friend. Perhaps both.

He was driving the kids to school every day and otherwise helping out around the house. It only felt reasonable to give him some time and space to contemplate his future in sailing. For now, the family would be able to live off Amanda's income as a doctor and some savings and she tried to resist the temptation to step in and save the day, something she knew she excelled at. The screws of Kevin's thinking seemed to be a little looser than normal, his thoughts and conversation a bit more cerebral and stream-of-consciousness, but she couldn't tell what that meant. As long as she had known him, he had never been one to slur his speech, never one to knock things over when he was drunk, and he wasn't doing that now. He was just talking more, and his thoughts were a bit more all over the place. In some ways, it was easier for her when Kevin was all-out manic, as she could then go into emergency doctor mode; the gray in-between was more difficult to navigate. She was feeling out of sorts, too, as the tragedy had shocked her as well.

Over the years, Amanda had inevitably learned a lot about sailing; she knew that no competitive career lasts forever and that as Kevin aged, it wasn't unrealistic to think that he could transition into a leadership role that would still keep him involved in the sport somehow. To leave sailing altogether was something neither he nor she had fully considered. She tried her best to give him room to think about questions that she knew she couldn't answer for him.

KEVIN

FIVE WEEKS AFTER the crash, Kevin officially quit his job onboard the *Artemis*, posted the words "Free at last" on his Facebook page, and changed his profile picture to a black-and-white photograph of him sailing at the 1985 Youth Championships. When asked about his plans, he told at least one person with the organization that he planned to take up oil painting. It was easy for Kevin to mark his last day of work, because June 16 is of significance to James Joyce fans: that is the day when people in and out of Dublin pay tribute to the author and *Ulysses*, with some making pilgrimages and others reenacting scenes from the book. Bloomsday. Perfect.

At least two people in leadership roles at the Artemis organization knew of Kevin's bipolar disorder, but it didn't come up in his conversations about leaving. Still, he worried about the stigma he could face in quitting, even after such a public crisis. Sailors aren't supposed to leave abruptly like that, at least not before serving out their two-year contracts. Even Kevin's father had cautioned him against doing it, saying that in the close-knit world of professional sailing, it was important not to burn bridges. Kevin also knew that the rumor mill would churn with both accurate and inaccurate conjecture. Whatever the facts of the crash and its aftermath, they weren't going to matter.

Kevin spent hours reading his old journal entries and love letters to Amanda. He'd forgotten what an outlet those missives had been over the years; revisiting them all these years later, he felt like a different person. Meanwhile, his children went about their summer, making a lemonade stand and taking an occasional gag photo with Kevin's Google Glass.

The America's Cup continued. The following month, Kevin made a handful of limited public remarks about Andrew's death on the website *Sailing Anarchy*. He recounted Andrew's congeniality as a teammate and wrote, "America's Cup 34 starts over, or for real, or just plain FINALLY. After all the controversy, and the meta-controversy about what started the controversy; after the divide between those who believe the world is owed the truth about the AC72 capsizes and those that believe it will never be known; after the fascinating discussions with manifold valid perspectives but one final and just decision . . . For me, today is still about the legacy of a great man and his family."

•

12 people like this.

 Susanne Lammot now I understand the significance of this picture ..
Like · Reply · November 10, 2015 at 11:21am

 Kevin Hall Aw Mum, it's just pixels on a screen - things don't have "significance" (do they?) 😊
Like · Reply · November 11, 2015 at 1:24pm

Facebook post (courtesy Kevin Hall)

On September 25, 2013, just weeks after the *Artemis* accident, the America's Cup had a winner with Oracle's "upset" of Team New Zealand. News outlets around the world eagerly repeated what the *Wall Street Journal* and others christened "one of the greatest comebacks in sports history." Somehow the richest team that entered the competition as the defending champion, with more time, resources and power in the event, had been recast as the underdog, its victory perceived as miraculous rather than merely surprising. In the press conferences that followed, there was little talk about the *Artemis* crash, Simpson's death, or any safety precautions or changes to the race going forward.

As summer shifted into fall, Kevin's expressions of his interest in time bending and reality increased. On Facebook, he posted thoughts about art, a video concerning global warming, the cover of Philip K. Dick's *Time Out of Joint*, and a photo he composed of a stairway to nowhere, an offbeat reference to Led Zeppelin's "Stairway to Heaven." That elicited a comment from his mother and a response from Kevin that was hard to deconstruct. Was it humor or an attempt to grapple with existence?

He posted a quote from Neil Gaiman's *The Ocean at the End of the Lane*: "How can you be happy in this world? You have a hole in your heart. You have a gateway inside you to lands beyond the world you know. They will call you, as you grow." And going full circle to his 1989 episode in Boston, the first experience with The Show, Kevin referred back to *Hamlet*, a work he still loved decades past high school. "Believe it or not one can live somewhere like this and still have some pretty tough struggles . . . Hangin' with Hamlet's ghost in Denmark." He engaged in long back-and-forth conversations on Facebook Messenger, riffing with stream-of-consciousness ramblings that he thought were an expression of his artist self coming out, the creation of meaningful work.

Kevin began to stay up late writing pages and pages of material— memoir, fiction, whatever he was in the mood for. He ingested books like a starving person at a buffet, among them Tom Payne's *Fame: What the Classics Tell Us About Our Cult of Celebrity*. In the book, Payne examined what he argued was a primal urge of humans not only to worship individuals, but to tear them down when they felt it was necessary. Those characters that people chose as their heroes revealed a lot about them, and about their views on mortality and immortality. When in The Show, Kevin had hungered to be a good hero out to save the world and inspire others through his actions. He saw himself as part of a lineage that went all the way back to the ancient Greeks and the *Iliad*.

Kevin pulled Lewis Carroll's *Alice's Adventures in Wonderland* off his bookshelf, not having revisited it for years. The next day, he received an email from the Dalí Society advertising an illustrated 1969 edition of Dalí's *Alice*, and he knew that that had to be a sign from the Director. Less than a week later, after watching *E.T.* with his children, he heard the John Williams score to the film on the radio when he drove them to school the next morning. He had listened to the classical station enough to know that they almost never played movie scores. It had to be another sign. A day or two later, Kevin walked into a bookstore looking for *Faust* and grabbed a copy of *Zero History* by William Gibson on his way to the drama section. Then, once in the drama section, he noticed that another William Gibson play, *The Miracle Worker*, was sitting right next to *Faust*. His brain began to short circuit as he wondered how the Director had known that he would be in the bookstore.

An even more significant sign came when Kevin asked a friend if she knew of a writing coach who could help him finally get in motion a dystopian science fiction book idea that he had. The writing coach his friend recommended turned out to be the former manager of Akiva Goldsman's production company, the man who had written the script for the 2001 film *A Beautiful Mind*. The film was an adaptation of Sylvia Nasar's biography of the same name of John Nash, a Nobel laureate in economics who had lived with paranoid schizophrenia. The film and the book had long been triggers for Kevin, and this real-life intersection seemed like yet another uncanny coincidence.

In the book, there's a moment when someone asks Nash how he, a mathematician, could believe that extraterrestrials were sending him messages. Nash's response was swift. "Because the ideas I had about supernatural beings came to me the same way my mathematical ideas did. So I took them seriously." Similarly for Kevin, moments from the crash flickered through his brain and with them, suspicions that it was all a conspiracy of some sort. There might have been a mass cover-up, and he himself might have been somehow implicated in the tragedy, and he had questions about the wind limit rules. There were things that even he, Simpson's friend and teammate, didn't know, but his thoughts of such things at a certain point were as untethered as Nash's.

A family vacation sounded like just the antidote for everyone to decompress and get their minds off the last few weeks. They decided to go to

Legoland, a theme park in Carlsbad, California, devoted to the playful bricks. Gordon, Susanne, Kristina, Bud, and their son would meet them there.

With his Google Glass in hand, Kevin had what he thought was a *great* idea, and he made sure the gadget was fully charged. Maybe this time, he thought, his entire family could join him and the Director.

It could be the greatest episode of The Show ever.

PART IV

FINALE

I have felt the wind on the wing of madness.
—CHARLES BAUDELAIRE, "Intimate Journals"

Try to love the questions themselves, *like locked rooms and like books written in a foreign language. Do not now look for the* answers. *They cannot now be given you because you could not live them. It is a question of experiencing everything. At present you need to* live *the question.*
—RAINER MARIA RILKE, "Letters to a Young Poet"

True heroism is minutes, hours, weeks, year upon year of the quiet, precise, judicious exercise of probity and care—with no one there to see or cheer. This is the world.
—DAVID FOSTER WALLACE (as reposted by Kevin Hall on Facebook, September 18, 2013)

AMANDA

AMANDA TOOK CONTROL of the rental SUV's wheel, towing Kevin and the three kids, all still under the age of ten, and their luggage, along. The drive to Legoland from Los Angeles International Airport takes about ninety minutes, if there's no traffic, which is seldom the case. They barreled south on the slate-colored snakes of concrete, past Long Beach, where Kevin had crashed his grandfather's car years earlier. For much of the drive, the ocean wasn't visible, but occasionally the twinkling blue of the Pacific beckoned from their right side, a mirror of what they had seen while living in New Zealand. However, scenery wasn't much on Amanda's mind at the moment.

Maybe, she thought, Legoland would provide the family time that could help calm Kevin's, and her, anxiety. In recent weeks, Kevin had turned a bit prickly, even the slightest comments being mistaken as criticisms or personal attacks. At the same time, Amanda was worried, thinking about her husband's stressors, and about the conversations that hadn't taken place just as much as the ones that had, particularly about Kevin's father, who would meet them at Legoland. The proverbial eggshells she and others felt they sometimes had to walk on around Kevin now felt like landmines.

At one point during their journey, Amanda took a photo of Kevin wearing a fedora and his Google Glass and posted it on Instagram with a caption: "midlife crisis." Kevin saw it and expressed his disapproval, so she took it down, but she was surprised that Kevin, usually easygoing, couldn't take what she had thought was a silly joke. Maybe it hit too close to home, she thought.

In the car, Kevin fiddled with his phone and read an email saying that his purchase of the rare, collectible Salvador Dalí *Alice* book online for $9,000 had gone through. Lushly illustrated, it represented an intersection of two fanciful minds that had long spoken to Kevin in their magical explorations of the psyche. Usually he and Amanda talked before making large purchases, yet this was the first she was hearing of it. They also avoided arguing in front of their children, but this news was too much for her. Kevin had spent a ludicrous sum spent on something nonessential, just after he had quit his job with nothing else lined up. What's more, he cut her completely out of the decision-making process.

In the car, time felt as though it was melting like a clock in a Dalí painting, and an argument erupted between the two of them, the children looking on. Amanda could feel her emergency doctor instincts kicking in, breaking the daunting, overwhelming tasks into a series of smaller procedures. If they could just make it through a couple of days at Legoland, she thought. If they could just make it through the first day. If they could just make it out of the car and into the Econo Lodge. If they could just make it to the theme park.

KRISTINA

PERCHED FACING A cacophonous highway, the Econo Lodge in Carlsbad, California, fused the aesthetics of a 1970s ski chalet, roadside motel, family vacation spot, and the theme parks in the area. The two-story complex was L-shaped, with rooms facing a parking lot that was typically filled with rental cars and vans, a stream of families coming and going. An oxidized red sign to the left of the lobby door read NIGHT WINDOW: RING BELL FOR SERVICE.

Amanda, Kevin, and their three children checked in to their hotel room, beige abodes with tightly made beds. From outward appearances, they could easily have been mistaken for any other vacationing family, in T-shirts and shorts, cameras out, luggage in hand. But the minute Kristina walked into her brother's hotel room and saw him, she knew that Kevin the dad, husband, and brother wasn't there. Perhaps more frightening, she felt that she was the only one who recognized that Kevin was manic, worse than she could ever remember seeing him.

In fact, the more she thought about it, the more she realized that while she had seen Kevin many times after The Show, she had never actually seen him *during* an episode. Looking at him now, the highs of his mania seemed far away. Kevin seemed angry, spitting venomous words through clenched teeth, not himself even on his worst day.

With their parents also due to arrive soon, she wondered if the missiles of blame would start to fly. She was really more concerned about how they could possibly handle Kevin while also taking care of four young children in an amusement park. Whenever she and Kevin had vacationed with their parents when they were children, their mom had drafted a Plan A, B, and C for various situations—flight delays, sour weather, closures, and any other contingency. Within seconds of arriving, it was clear to Kristina that no one even had a Plan A for Kevin's script flipping.

Kristina didn't think of herself as a pessimist, but her assessment of the current situation seemed on point. Legoland was going to be a disaster.

AMANDA

AS THE HALLS packed into their rental car and made their way from the hotel toward the sprawling parking lot of the theme park, large block letters spelled out WELCOME and a bright, crayon-colored edifice beckoned. They turned off Legoland Drive and parked, the children skipping ahead in excitement, Gordon and Susanne excited to see them.

Similar in spirit to other amusement parks in Southern California, Legoland bills itself as a fun attraction for families, its own fantasyland built of brick and plastic. At the center of its round 128-acre grounds is a pastoral lake surrounded by awe-inspiring Lego displays, including a large multicolored dragon and replicas of the Taj Mahal and the Sydney Opera House. Groups of tourists putter around in small boats, oohing and aahing as they pass by the intricate creations. Elsewhere in the park are Lego recreations of Egyptian tombs, chunky gray-brick knights, pirates with peg legs, stunning scale models of U.S. cities, and water parks with slides, among other things. Upbeat music blares from unseen speakers and brightly colored signs direct visitors down smoothly paved paths, past landscapes populated with Lego rabbits and Lego deer.

As Amanda tried to funnel the excitement of their children, she wondered if the day might be better managed if the group split up. More specifically, it might be a good idea to let Kevin wander off on his own so that his sour mood wouldn't temper that of the children. Amanda reasoned that within the confines of the theme park, Kevin couldn't stray too far.

He agreed to the plan and they arranged a meeting time and place. The park was also sure to be loaded with security cameras and staff, hopefully ensuring that Kevin couldn't do too much harm to himself or others. He had his cell phone and Google Glass with him, too, if they needed to get in touch.

Amanda also wanted to protect her children from seeing their father so unhinged. She stoically smiled for snapshots as she and the children explored the park with Gordon, Susanne, Kristina, and Bud. Amanda couldn't remember the last time she had tried so hard to achieve a smile.

Kevin set off on his own, armed with his Google Glass and a brand-new, bigger-than-ever mission from the Director.

KEVIN

BEAUTIFUL, BEAUTIFUL, BEAUTIFUL. The Lego models were beautiful. The uniforms of the Legoland staff were beautiful. The trash they picked up was beautiful. The trashcans that held the trash were beautiful.

As Kevin explored the park wearing his Google Glass, it only made sense that people stopped him and commented on his new gear and asked him questions about it, as they were still rare. He was on The Show, after all, so the attention he was getting from the extras and supporting cast felt perfectly logical. In response, he told the questioners an assortment of things, among them that he was wearing the spectacles because he was working on "a project," and invited strangers to talk about it with him. They nodded, enforcing the idea in Kevin's mind that this was a worldwide show. Of *course* they were interested. They were part of the narrative, too, all souls linked together at Legoland by destiny, meant to be there as part of the new world order.

The Director wanted Kevin to keep the Google Glass on and go to the bathroom. Sure, the sight might arouse suspicion and privacy concerns from others, but Kevin complied. Thankfully, no other patrons were inside to object. He stood in front of several mirrors. Because he had been toying with the Glass for a couple of months, he now understood why this episode was important. It was pivotal in the history of The Show. For once, *he* would be allowed to do some of the directing, and that level of control made him feel tremendous. He could weave in the recent advancements in social media and mobile technology, as more and more, Kevin had heard about how people were streaming their lives using services like Twitch and video blogs. All the previous episodes were part of a historical narrative leading to this one, which made Kevin a trailblazer on that front with The Show.

It was all making some sense and now, in 2013, it was all coming together. Once again, Kevin had an overwhelming sense of sureness. This was precisely what he was supposed to be doing.

He left the bathroom and made his way to a part of the park that was a winding, paved road lined with Lego busts; LEGOLAND BLOCK OF FAME, a red and blue sign read. Shaded and serene, the road felt more fitting for an English garden than a theme park. He walked past columns topped with chest-level Lego renditions of famous heads: Winston Churchill grimacing with a cigar, the Queen of England with pursed red lips, Shakespeare with a thin mustache, Einstein with thick gray Lego eyebrows. There was also a suited Lego Arnold Schwarzenegger, the action star turned governor of California, and a Lego Marilyn Monroe with stylish waves of yellow hair fashioned of bricks.

Then Kevin spotted a Lego Salvador Dalí. That *had* to be a sign that he was on the right track. Not only did he love Dalí, he had trained for the Olympic trials by the Salvador Dalí museum in Florida with Morgan.

Lego Salvador Dalí

And, of course, it was a reference to the argument he and Amanda had had just the day before in the car over his book purchase. Kevin stood in front of the bust in awe.

Next, Kevin made his way to an exhibit about the history of music told through Legos. This also seemed like too great a coincidence to be just random chance. The Director must have put it there, knowing that Kevin loved music and singing, and for years had found clues and meaning in song lyrics.

With the Google Glass, Kevin could be on the other side of what he now thought of as the rabbit hole (from *Alice*, of course) and share with the audience the things he was seeing even as he himself was being filmed. Depending on what the Director wanted to do, Kevin's view could be transmitted on screen as a thumbnail within a larger screen, or the screen could be split to show multiple perspectives at the same time. What Kevin did with the Google Glass was performance art, evocative in his mind of William Gibson, the speculative science fiction writer whose work

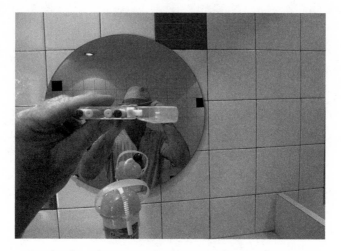

Google Glass photo at Legoland (Kevin Hall, November 2013)

Kevin had seen recently at the bookstore and who was credited with helping pioneer the subgenre of cyberpunk.

From an art creation standpoint, the mirrors of Legoland fascinated Kevin, and he delighted in seeking them out, creating one pseudo-selfie after another, feeling as if he was in an artificial metaparadise, or, even more profoundly, HOME. Whenever a song he liked came over the theme park speakers or on his Spotify playlist, it seemed like a sign that he was on track with The Show. He sang along to some of the tunes as he roamed the park and noticed a few fellow patrons staring at him. Unlike the other extras, they didn't get it, he thought.

Kevin turned down a winding path and there it was: a Lego replica of the Golden Gate bridge stretched across the pond, its bright red bricks shining in the California sun. That *had* to be another sign, especially since on the water was a boat, and not just any boat, but what appeared to be a J-class yacht, a type associated with the America's Cup. Kevin felt spooked. What was it doing there? The boats used in the competition must have been packed up by now—the Director was off if he was trying to make a scene. Or, was it a callout to the crash and Simpson's death? Kevin's future in the sport? This episode was laced with even more meaning than Kevin could have predicted and he struggled to take it all in.

Every now and then Kevin thought he caught glimpses of his father in the park, usually grimacing or frowning at him. He didn't understand why his dad was being such a bummer. Couldn't he see that Kevin, for once, was just trying to be himself?

KRISTINA

AFTER KEVIN PARTED from the others, Kristina turned to Amanda and asked what they should do. They both agreed that Kevin needed to take his meds, but they feared an explosion of anger if they broached the subject with him.

Maybe they could crush his pills up and sneak them into his food somehow? It was a long shot and the very idea that they were talking about it made them both feel as if they, too, were going crazy.

KEVIN

THAT NIGHT AT the Econo Lodge, Kevin walked into the bathroom, flicked on the light, and hopped into the empty bathtub, fully clothed, with a copy of D. T. Max's acclaimed biography of David Foster Wallace, *Every Love Story Is a Ghost Story*. His son Rainer was asleep in his bed with his arms outstretched in what Kevin perceived as a "Jesus-like" pose—something he had never done before. Strange, Kevin thought, recalling reading the Bible in the bathtub at the motel near Logan Airport with Amanda more than a decade earlier. With the whole family in the cast, now the stakes for this episode suddenly felt greater than ever.

Reading the Wallace biography made Kevin feel again as though he had a friend with him in the episode who understood it all. He took out a pen and underlined copious passages, making notes in the margins, the words and ideas bouncing around his head rapidly as he tore through the pages into the quietest hours of the night. Underlining the text seemed like an effective way to signal to viewers that certain parts of the book were really resonating with him. They could follow along at home.

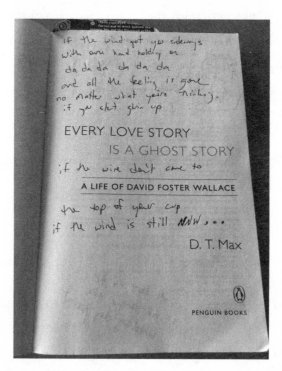

Kevin's copy of *Every Love Story Is a Ghost Story* (courtesy Kevin Hall)

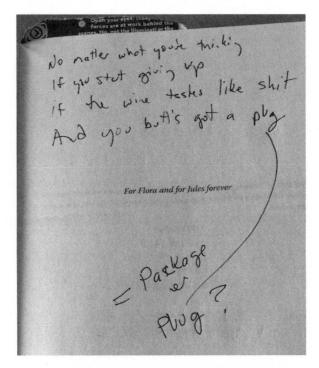

Margin notes (courtesy Kevin Hall)

The mathematician in Kevin was astounded by Wallace's ability to organize, communicate, teach, and make thrilling abstract concepts like infinity sing. Wallace didn't just understand those concepts deeply, he could translate them, be a bridge from one world to the rest of us, Kevin thought.

Inside the front cover Kevin scrawled some of the lyrics from Jack Johnson's song "Brushfire Fairytales" along with some musings of his own. *Been there, done that,* Kevin scrawled at the bottom of a page detailing Wallace's four-week stay at McLean. Max wrote that Wallace's stay there changed his life, not because it was his first or most serious crisis, but because "he felt now as if he had hit a new bottom or a different kind of bottom."

Curled up along the margins, Kevin added stray sentences:

Reality is that which, when you stop <u>believing in it</u>, doesn't go away

1. What is real? 2. What is human?

Kevin also underlined a line from *The Velveteen Rabbit* that Max cited: "Real isn't how you are made," the Skin Horse tells the Velveteen Rabbit, "it's a thing that happens to you." It had echoes to Kevin, too, of Dick's work about "How to Build a Universe that Doesn't Fall Apart Two Days Later," all of his literary heroes coming together as one.

The next day, things only got worse.

•

On the second day of their excursion, Kevin emerged in great spirits from the 4-D Lego movie with his children. Inside the theater, there had been smoke, sound, and sensory excitement—the chairs they had sat in had even moved according to the action on screen. All was going according to plan in this family togetherness episode of The Show, featuring them all in an interactive performance piece, Kevin thought. The kids that had been cast as his had been prepared perfectly—they were adorable and playful with their dad as they romped through the park together.

Next, it was time to go to the gift shop for the part of The Show that was all about the role of capitalism in children's lives. Kevin's kids, right in character, asked if they could take a look inside. Kevin walked in, dressed in shorts, bucket hat, T-shirt, and shades, and began singing at

Leo, Kevin, Rainer, Stevie (courtesy Kevin Hall)

the top of his lungs "That I Would Be Good" by Alanis Morissette, the song he and Amanda had danced to at their wedding.

He held up a Lego set of the Sydney Opera House, making sure the cameras had a good view, thinking that his gesture would lead to an influx of callers ordering their own sets. It was not a cheap set, around $500, but he was getting ready to pay for it when Amanda stopped him and explained that they had already purchased several sets for the kids as birthday and Christmas gifts. He argued with her. Why didn't she understand that they needed *this* set? That The Show, in fact, depended on it?

They compromised and settled on a book, *Beautiful Lego*, which had lavish full-color photographs of Lego creations: faces, snakes, snails, cupcakes, typewriters, trucks.

Reluctantly, Kevin put the Sydney Opera House set back on the shelf and made his way out of the park with his family. He felt very proud of himself for complying with Amanda's wishes.

AMANDA

IT WAS LIKE having a fourth child.

Her three actual children had enjoyed themselves at Legoland, but they were ready to leave, dinner and rest beckoning. Kevin, on the other hand, was arguing with her about whether or not he could buy a Lego set. Setting aside that he had just quit his job, aside from the fact he had already spent too much money on a Salvador Dalí book, he was a grown man begging for a Lego set.

She thought about dinner the night before, when the family had gone to a pizza place where Kevin behaved like a babbling idiot, singing to himself outside in the parking lot in a voice loaded with emotion, on the verge of tears. At the table with the rest of the family, he had been obsessed with rearranging the silverware on the table into patterns and shapes.

It was time for an intervention.

GORDON

KEVIN'S BEHAVIOR WAS embarrassing and, even more than that, disappointing.

Gordon's son-in-law, Bud, had taken the four grandkids to another hotel room to babysit so the other adults could confer about what to do. They agreed upon the goal of persuading Kevin to check in to an institution.

Kevin never told anyone, Gordon thought angrily, when he was going to go off his meds. Instead, time and time again, he left others to deal with the wreckage that his mania left in its wake. It was one thing if he wanted to screw up his own life with his mental illness, but now he was a husband, a father, a provider. People were depending on him. Gordon couldn't understand why Kevin resisted taking a pill that everyone told him would help him. Why was that so hard?

He thought of a photo he had snapped of Kevin at Kristina's MBA graduation from Portland State University several years earlier. In the photo, Kristina was beaming, Kevin's eyes wide as saucers. How could Gordon have missed that at the time? Gordon later described Kevin's face in the photograph as looking "practically on fire."

Having a common interest in business had helped Gordon bridge the chasm between him and Kristina, making them closer in adulthood than they had been when she was a child. It also helped that she had finally, at age thirty, quit smoking. Oddly, he felt that he could talk with her more easily at times than with Kevin. How strange that it was the daughter who had been a hippie, a party child in high school and college, would end up becoming the stable small business owner. Yet his son, the meticulous champion and Olympian, gave him more emotional stress.

The idea that the whole family could get along together at Legoland had felt nothing short of manufactured to Gordon from the beginning. Then, Kevin had wandered off, and yelled and argued with Amanda, something Gordon had never seen him do before. Gordon had noticed the look in his grandchildren's eyes, mirroring his own fright and surprise, and had told Kevin that he was out of line, to no avail. Gordon had worn his disappointment and shame in his face. Anger, too. All the time and money spent to pull the family together and his son didn't even have it in him to take his medicine.

In 2001, Gordon had told Amanda that Kevin was off his desk and onto hers. At Legoland, it felt as if Kevin was back on his desk again. This wasn't what he had signed up for.

KRISTINA

KRISTINA WATCHED AS her brother paced back and forth in the hotel room, muttering. Some things were audible; others, words beyond meaning tossed into the air. She could see that her father was angry about Kevin's mania, that he felt he once again was being put in the position of being the bad guy. Her mother remained mostly silent, politely listening, recognizing the insufficiency of words.

As Kevin half-listened to his family's talk of his going to a hospital, he asked whether, if he started taking his medications, he could avoid having to be admitted. He also wondered to himself if the Kevin on The Show was supposed to have a mental illness, maybe as a way to stir up advocacy. Kevin suggested that he could stay at a hospital that had a sound studio so that he could record some things. He thought he recalled one in the Pasadena facility where he had stayed years before, even though it was far from where he and Amanda and the kids were living now in Berkeley.

This wasn't a bargaining meeting, Gordon said. This was a declaration that Kevin was going to have to go to a hospital and that he would be expected to take his medication right now whether he liked it or not. Gordon spoke to Kevin about how he had responsibilities, he had children, a family. The father and son circled each other, weaving invisible threads of logic, patterns in the air.

Listening to her father and brother, Kristina thought about how different her and Kevin's childhoods had been, in spite of being siblings growing up in the same home. Kevin had conformed to their parents' expectations, whereas Kristina had done anything but. So often it is forgotten, she thought, that siblings often end up sharing only some of their genes and that their experiences in their environments growing up can vary widely. Family and home, in fact, are not monolithic and can be the site of a variety of early Darwinian fights of human development. Kristina had fought to find space that Kevin hadn't already claimed, and that, perhaps ironically, ended up creating an openness in her that was serving her well in adulthood, particularly in stressful moments like these.

Kristina had had ordinary jobs as a kid and teenager like delivering newspapers or waiting tables, while her brother had had prestigious, yet competitive, sailing on which to pin his identity. She had gone to parties and been forced to make her own friends, whereas just about all of Kevin's closest confidants were fellow sailors and he had far less spare time to hang out with them. Later-borns were seventeen times more likely than first-borns to adopt a revolutionary point of view, but firstborns craved digging deeper into the status quo, often bending and examining it in new and fascinating ways.

Kevin inexplicably snapped at Kristina when she used the phrase "on the same page." It was virtually impossible to tell what his triggers were. It felt as if they were going around and around and around with him on the merits of his going to a hospital not in Pasadena, but in the Bay Area, where he would be near home. There was no easy cure, chemical or otherwise.

Behind the façade that Kristina knew she was wearing, a piece of her inner little sister maintained a presence. Never mind that she had found a great husband, raised a curious and bright son, and started her own successful business. Once again, it was all about her big brother.

It was the Kevin Show. And Kristina and everyone else were nothing but supporting actors.

KEVIN

THE IDEA OF staging an intervention scene for The Show worked, he supposed.

This dialogue in the hotel room was testing him, splitting him in two. Being on The Show in Legoland was fun, although more and more, Kevin could see how a plot involving his going to a hospital could provide an immense public service by raising awareness about mental illness.

The David Foster Wallace biography he had binge-read in the bathtub the night before reverberated in his head. Echoing Wallace's writing about imposter syndrome, Kevin told his family that he felt like a fraud. A fraud as an athlete, as a husband, as a father. He had been faking it for years. How could they not see that?

He agreed to go to a hospital in the Bay Area after they returned home the next day.

It was difficult for those in the room to know if he really meant it or not.

AMANDA

AS ADVERTISED, DINI'S by the Sea had a wall of windows that looked directly onto the vast, glimmering blue Pacific Ocean, a view that looked more like a painting than reality. A local bar and restaurant featuring seafood, steak, and burgers, the restaurant was flanked by flat screen TVs and a long bar bedecked with surfboards.

It felt miraculous that they had persuaded Kevin to go to the hospital the next morning. So perhaps it wasn't surprising that when a waiter came to their table, some of the adults ordered beer or wine to go with their dinner.

Kevin ordered a Guinness.

Amanda was surprised when she heard her husband speak up.

She wondered what he was thinking. Then she realized that he wasn't. He was already looped out of his mind and now he wanted to have alcohol. She could feel another conflict sprouting before them.

She had to say something. She calmly told Kevin he couldn't have it.

He erupted, pounding his fist on the table and yelling. Their three children stared at their father with fright—a contorted, angry version of him having emerged. The roar of his voice, the overwhelming presence of his body, the reddening of his face, garnered glances from fellow patrons as well.

Kevin stormed away from the table to the bar nearby.

KRISTINA

KRISTINA SURVEYED THE table. Amanda needed to tend to her frightened children. Her father's faced looked too angry and frustrated to offer any kind of aid to Kevin. Her mother, too, looked shocked. A waitress came over and asked if everything was okay. The family nodded yes, yes, yes, everything was fine, a collective fib they could all agree on.

Her brother needed an ally. Calmly, Kristina made her way over to the bar, where Kevin sat with his back to the rest of the restaurant, sipping his beer.

He was still wound up, seething in a new way. She struggled with what to say to him, knowing that if her voice had a tone that was anything short of calm, considerate, and empathetic, he could erupt. Hell, even the most tranquil approach might make him flee.   .

She was there to help him, she said. She was an ally, on his side. She and Kevin compromised on his being allowed to have one beer, provided that he return to the table and act sedately. To Kristina's surprise, this worked.

Kevin made his way back to the table, a slightly calmer version of the man who had stormed off a few minutes earlier.

The children were confused by their father's outburst and wondered if he was mad at them. Kevin and Amanda tried to explain that that wasn't the case. The toxic mood still hung in the air, but it had dissipated slightly.

Kevin thought it was nice that his little sister, his parents, and his own wife and children were finally getting some screen time, too.

SUSANNE

MORE THAN TWENTY years had passed since Kevin's first episode, yet it felt as though nothing had changed. Susanne offered to change her plans in order to fly with Kevin and his family to the Bay Area and help Amanda with the children and logistics instead of going home to Ventura. She would drive him up the highway to the airport, Amanda and the kids in a separate car.

Susanne remembered the exuberance of Kevin's junior and senior high school years, and how he would stay up late at night in his darkroom developing photographs even after a long day of sailing and schoolwork. She wondered now whether that had been just the excitement of youth or an early sign of mania, where the gray had started and the black begun. As a teenager, too, Kevin would go flying, sometimes with his father, who taught him about aviation in much the same way he'd taught him about sailing: with a focus on detail and precision. Kevin flew occasionally during college, but in adulthood, as sailing took over, he eventually let his instrument pilot's license lapse. If flying wasn't an attempt at trying to feel closer to the sky, away from the earth, and to escape reality, she didn't know what was.

AMANDA

SOMEHOW, SHE HAD finally gotten some medications into him, but it was unclear how long it would take for them to take effect. How Susanne had managed to get him to the airport without anyone's getting hurt along the way was one of the great miracles of the weekend. It appeared the elixir was putting Kevin in the backseat with Eminem's "The Real Slim Shady" on repeat, apparently allowing him to smoke the occasional cigarette. As the family walked through the brightly lit and buzzing corridors of the airport, Amanda felt relieved when Kevin chose to pass the baggage carousels without darting off and onto the tarmac as he told her he had done in Tokyo.

Once they all boarded the plane and were up in the air, Kevin sat in his seat with what Amanda felt was suspicious calmness. Every second that passed felt like a victory.

The plane touched down at San Francisco International Airport.

They had made it home.

SUSANNE

As she led her son in through the doors of the mental institution, Susanne realized that Kevin was still wearing his Google Glass.

KEVIN

The drugs were starting to kick in the way they usually did, radiating a sense of almost contagious relief to those around him, even though they hadn't also ingested them. Kevin slowly started to realize where he was, but he still didn't have a clear idea who he was or how he had ended up in a hospital. As he was coming down, he read a Stephen King book, not for literary pleasure or to pass the time, but for clues. Maybe this scene had been designed to offer him hints on how to get out of the hospital, or maybe the book contained a code that needed to be cracked.

Reality returned and the fantasy of The Show receded. Worse than the loss of The Show itself was the realization that, once again, it had all been a lie manufactured in his own head. His jaunt to Legoland hadn't done anything to save the world. Not only that, all he had done was inflict emotional pain on those he loved the most, perhaps this time to a new degree. The guilt of the vacation weighed on his shoulders like an unwanted, wet backpack. Having lost track of the number of times he had been in hospitals didn't help, either.

A doctor came in and introduced himself. In chatting with him, Kevin found that he had studied with Dr. Joel Gold, the same man Kevin had written to regarding the "Truman Show" delusion and who had also been in his year at Brown. It was hard, at first, not to wonder whether this was another sign from the Director that The Show was still going.

As Kevin came down and the drugs started to kick in, Amanda and the doctor both agreed that this was another uncanny coincidence.

•

Amanda visited Kevin in the hospital and they talked about their children. Legoland had marked the first time that the children had witnessed their father's mania in full force, but Rainer was now nine years old, old enough to understand that something was amiss.

Kevin thought of when he was Rainer's age. Back then, he had believed that there was an absolute right and wrong, success and failure. Some of that he felt had been because of his parents and a culture that had made him feel that one's worth came from being as close to the line of achievement as possible. Now, doubts that had been slowly building up in his mind for years came crashing down on him as a revelation: there was no line, and if there had been, there was more to life than coming close to it. Or, more closely tied to the crash, what good was an Olympic gold medal if one was dead?

Kevin and Amanda knew they faced a decision. Should they tell Rainer about Kevin's madness? Kevin could hold his emotions in, the way he felt his own father had, or he could try to explain to his children his relationship with the Director, the false comfort of The Show, and the implications of his mania. He could tell them what he really thought about failure and the quest for perfection and the gold. Tell them that he hoped they would go through their teenage years and lives sheltered from his tempest, but also not afraid to find their own strength in vulnerability.

It had been thirteen years since Kevin had been an inpatient. All this time later, regardless of now being an Olympian, a husband, a two-time cancer survivor, and, most important, a father, The Show was still with him. The Director was still finding new and creative ways to interrupt all that he had built, all that he had fought for.

He chose to tell the children about all of it.

Amanda agreed. They would bring the children to the hospital and explain to them what had happened. It wouldn't be easy, but it felt right. Kevin also thought about his battle with medication. The way he later put it: "The world is round, yet I am flat."

During the children's visit, Rainer described what he had seen in his father at Legoland. He had thought his dad was acting just like one of the children. Kevin listened to his son, then began telling him his story as openly and honestly as he could.

GORDON

A COUPLE OF weeks after Legoland, the family reassembled for Thanksgiving. They hadn't spoken much since their vacation, but it wasn't long before the subject came up again, however awkward. Gordon told Kevin how he had felt at Legoland: disrespected.

Kevin was shocked. He asked him to repeat what he had said. He wanted to be sure that he had heard it correctly. *Disrespected?*

In his characteristic, even-paced tone, Gordon explained that he felt he had wasted his time and hard-earned money to be part of Kevin's indulgence, his mania that he didn't seem able or willing to control.

Years after Kevin's first hospitalizations, Gordon still maintained that his son did only the bare minimum necessary to stay out of the hospital; he wasn't making a commitment to his family. He also felt that the manic Kevin resembled a used car salesman in his pushiness and ability to persuade others to do things against their will. He felt manipulated by what he interpreted as Kevin's continual attempts at sabotage.

Susanne held a much different view. She felt that Gordon wasn't interested in trying to understand what things were like for Kevin. He didn't want to understand the rare form of suffering that their son had been struggling with for years. Her own attitudes toward medication, mental health treatment, and therapy had migrated much toward Amanda's more holistic approach, including in her own medical practice. While she didn't pretend to completely understand what was going on in Kevin's head, she was at least curious to find out more. That was a conversation, it seemed, that Gordon, for whatever reason, wasn't interested in having.

KEVIN

KEVIN'S THOUGHTS ROLLED on a separate track as his father kept talking. He wanted to ask him how he felt about not having any biological grandchildren from him, but he didn't bring the subject up. "I didn't need to hear [that] my ancestors feel disrespected, too," he later said.

Kevin had been trying to explain his mania to his father for years, but Gordon still regarded it as a simple matter of whether or not Kevin took his medication. He thought Kevin just didn't have enough willpower and that it was Kevin's choice to mess everything up, when in actuality,

Kevin wanted to scream at the top of his lungs that he was trying, trying harder than any of them could ever imagine.

When Kevin was growing up, he had thought that having intelligence entailed having a certain level of empathy. Now he was learning that the two didn't necessarily go together, that one could be bright but not kind, as well as the other way around. And that mismatch could have a disastrous effect on others, even though many people, including his father, weren't intending to do any harm. Kevin's father seemed to know factoids about every item in a room—he was a walking library filled with nuggets of information that he could pull down from shelves. Or, like those people who can keep an accurate Scrabble score in their head during a game, as well as the point tallies of everyone else playing. But to Kevin, facts were just that—facts—devoid of a soul or sensorial experience.

Kevin had spent most of his adult life not really understanding what "normal" felt like. That is, if normal even existed—maybe it was a mere construct or myth. Often when he was on medication, he felt that something was missing, as if he wasn't his real self. Yet he still had to wake up and be a dad every day. The narrative of being the victim, a helpless loon in a psych ward, is a powerful one, Kevin thought, but ultimately one that wasn't helpful. No one ever talked about his diagnosis as an opportunity to learn or explore what it meant to be human—just as a problem.

Right there, Kevin later wrote, "hidden in the evasive name of the condition is the truth. There are two sides to the story. Maybe stopping the medicine is an attempt to cure something far more painful and scary than the fear of losing one's job, friends, or even sanity."

What if he wasn't broken after all?

AMANDA

AMANDA SAT DOWN at her laptop and began to write a letter to her father-in-law. For years, she had urged Kevin to try to reconcile his tension with Gordon. She had long felt frustrated with Gordon's lack of understanding, or lack of *wanting* to understand, his son. Kevin's mania. It wasn't just going to go away, ever. Gordon, like Amanda, needed to learn how to live with that, how to work with it rather than against it. Amanda wrote that part of what wasn't evident to Gordon was "that Kevin's life-long struggle for self-love is what is keeping him alive—keeping him here as a father and a husband." She clicked send.

Gordon responded with an hour-long phone call to Amanda. Upon hanging up, she realized that the content of her letter hadn't sunk in and that Gordon wasn't likely to change his views. At least for a while, Kevin's desire to maintain some space from his father seemed like a good idea. The therapist he and Amanda had recently started seeing in Auckland agreed. The two men weren't likely to connect anytime soon, and the stress of interacting with Gordon could add yet another weight on a recovery that still felt fragile.

After Legoland, she and Kevin developed a checklist, written from Kevin's point of view, for the kind of behavior that signaled that he was heading toward The Show and away from reality:

1. I want music in the house more than usual
2. I sing more passionately, and better, than usual
3. I am more chatty
4. I am more interested in other people, and their lives

5. I am more interested in different books, movies, exploring the web
6. I am more creative and fun as a father
7. I am more interested in sex
8. I am more interested in my own appearance, clothes, the news
9. I think people on the street look a little like famous people
10. I trust everything is going to work out, and life is easy . . .

They also developed a checklist for the kind of behavior that signaled he was firmly rooted in reality:

1. I haven't put on music for weeks
2. I have to force myself to read the one book I have going
3. I talk slowly and don't barge in with an unsolicited conversation
4. I am too emotionally lazy to be irritated by anything, even things which should irritate me
5. I get plenty of sleep . . .

In some ways, dealing with a "good day" was the tragedy of it, as Kevin and Amanda found themselves second-guessing whether it really was a truly positive moment in the ordinary sense or if Kevin was spinning up toward an episode. They both knew that the checklists were far from being a solution. In her more than twenty years of knowing Kevin, Amanda was the first to admit that there would never be a way to know for sure when he was heading toward an episode, or to find a "cure" or "quick fix." At least identifying his patterns was a start.

KEVIN

KEVIN, AMANDA, AND their children moved back to Auckland from the Bay Area. The skyrocketing Northern California real estate market had served them well in unloading their house there, and after years of being nomads, they sought to have a more permanent home.

The world around them was changing as well. More and more, online campaigns such as the hashtags "#sicknotweak" and "#imnotashamed" were becoming shorthand for people "outing" themselves as having been diagnosed with a mental illness. Other people wrote blogs chronicling their battles in detail. In 2013, the same year that Kevin sailed on the *Artemis* and had his Legoland episode, the nonprofit Project Semicolon was launched, its name derived from the punctuation used "when an author could've ended a sentence but chose not to," the group's website read. "You are the author and the sentence is your life." Many in the movement draw semicolons on their skin as reminders that life does go on. Kevin took it a step further and got a semicolon tattooed on the top of his wrist.

Largely thanks to social media, some people with mental illnesses were feeling connected to each other in new ways, including Kevin, who started to use Facebook to call on help from friends and family, many far-flung from his years of international travel. Reading the posts of others who had gone through struggles like his own made Kevin think of Arthur Schopenhauer's notion that when the mind, body, and soul are faced with severe trauma they look for ways to cope. He began trying to deconstruct what his initial trauma might have been and how The Show might have become the means by which he tried to handle it, slowly helping to shift his relationship with social media from one of it acting as a trigger to becoming an ally.

The culture at large was becoming more interested in the nature of bipolar disorder as well. More nuanced depictions of people who had been diagnosed with it were appearing in critically and commercially successful shows and movies such as *Homeland, Six Feet Under*, and *Silver Linings Playbook*. Celebrities not only began to identify themselves as having been diagnosed, but were beginning to talk about it in more detail—among them the actress Carrie Fisher, who wrote about her bipolar disorder in several memoirs. While a stigma remained, the term was slowly but surely entering the mainstream Western lexicon and inspiring more people with diagnosed, or suspected, mental health issues to talk more openly about their experiences.

As time stretched away from the crash, from Legoland, from the psychiatric hospital admission with the Google Glass, Kevin further dissected the questions of who the Director was and what purpose, if any, he was going to serve in his life going forward. Was it as Freudian as the Director being a manifestation of his father? Was the Director a supporter? An oppressor? A coach? A version of himself, an alter ego of sorts? Some combination of all those? Kevin felt that he needed a visual reminder of his "Truman Show" delusion, something that he could look at every day that would remind him of his own reality rather than that of The Show. With Amanda's blessing, he designed a television set tattoo that would live on his inner arm. The antennae were asymmetrical, to make sure he could clearly see the *L* in the scene—to go with an *O, V,* and *E*. The *O* was the outline of the screen, the two legs of the *V* were attached to the bottom, and there were four *E*s.

The *E*s framed the television set and were inspired by the shorthand that James Joyce had used when writing *Finnegans Wake* to keep himself oriented while weaving together several narrative threads and trying to come to terms with his daughter's schizophrenia. In the book, Joyce played with the idea of fours over and over again: four seagulls, four old men, four waves, four provinces of Ireland, four seasons, four points on a compass. Kevin wanted the tattoo, with its four sides, to remind him that his life was best lived when he was in the middle, that moderation was the goal.

Importantly, too, the *E*s pointed outward and formed a border. If he ever felt a whiff of the Director or caught a peek into The Show, he was to stare at his tattoo, the television, to keep him focused, literally, on the right channel.

Increasingly, Kevin and Amanda try to broach Kevin's "Truman Show" delusions with friends. The moniker gives them a built-in reference to the film, but Kevin often also explains his delusions by referencing the CCTV cameras in London or the increased presence of street cameras in New York City. "That's how I feel when I'm in The Show," he says. "All the time."

When Kevin and Amanda talk to their children about their father's mental health, they often use the Pixar film *Inside Out* as a tool to help them in describing how sometimes their father's train of thought goes "off the track." In the film, a girl named Riley lives with five personifications of her emotions—Sadness, Fear, Disgust, Anger, and Joy—who live in her brain's headquarters and influence her actions. Her memories are stored as multicolored gumballs, and there's an ongoing battle to keep Sadness away from her brain's console, a parallel plot to Kevin's at times. The narrative is even more complicated when thinking about the compassion Kevin received from law enforcement. It's a sharp contrast in an era of police shootings and headlines about Trayvon Martin, Eric Garner, and far too many other names that are in the news as their middle child, Leo, comes

Kevin Hall's tattoo

of age half-black. "Do we have to worry about Leo just walking around in a sweatshirt?" Amanda asked.

Like many people who have had manic episodes, Kevin says he wouldn't trade his diagnosis in if given the chance, because he's accessed parts of his brain that the vast majority of people can only imagine. Kevin has to constantly remind himself that as exciting as an episode can be, its consequences for his real-life supporting cast are too devastating to be worth it. His lows, too, can be contagious. Every day, Kevin wakes up and is tested.

Since returning to New Zealand, Kevin still has had visits from the Director. In the fall of 2015, he had an episode that was *Ulysses*-themed in which he purchased a one-way ticket from Auckland to Dublin and made endless loops on the ground with the cables of his cell phone chargers. Amanda drove around all night trying to find him. He recalled Joyce's quotes and took them to heart. "For myself, I always write about Dublin," Joyce said, "Because if I can get to the heart of Dublin I can get to the heart of all the cities of the world. In the particular is contained the universal."

The universal sounded pretty good to Kevin as he boarded the plane. He wanted to be swept away and escape, feeling as though he was letting his family down again. That pain of having to choose between what he saw as his false self and "true self," became unbearable. But when he heard Coldplay's "Fix You" on his Spotify playlist and the line "Lights will guide you home," he realized he had made a mistake. He ran out of the plane before it took off, reconnected with Amanda and his children in Auckland, and entered a hospital shortly thereafter.

In May of 2016, Kevin spent several days on suicide watch, a down period he attributes to the difficulties he experienced in trying to figure out his post-professional athlete identity. During this period, he and Amanda benefited from cognitive behavioral therapy, an evidence-based way of developing personal coping strategies and problem-solving techniques. It is a hyperpractical approach and a departure from the older Freudian style of hopping onto the couch and talking about sexual proclivities developed during childhood. Kevin did not sail until more than a year after the *Artemis* crash, and even then it was just him testing out his Moth with some friends, not a competition or preparation for one. Although he enjoyed the physical sensation of being out on the water, the experience didn't make him miss racing at all.

Today, Kevin still sails occasionally, but derives pleasure from writing, spending time with his family, and doing some sailing coaching. He's excited about the prospect of helping guide someone else on their path through the sailing circuits and sharing his years of experience with those just starting out.

Kevin has said on more than one occasion that being a stay-at-home dad is more difficult than being an Olympian. "When you train for the Olympics, it's all about you," Kevin wrote. "When you're a stay-at-home dad, it's never about you." He says he could make sense of his bad days on the water, but his challenging days raising kids are far less logical. The only thing less predictable than the water, it seems, is the behavior of children. "When you say you're an Olympian," Kevin says, "people think you're amazing. A badass, a model citizen, an inspiration, worthy. When you say you're a stay-at-home dad people wonder what you did wrong to lose your job and whether you ever wore the pants at all."

The Hall children have sailed some, including through a New Zealand school program that Kevin sometimes volunteers with. He enjoys spending time with his kids on the water but is anxious that he might begin pushing them too hard. He doesn't want them to feel as though sailing is their only means of achievement—or to flame out early and lose their joy of the sport. "I loved it so much as a kid," he says. "I just want to be supportive." During a recent fun run on one of Auckland's beaches, two of the Hall children were giggling toward the back of the pack. "We were thrilled," Amanda said.

When Kevin sits on his couch describing his current position in sailing, he speaks of *Moby-Dick*, Herman Melville (who many scholars today believe may have had bipolar disorder), and his protagonist Ahab, forty years at sea. For Kevin, too, it has been forty years at sea and counting, and maybe he has proved what he wanted to in that time after all. Maybe his own quest, like Ahab's, has been about something other than just the impassioned hunt for the whale, or an Olympic medal. Instead of questioning his passion for sailing, Kevin is now questioning the fanaticism itself. But unlike Ahab, he's losing interest in making his life about executing a revenge plot against an internal or external enemy of some sort. For both him and Ahab, the ship quite literally snapped, but Kevin is determined that his life beyond the water not be marked by melancholy or mania. "Thus sailing with sealed orders," Melville wrote in *White Jacket*, "we ourselves are the repositories of the secret packet, whose mysterious contents we long to learn. There are no mysteries out of ourselves."

Kevin and Amanda talk about what they've been through in and out of The Show, as she reminds him over and over again that she knew what she was getting into from the start. She chose it then and continues to choose it every day. She wants a world with Kevin in it, and in it as her partner.

Kevin has started writing about his experiences in and out of The Show and is both committing his story to, and confronting it on, paper. "I want people to know you can be a little crazy and have a good, real life, too," he says. He knows he's not alone in the surreal becoming real, and the other way around. Life continues to surprise, and whether Kevin spends his days on the water, in front of the laptop screen, helping his children with homework, or doing something else altogether, he resists the temptation of the Director while trying to maintain that same feeling of connected bliss he felt on the water as a kid. The Director may never go away permanently, but can he at least please hang back for a while?

Kevin is needed, and loved, back on the shore.

MARY

IT'S HARD FOR me to say when my Great Aunt Lettie first started hearing the voices in her head.

For years, my mother and several other friends and family members who had known Lettie when she was alive recounted to me tales of attending the séances held in her Oregon farmhouse basement. Lettie said that she could hear the voice of Roger, her son who had drowned at the age of ten in the Santiam River. From his death in the 1950s until her own in 1981, she said that she could hear Roger's voice, even if no one else could.

Television and radio played a part, as the perfect time to communicate with the voices of the dead, Lettie said, was after *Lawrence Welk*, as the vibrations were the highest. She often laid out sacred objects of Roger's to help conjure his voice: red puppets he had played with; his favorite type of apples, picked fresh; a postcard-sized framed pencil drawing of two cats that once hung above his small bed.

My mother went on to study psychology and work with people who, among other things, said they heard voices and were struggling to keep a steady hold on reality. Instead of being spooked, or romanticizing Lettie's struggle, my mother became curious and made it her job to try and understand them. People who heard voices were not presented to me as a child as dangerous or scary. They were friends, neighbors, fellow citizens. Often, they were suffering, needed help, and lacked support. They had a different story to tell, but it was still that—their own story. They were, literally, in our blood.

Perhaps it was no surprise then that by the time I began reporting *The Kevin Show* in the summer of 2014, the annals of crazy had become my microniche on the sports desk at the *New York Times*. It was then that Andy Lehren, a colleague of mine there, breezed by my desk one day and mentioned that he had heard of "an Olympic sailor with some weird mental illness," I reluctantly, and skeptically, made some calls. While reality television was more than ubiquitous at that point, as was social media and our collective push toward being our own publicists online, I had no idea how the themes of the story would only amplify more loudly over the ensuing years.

Fast-forward to November 2016, when, with the aid of Russian hackers, Donald J. Trump, a reality television star with no political credentials and an exhaustive platform of racist, homophobic, sexist, and otherwise bigoted ideals, won the U.S. presidency. Among other things, he used the idea of a distorted reality (now, infamously, "fake news") as a weapon with lasting impact. The surreal became real.

One of many things that fascinated me about the election as I reported *The Kevin Show* was the flippant use of mental health terms like "crazy" or "from the loony bin" or "insane" to describe Trump. Marisa Lancione, a blogger with bipolar disorder who frequently writes about her experience on *Mad Girl's Lament*, has called for people to stop calling Donald Trump mentally ill, noting that "when we equate a person like Trump with mental illness we're creating a false equivalency." While Trump's behavior is far beyond societal norms (the diagnoses of sociopath or narcissistic personality disorder are most often bandied about), Trump isn't representative of the mental health community, most of whom don't share his misogynistic, bigoted, and xenophobic views.

It was against this tumultuous backdrop that in the fall of 2016, the Halls moved back to the United States from New Zealand. Amanda would be closer to her roots and her family and Kevin could find more coaching opportunities. Being stateside also meant that they would have a more robust support system as Kevin continues his transition from professional athlete to writer, coach, and mentor. After packing up their boxes, children, and their dog, they settled in Hudson, New York, just a short train ride up from where Kevin had his Grand Central episode years ago.

It hasn't been easy. Kevin was hospitalized once during the winter. He considered killing himself because of an overwhelming feeling that he was going to let his family down and never be a good enough dad, that life as himself was impossible. "I wasn't psychotic," Kevin said. "I just wanted not to wake up." He spent his time there copying passages from *A Portrait of the Artist as a Young Man* and *Moby-Dick* and earned the nickname of Yoda from his fellow patients for his wisdom and insights. And his sense of humor remained intact. With Trump in office, Kevin said, "at least my mental illness is trendy."

In the hospital, Kevin once again asked doctors about how medications worked and if he could learn more about gradually getting off of them. He was told that would be virtually impossible. One of his dialectical behavior therapy groups focused on identifying patterns and giving ways to help cope with stress, and with these new tools in hand, Kevin decided to go medication-free on his own.

A few days after he was released, Amanda heard Kevin singing in the shower—a sign that he could be spinning up—and asked him about it.

Kevin told her he was off of his meds and that he was willing to die trying to stay off of them. He said he felt that, for twenty-eight years, he had lived "chemically incarcerated." Amanda took a sip of wine and told Kevin she knew that he could do it, pointing to his drug-free run ahead of the Olympic trials years ago. They knew more now than they knew then. "We'll do it together," she said. "I love you." Then, not long after Kevin's release, he received the news that his father, Gordon, with whom connections were still strained, had died suddenly while riding his bicycle in California.

Just two days before, Kevin had talked to Amanda about being ready to see him again. He had spent the moments before Gordon's death listening to John Denver and the Beatles, albums he knew his father loved. "I felt like I spent a day with him," Kevin said. Amanda received the call from Kristina that Gordon had passed away, and when she told Kevin, he said that although he felt sadness, he maybe even experienced a sense of relief. "I collapsed and I picked myself up," he said. "He was a good man. He believed in justice and trying hard, being responsible, and owning your own behavior. I'm glad I have a lot of that in me."

Kevin reports feeling grounded, healthy, connected. He wonders: How many of his "relapses" were due to the drugs rather than his own mind? How has his brain changed and grown since his original diagnosis in Boston? He's increasingly feeling comfortable talking to friends and family about his mental health odyssey, but what of others who still feel stigmatized?

The conversation around medication and treatment can get wonky, jargon-filled, and politically loaded pretty quickly. But it's a critical one; half of all Americans will have a mental health crisis, according to the Center for Disease Control and Prevention, and it would be virtually impossible to draw up one single type of treatment path for every one of them. Thinking about mental health in terms of our legal system, prisons, schools, workplaces, homeless shelters, and beyond can be dizzying, and the desire for a quick and easy fix is often well-intended; it's hard to experience suffering or see it in others, to say nothing of its unwanted companion, helplessness. Many solutions, including Kevin's evolving treatment, are long and arduous; medication or no, they involve investments of patience and compassion. If only it were as simple as taking pills.

Aunt Lettie lingers in my mind; it's hard not to think of her communicating with Roger as her own way of coping with an unfathomable tragedy, along with her own difficult childhood. I now find it remarkable and fortunate that she was received by family and friends who asked questions, and lived a life of her own on the farm, in spite of what were widely perceived as heavy eccentricities.

It would be foolish to pretend that Kevin's story, or that of any one person, contains all of the answers. In some ways, it leaves me with more questions than when I set out with my first phone calls. I spent more than three years reporting a story about a man who called himself (jokingly) "the village idiot" only to find myself at times more confused by the village than its purported nutcase.

Kevin is rethinking the narrative of his own diagnosis, instead wondering if what he experienced in Boston was more of a spiritual crisis rather than what he feels may be the overly simplistic label of bipolar disorder. The problem with the label of a diagnosis, Kevin said, however well intended, is that it leads some people to believe they're permanently defective, and it may serve the labelers more than the labelees. (He also points out that while he can't recommend a solution for everyone, and that in many cases drugs have saved lives, John Nash stopped taking his psychiatric medication in 1970, a fact that was in the book *A Beautiful Mind*, but not in the feature film adaptation.)

"The message is 'We know exactly what's wrong and you must stay within the *DSM* and comply with our regimen,'" Kevin said. "And here are all these other broken people who go on to do things. It's a setup that doesn't empower you. I'm not broken. How about 'You're human and you're trying to handle something. Let's heal you so you can have your life.'"

The descriptions and implications of Kevin's delusions have stuck with me, even though I wasn't present for any of them. They've also become a filter through which I now see the world, as I'm continuously fascinated with our (and, at times, my own) willingness to invade a sense of presence to create that perfect Instagram, however staged it may be, even as we're often missing the very things we're supposed to be capturing: our lives. It's becoming harder and harder not to think that for many of us, every corner of the world is a photo set. Now some lives are actually ending in selfie deaths: people falling into canyons through the inattentive use of the gadgets. At best, however, filming can bear witness to racial discrimination, sexual harassment, or other ills that now can be chronicled with justice-seeking voices. This is not to be dismissed. But at worst, there's Steve Stephens, who posted video of his murder of a man on Facebook in April 2017 and even more grimly, how millions of people watched. How prescient Susan Sontag was when in 1977 she wrote that cameras are "fantasy machines whose use is addictive."

When our screens are up, and we're all somehow creating our own versions of The Show, how connected are we, really? How are we to draw the line between what is real and what is distorted? What is sane or crazy in our own version of heeding the Director? Isn't everything—language, culture, customs, societal norms—made up? Yet we choose this, day in and day out, many of us acknowledging that our engagement with a distorted reality often makes us less happy, adding a strange, masochistic tone to the behavior of our current moment. None of this is new. For Lettie, it was a radio show of sorts. For Kevin, it was television with a dash of Google Glass. For many of us, it's social media.

Roger's cat drawing from the séances passed from Lettie to my mother, and then to me after her death in 2004. I still keep it on my desk in New York as a reminder that the Director, whether being beamed into Lettie's farm, in Legoland, in our own head or that of someone we know or care about, isn't ever really that far away.

Kevin considers his children who are growing up in today's complicated digital landscape.

"The message is 'We measure whether your fake show is watched more than my fake show,'" Kevin said. "I'm glad I didn't have to go through that, too. It was all in my head. But now it's real and terrifying. It's hard to shake a nineteen-year-old who has been raised with every fiber of his existence in a meritocracy machine construct, then say 'None of that matters.'"

How fitting, then, that it was the age-old storyteller Shakespeare whose work made a cameo in Kevin's first episode in Boston. All the world is a stage more than ever before.

Maybe Truman Show Disorder isn't as rare as we think.

A NOTE ON SOURCES

THIS BOOK IS the result of hundreds of hours of interviews with more than fifty people, a review of hundreds of pages of medical records, research, reports, journal entries, correspondence (handwritten and digital), sailing footage, police reports, and a variety of other documents. Given the nature of the topic and some of the incidents described, not every single detail was confirmable by two or more sources. To the best of my ability, I have tried to detail that in the endnotes, along with where and how I came about information. Not even the best work of journalism can be a perfect work of the truth, rather a version of the truth, an irony that's not lost on me as I write a book about a man who grapples with reality. If anyone has suggestions for how better to report out someone's inner world, I'm all ears.

In addition, per *Wall Street Journal* and *New York Times* ethics policies, I have not, nor will I, accept funding from conflicted parties, such as pharmaceutical companies, Scientologists, or any political organizations.

RECOMMENDED READING AND MENTAL HEALTH RESOURCES

The world you see is just a movie in your mind.
—JACK KEROUAC, *The Portable Jack Kerouac*

FIRST AND FOREMOST, I highly recommend Kevin's memoir about his own experience, *Black Sails White Rabbits*, which is cited throughout this text. You can find out more about the book and Kevin's latest work on his website, kevinahall.com and the audio book of *Black Sails* is a particularly vivid way of getting into the story.

Joel and Ian Gold's book *Suspicious Minds: How Culture Shapes Madness* is the definitive work on the "Truman Show" delusion, as well as a fascinating exploration of how cultural influences can inform madness. It was the brothers Gold's work that first tipped me off to Kevin's story, and their contributions to the field have been enormous.

At the risk of stating the obvious, *The Truman Show* is a must-see film, but also one of the best rewatches for those looking to revisit the rare film about technology that truly stands the test of time.

MENTAL HEALTH MEMOIRS

Manic by Terri Cheney
Wishful Drinking by Carrie Fisher

Marbles by Ellen Forney

An Unquiet Mind by Kay Redfield Jamison

The Center Cannot Hold by Ellyn Saks

Darkness Visible by William Styron

BOOKS ABOUT MENTAL HEALTH

The Alchemy of Mind by Diane Ackerman

Am I Bipolar or Waking Up? by Sean Blackwell

Psychosis and Spirituality: Consolidating the New Paradigm edited by Isabel Clarke

The Brain by David Eagleman (book and documentary series)

Illusions of Immortality: A Psychology of Fame and Celebrity by David Giles

Spiritual Emergency: When Personal Transformation Becomes a Crisis edited by Stanislov Grof and Christina Grof

The Stormy Search for the Self: A Guide to Personal Growth through Transformational Crisis edited by Christina Grof and Stanislov Grof

Outside Mental Health: Voices and Visions of Madness by Will Hall

The Antidepressant Era by David Healy

Rational Mysticism by John Horgan

The Varieties of Religious Experience: A Study in Human Nature by William James

Exuberance by Kay Redfield Jamison

Touched with Fire: Manic-Depressive Illness and the Artistic Temperament by Kay Redfield Jamison

To Walk on Eggshells by Jean Johnson

Myths about Suicide by Thomas Joiner

The Red Book by Carl Jung

A Farther Shore: How Near-Death and Other Extraordinary Experiences Can Change Ordinary Lives by Yvonne Kason and Teri Degler

The Emperor's New Drugs: Exploding the Antidepressant Myth by Irving Kirsch

After the Ecstasy, the Laundry: How the Heart Grows Wise on the Spiritual Path by Jack Kornfield

Shrinks: The Untold Story of Psychiatry by Jeffery A. Lieberman

A Beautiful Mind by Sylvia Nasar

Healing the Split: Integrating Spirit Into Our Understanding of the Mentally Ill by John E. Nelson

Fame: What the Classics Tell Us About Our Cult of Celebrity by Tom Payne

Far Side of Madness by John Weir Perry

Trials of the Visionary Mind by John Weir Perry

Breaking Down Is Waking Up: The Connection Between Psychological Distress and Spiritual Awakening by Russell Razzaque

What Is Self?: A Study of the Spiritual Journey in Terms of Consciousness by Bernadette Roberts

Far from the Tree and *The Noonday Demon* by Andrew Solomon (Solomon's work for the *New York Times Magazine* and his TED talks are also invaluable)

The Healing Wisdom of Africa by Malidoma Patrice Somé

Born to Rebel: Birth Order, Family Dynamics, and Creative Lives by Frank J. Sulloway

Out of the Darkness: From Turmoil to Transformation by Steve Taylor

The Body Keeps the Score by Bessel Van der Kolk

Crazy Like Us by Ethan Watters

Unshrinking Psychosis by John Watkins

Rethinking Madness: Towards a Paradigm Shift in Our Understanding and Treatment of Psychosis by Paris Williams

The Outsider by Colin Wilson

I Contain Multitudes by Ed Yong

BOOKS ABOUT TESTICULAR CANCER

The Emperor of All Maladies by Siddhartha Mukherjee

BOOKS ABOUT SPORTS, SAILING, AND THE OLYMPICS

The Champion's Mind by Jim Afremow

The Sports Gene by David Epstein

Players by Matthew Futterman

The Games by David Goldblatt

Winging It by Diane Swintal

POP CULTURE IN KEVIN'S DELUSIONS

LITERATURE

Beethoven's "Immortal Beloved" letters

Time Out of Joint (a nice *Hamlet* shout-out in the title) and the other works of
     Philip K. Dick

They by Robert A. Heinlein

Finnegans Wake, A Portrait of the Artist as a Young Man, and *Ulysses* by James
     Joyce

Every Love Story Is a Ghost Story: A Life of David Foster Wallace by D. T. Max

Moby-Dick by Herman Melville

The Crying of Lot 49 by Thomas Pynchon

The works of Rainer Maria Rilke

Hamlet by William Shakespeare

The works of Kurt Vonnegut (the short story "Harrison Bergeron" in particular)

"Good Old Neon" (short story), *Infinite Jest, The Pale King* by David Foster Wallace, as well as his other fiction

MUSIC

The works of Alanis Morissette

"Lithium" by Nirvana

"ÜBerlin" by R.E.M. (along with all of the R.E.M. catalog)

"And She Was" by the Talking Heads

FILMS

12 Monkeys

A Beautiful Mind

E.T.

The Firm

The Frame

Inception

Ink

The Matrix

North by Northwest

Total Recall

Trading Places

Wicker Man

PODCASTS

The Mental Illness Happy Hour with Paul Gilmartin (mentalpod.com) likens itself to a patient waiting room and is a great, approachable resource.

Hidden Brain on NPR, an excellent, thorough examination of many issues in and around the mind. (npr.org/hiddenbrain)

WNYC's excellent *Radiolab* (radiolab.org) and *Death, Sex, and Money* (wnyc.org/shows/deathsexmoney).

WBUR's *Dear Sugar* (wbur.org/dearsugar).

MENTAL HEALTH RESOURCES

In case this isn't already abundantly clear, this book is *not* a substitute for psychiatric care. Nor is it intended to be the definitive word on what it means to live with mental illness. Instead, the hope is that it will serve as a jumping-off point for a larger conversation about how our minds and the minds of those we care about function.

National Institute of Mental Health (nimh.nih.gov)—The leading federal agency for mental health research.

MentalHealth.gov—The U.S. Department of Health and Human Services portal for access to government mental health resources.

The National Suicide Prevention Hotline (suicidepreventionlifeline.org), 1-800-273-8255—offers confidential, nationwide support for those going through emotional crisis. Additional resources are available for military veterans, youth, Native Americans, LGBTQ+, and disaster survivors, as well as their friends and families.

The Anxiety and Depression Association of America (adaa.org)—Access to support groups, therapists, podcasts, apps, and volunteer opportunities.

Depression and Bipolar Support Alliance (dbsalliance.org)—Peer-directed nonprofit with educational resources and support for those with mood disorders.

Each of Us (eachofus.eu) and Time to Change (time-to-change.org.uk)—European anti-stigma campaign, with an emphasis on testimonials and changing the language around mental illness.

Shades of Awakening (shadesofawakening.com)—A group Kevin recommends that delves more into spiritual crises, with a robust online community.

The Icarus Project (theicarusproject.net)—With a nod to Greek mythology, the Icarus Project "seeks to overcome the limitations of a world determined to label, categorize, and sort human behavior."

Project Semicolon (projectsemicolon.com)—A nonprofit committed to suicide prevention through public awareness, educating communities, and equipping individuals with the right tools.

ADDITIONAL GROUPS

The Men's Health Initiative (mhinitiative.org)—A nonprofit "dedicated to promoting healthy behaviors among our fathers, sons, brothers, and other loved ones while advancing the academic and scientific fields of men's health."

Testicular Cancer Society (testicularcancersociety.org)—A survivor-focused support community for those who have been diagnosed with testicular cancer that provides education, awareness, and events.

The Andrew Simpson Sailing Foundation (andrewsimpsonfoundation .org)—A U.K.-based foundation that provides sailing instruction and other opportunities for youth worldwide.

The Joseph Campbell Foundation (jcf.org)—A nonprofit devoted to keeping the work of the iconic mythologist alive.

CLOSING CREDITS: THANK-YOUS AND COFFEE SHOPS

The poet Paul Valéry wrote that anyone preparing to venture into the interior of the psyche had better go "armed to the teeth."

And armed with a militia of wonderful, kind people, I continue to be. I'm beyond thankful for the cheerleading and support I received in working on *The Kevin Show*.

First and foremost, I've never asked more of sources than I have of Kevin and Amanda Hall. They endured an ungodly amount of interviews, often about the deepest corners of their lives. Kevin especially took a huge leap of faith and entered the strange world of being interviewed by a journalist and trusting someone with his story, no small feat in any case, but particularly impressive considering the subject matter. Through the entire process they were patient, candid, clear, and I can't express my gratitude enough. That extends to their children, Rainer, Leo, and Stevie, as well as other members of the Hall family who agreed to be interviewed: Kristina and Bud Culbertson, Susanne Lammot, and Gordon Hall before his passing in 2017.

In addition, several other people tied to the story generously offered their time and insight. Thank you to Morgan Larson, Zach Leonard, Richard Feeny, Ray Davies and Emirates Team New Zealand, Sarah O'Kane, Sanda Golopentia, Stephanie Gisondi-Little, Dr. Joel Gold, Michael Rovito, John Rousmaniere and the New York Yacht Club, Dr. Andrew

T. Nathanson, Mike Craycraft, Judi Clements and Sophia Graham at the Mental Health Foundation in Auckland, Tim Brown, Emma Mackley, John R. Suler, David Krauss, Tommy Dodson, and many others. Thank you to the research staffs at the New York Public Library and the Brooklyn Public Library.

In addition to Kevin, I spoke with dozens of people who have been diagnosed with bipolar disorder, including some who had Truman Show–like symptoms, but wished not to be named. I also spoke at length with many friends and family members of people who have been diagnosed with a variety of mental illnesses. You know who you are. Telling your stories helped me tremendously in developing my understanding. Thank you.

My family is the best. Huge thanks to my dad, Myron, my older brother, Andy, and my nephew, Quint. My late mother, Carol Morse, was a family psychologist and without a doubt planted all this interest in mental health and what makes humans tick in me at a young age. Additional thanks are owed to: Aunt Ronda Pilon and Uncle Bob Roschke, Aunt JoAnn Morse, Michael Morse, the Guernsey family (Carol, Daniel, Aidan, and Owen), Aunt Linda Renfro and Uncle Guy Renfro, Uncle Jim Pilon and Aunt Carol Ashley, Grandma Maxine Pilon, Auntie Jan and Uncle Steve. They provided everything from meals to couches to ears and understanding.

Deborah Schneider, my power literary agent at ICM, continues to be a force and I'm indebted to her for her insight and support. Thanks are also owed to Will Watkins, Josie Freedman, and Melissa Orton at ICM, as well. My lawyer, Kim Schefler, is a badass.

Once again, I can sing the praises of Bloomsbury. A huge thanks to the entire crew there, including Nancy Miller, Sara Mercurio, Sara Kitchen, Callie Garnett, Lea Beresford, Laura Phillips, Christiane Bird, and George Gibson.

The *Wall Street Journal* and the *New York Times* newsrooms taught me how to be a journalist and I thank them for that and the continual friendships I have there. A special thanks to Andy Lehren, my friend and colleague at the *Times* who first tipped me off to Kevin's story.

Thank you to the newsrooms who have also embraced me as a freelancer these last couple of years and my "Kevin Show" deadlines: the *New Yorker, Esquire, Bloomberg Businessweek, Wired, Vice,* NBC Sports, the *New Republic,* Reuters, ESPN, *Bleacher Report, Entrepreneur,* and others. During my reporting of this book, Gawker.com died, but it will forever be alive in my heart.

There were many friends to me and this book. They include Samantha Wolf, Ben Ryan, Oliver Wolf, Jillian Goodman, Jason Feifer, Emily Steel, Clarissa Williams, Elsa Kaminsky, Maya Lau, Travon Free, Jason Zweig, Pip Ngo, Colleen Clark, Jeremy Greenfield, Elle Reeve, Seth Porges, Diane Nabatoff, Irma Akansu, Anna Karingal, Pam Capalad, Dramatic Dyalekt, Christina "Lopez" Lipinski, Francine Dauw, Jon Levy, Jan Messerschmidt, Wendy Frink, Steve Eder, Hamilton and Rufus Pug, Lauren Perlgut, Carrie Sin, Will Martin, James Andrew Miller, the NBC Sports Olympics crew, Natti Vogel, Lauren Giudice, Jeremy Redleaf and Ben Bechar and our magical Mystery Dinner guests, the various Pierces, Jennifer Wright, Maricor Resente, Susanne Craig, Taylor Katai, Suzanne Zuppello, Jenny Li, Eric and Raven Stralow, Salman Somjee, Rana June, Philip Green, Carla Correa, Bob Sullivan, Troy Pospisil, Dorna Moini, Ron Lieber, Vanessa Livingston, Adam Spiegel, Halley Theodore, Caitlin Burns, Alex Amend, Dara Rosenberg, Peter Feld, Barry Newman, Lindsay Kaplan, Richard Blakeley, Rachel Fershleiser, Rob Dittler, Nick Douglas, Cole Stryker, Hugo Lindgren, Lauren Ruff, Ryan McNeil, Aviva Slesin, Matthew Williams, Nick and Julie (and Malou!) Koch, and Fry and Anthony Miale. Thank you to the Invisible Institute, my awesome book club, Forward/Story, Cave Day, Croissant, and the CUNY Graduate School of Journalism. A huge gracias to Alicia Marvan and the Guapamacataro fellowship y mis amigos en Michoacán. I still miss David Carr, but am glad that his wise words about journalism, books, and life still dance around my mind.

Then, there were the saints who agreed to read early versions of the book: Kari Ensor, Lauren Appelwick, Charles Schaeffer, Annie He, Irma Akansu, Kas Ghobadi, Erin McGill, Sophia Muthuraj, Jen Simonian, Liz Stork, and Aviva Slesin. Thank you.

Thanks are owed to the Apple Store employees at the World Trade Center and Fourteenth Street locations in Manhattan, who, without judgement, replaced up to five of my laptop keys at a time when I broke several during the writing of this book.

Robert Caro probably doesn't remember randomly meeting me on the Upper West Side, but his offhand writing advice to me changed my approach to this story and the way I write forever. Thanks for that.

I'm a proud graduate of New York University and Winston Churchill High School in Eugene, Oregon. (Go, Lancers!)

COFFEE SHOPS

Whatever you're tipping your barista, it's not enough. I'm thankful to these places for giving me caffeine and comfort during the writing of *The Kevin Show*.

NEW YORK

Kos Kafe, Konditori (multiple locations, but 5th Ave Park Slope receives a gold star), Venticinque (RIP!), Gorilla Coffee (Bergen and Fifth Ave. locations, RIP to the latter), Brooklyn Roasting Company, Hungry Ghost,

Postmark Cafe, Cafe Regular (all locations), COFFEED (Sixth Ave and 16th), Gregory's Coffee, Root Hill Cafe, Bryant Park, Grounded, Tilda, 61 Local, Uptown Roasters (South Slope), Budin (Greenpoint), Oren's, Think Coffee (various locations with a shoutout to 8th Ave and Mercer St.), the Bean (on Broadway), Culture Espresso, Cafe Reggio, the coffee shops at McNally Jackson and Housing Works, as well as the Ace Hotel, Soho House, and The Uncommons

EUGENE

16 Tons, Allan Brothers (both South Eugene and 5th Street locations), Perk (gold star because the baristas yell to everyone in the shop when "the parking meter lady" is afoot and their wifi password is a Devo reference), Vero, Wandering Goat, Espresso Roma, Coffee Plant Roaster (West 11th)

PORTLAND

Stumptown, the World Cup Coffee and Tea at Powell's. Powell's continues to be my Vatican. Thank you.

SEATTLE

Victrola (Beacon Hill), Fremont Coffee, The Conservatory (Georgetown), Arsenio Coffee, Little Oddfellows in the Elliott Bay Book Company

SAN FRANCISCO/BAY AREA

Spasso (Oakland), Cup a Joe Coffeehaus (Sutter St), Papillon (Lafayette), Cafe Sapore

LOS ANGELES

Kaldi Coffee, Collage Coffee (Venice Beach), Rise N Grind (Hollywood), Stories LA (Echo Park), H Coffee House, Urth Caffe

HOUSTON

Slowpokes (bonus points for the sloth theme)

ATHENS, GA

Jittery Joe's

LOUISVILLE

Quills

WASHINGTON

Filter

KEY WEST

Sippin Coffee House

AUCKLAND

Vanilla Cafe, The Coffee Club, Henri, the Corelli Club

CANADA

Locomotive Espresso (London), Nova Cafe (London)

MEXICO CITY

The Urban Corner

REYKJAVIK

C is for Cookie, Reykjavik Roasters, Kex Hostel, Stofan Cafe, Cafe Haiti, Cafe Babalu

THAILAND

Rocket Coffee (in Silom, Bangkok), Archers (Chiang Mai), Pakhinai Cafe Chiang Mai, Nes Coffee (Chiang Mai), Tiamo Cafe (Ko Samui)

CAMBODIA

One More (Phnom Penh), TJ Cafe (Phnom Penh), Bun's Baguette (Phnom Penh), Artease (Phnom Penh), the Foreign Correspondents Club (Phnom Penh), Joe to Go (Siem Reap), Cafe Central (Siem Reap), Missing Socks (Siem Reap), which receives bonus points because I got my laundry done there at the same time.

An assortment of the Coffee Bean, Starbucks, Au Bon Pain, and Pret a Manger locations were in the mix, too.

If I forgot anyone, I apologize. And I love you!

NOTES

PROLOGUE

had snapped at once   Kevin Hall author interview, January 23, 2015.

Kevin and his teammates   Adam Fisher, "What Went Wrong in the Deadly America's Cup Crash," *Wired*, May 9, 2013, https://www.wired.com/2013/05/americas-cup-crash/.

$140-million *Artemis*   The $140 million number is an estimate for the cost of mounting the campaign. Eric Sorenson, "The Cost to Compete in the 34th America's Cup," *Scuttlebutt*, September 26, 2013, http://www.sailingscuttlebutt.com/2013/09/26/cost-compete-34th-americas-cup/.

dwarfed by the *Artemis*   San Francisco Police Department. Incident Report number 130 318 063. Matthew J. Mattei and Keith R. Matthews, reporting and responding officers. San Francisco Police Department, May 9, 2013, 83 pages.

PART I: MEET KEVIN HALL

Kevin wasn't especially well coordinated   Kevin Hall author interview, February 11, 2016, and emails to author about backstory of The Show, February 2016.

"Because no one remembers the past."   Joan Didion, *Slouching Towards Bethlehem* (New York: Farrar, Straus and Giroux, 1968), 4.

a Canadian by birth   Susanne Lammot author interview, March 27, 2016.

a slump in the early 1980s   The early 1980s recession in the United States began in July 1981 and ended in November 1982, and it had further lasting impacts, particularly in the world of banking and lending.

studying a second language   Kevin Hall author interview, November 6, 2014.

completely disintegrated   Susanne Lammot author interview, March 27, 2016.

coming out of nowhere   Kevin Hall author interview, November 6, 2014. Kristina Hall author interview, January 31, 2016.

debts from the boat business   Kristina Hall author interview, January 31, 2016.

sometimes resulting in a win   Gordon Hall author interview, April 28, 2016. Kevin Hall author interview August 12, 2014. Richard Feeny author interview, October 27, 2015.

with him every day as teammates   Richard Feeny author interview, October 27, 2015.

Bob Dylan song lyrics   Ibid.

attended class consistently and punctually   Sanda Golopentia author interview, June 28, 2016.

renderings of complex algebraic equations   The student's name is Cassidy Curtis, according to Kevin, confirmed here: www.math.brown.edu/~banch off/BHE.pdf.

more practical than French literature   Kevin Hall author interview, February 11, 2016, and emails to author about backstory of The Show, February 2016.

Kevin eagerly signed up   Sanda Golopentia author interview, June 28, 2016.

"have to get away from where you are"   Marguerite Duras, *The Lover* (London: Harper Perennial, 2008).

entered his head before college   Kevin Hall author interview, February 11, 2016, and emails to author about backstory of The Show, February 2016.

bad case of herpes zoster   Kevin Hall author interview, January 31, 2016, and emails to author about backstory of The Show, February 2016. Confirmed by his sister, Kristina Hall, in an interview with the author, January 31, 2016.

probably would fail at something   Kevin Hall author interview, November 11, 2014.

locked in an intense dance   Alison Wood Brooks, "Get Excited: Reappraising Pre-Performance Anxiety as Excitement," *Journal of Experimental Psychology* 143, no. 3 (June 2014).

regaining control of the room   Kevin Hall author interview, July 5, 2015.

sounded like a good idea   Ibid.

a way of thinking   Ibid.

gift from a source beyond   Kevin Hall author interview, February 11, 2016, and emails to author about backstory of The Show, February 2016. Given the nature of the event, tracking some eyewitnesses was virtually impossible. Also based on interviews with Kristina, Susanne, and Gordon Hall.

PART II: THE HIGHS

couldn't have been more excited   Ibid.

the role he was to play on The Show   Ibid.

the right choice to be the star   Ibid.

the setting of the hit television show *Cheers*   The actual *Cheers* bar, used for exterior shots, is the Bull & Finch pub in Beacon Hill.

a homeless man had frozen to death   Pine Street Inn. http://www.pinestreet inn.org/about_us/history

Beacon Hill, a historic neighborhood   Kevin Hall, *Black Sails White Rabbits* (Createspace Independent Publishing Platform, 2015).

love interest of Prince Hamlet   Kevin Hall, "William Shakespeare: *Hamlet*," October 24, 1986. Generously provided by Kevin Hall.

go find Ophelia *together*   Kevin Hall, *Black Sails White Rabbit*, (Createspace Independent Publishing Platform, 2015), 19.

The Dead community embraced her   Kristina Hall author interview, January 31, 2016.

a new, thirtysomething boyfriend   Ibid.

birthday weekend with her mother   Kristina Hall author interview, February 2, 2016.

with no beginning and no end   Kevin Hall journal entry, December 26, 1989.

also known as bipolar disorder   I've stewed over which term to use in this book, "manic depression" or "bipolar disorder." I use them both throughout, as various people have told me their preferences either way, but will largely default to "bipolar disorder," per the National Institute of Mental Health: nimh.nih.gov/health/topics/bipolar-disorder/index.shtml. The objections to either term make sense, as often people complain that the term "manic depression" can set folks off with the charged word "manic," but others complain that "bipolar disorder" sounds too technical, detached. Jamison and Hall both prefer "manic depression."

between 1 percent and 2.6 percent   Colby Itkowitz, "Unwell and Ashamed," *Washington Post*, June 1, 2016, http://www.washingtonpost.com/sf/local/2016/06/01/unwell-and-unashamed/?utm_term=.c035d48be469. Whitaker, and others, have questioned the ballooning numbers for bipolar diagnoses. See chapter nine of *Anatomy of an Epidemic*, titled "The Bipolar Boom," in which Whitaker writes: "Although the quick-and-easy explanation is that psychiatry has greatly expanded the diagnostic boundaries, that is only part of the story. Psychotropic drugs—both legal and illegal—have helped fuel the bipolar boom."

significantly more likely to be misdiagnosed   Kay Redfield Jamison, *Touched with Fire: Manic-Depressive Illness and the Artistic Temperament* (New York: Free Press, 1993), 17.

chaotic patterns of personal and professional relationships   Ibid.

bipolar disorder played a role   Hemingway's granddaughter, Mariel Hemingway, is a mental health advocate, and Barbara Kopple made a film about her family's experience with mental illness called *Running from Crazy*. You can find out more here: http://www.wnyc.org/story/how-mariel-hemingway-practices-wellness-shadow-her-grandfathers-legacy/.

the lifetime rate of attempted suicide   Some have put the lifetime suicide attempt rate even higher, 25 to 50 percent: ohsu.edu/xd/education/schools/school-of-medicine/departments/clinical-departments/psychiatry/grand

-rounds/upload/Suicide-and-Suicide-Prevention-in-Bipolar-Disorder_25Sept
12.pdf.

considered people with schizophrenia to be dangerous   Wendy Cross and
Ken Walsh, "Star shots: self disclosure and celebrity in bipolar disorder,"
Research Online, University of Wollongong, 2012, ro.uow.edu.au/cgi/view
content.cgi?article=4115&context=hbspapers. Slowly but surely, the law has
begun to catch up, particularly as regards workplaces. The Americans with
Disabilities Act of 1990 prohibits discrimination based on disability,
including mental illnesses such as bipolar disorder. In 2012, the Equal
Employment Opportunity Commission won a lawsuit against the Cash Store
for failing to provide reasonable accommodation for a man working there
who had disclosed his bipolar disorder and was denied time off work to
adjust to a change in medication from his psychiatrist, and several similar
cases are working their way through the courts.

far more likely to be victims of violent crime   There are several studies on
this, but in my research, I looked at Heather Stuart, "Violence and mental
illness: an overview," *World Psychiatry* 2, no. 2 (June 2003): 121–124, ncbi.nlm
.nih.gov/pmc/articles/PMC1525086/; Richard A. Friedman, "Violence and
Mental Illness—How Strong is the Link?" *New England Journal of Medicine*
355 (November 16, 2006), http://www.nejm.org/doi/full/10.1056/NEJM
p068229#t=article; work from the Treatment Advocacy Center, treatment
advocacycenter.org/storage/documents/final_jails_v_hospitals_study.pdf;
and the Harvard Medical Health Letter, health.harvard.edu/newsletter_article
/mental-illness-and-violence.

"breakthrough drug for depression"   Twenty years later, rival *Newsweek* ran
the headline ANTIDEPRESSANTS DON'T WORK on its cover: healthwyze
.org/reports/412-special-investigative-report-l-tryptophan-lactic-acid-prozac
-and-naturally-treating-depression-the-holistic-way.

"encompasses the extremes of the human experience"   Kay Redfield
Jamison, *Touched with Fire: Manic-Depressive Illness and the Artistic Temperament* (New York: Free Press, 1993), 47.

reduced the suicide attempt rate Ibid., 16. For more on lithium's use compared with a placebo group, see R. J. Baldessarini, L. Tondo, and J. Hennen, "Effects of lithium treatment and its discontinuation on suicidal behavior in bipolar manic-depressive disorders," *Journal of Clinical Psychiatry* 60 (1999), ncbi.nlm. nih.gov/pubmed/10073392. Many patients stop taking lithium, complaining that it dulled their movements and minds. Jonathan Himmelhoch and Ross J. Baldessarini are among those studying the effects of lithium and its withdrawal.

"cigarette smoke and contradictions" Kevin Hall journal entry, December 26, 1989.

the way it impacts artists Kay Redfield Jamison, *Touched with Fire: Manic-Depressive Illness and the Artistic Temperament* (New York: Free Press, 1993), 5.

elite athletes are more prone Ann Kearns Davoren and Seunghyun Hwang, "Mind, Body and Sport," NCAA, October 8, 2014, http://www.ncaa.org/sport -science-institute/mind-body-and-sport-depression-and-anxiety-prevalence -student-athletes.

picking up on subliminal cues Michelle W. Voss, "Understanding the mind of the elite athlete," *Scientific American*, June 1, 2010, scientificamerican.com /article/understanding-elite-athlete/.

because he was institutionalized Sanda Golopentia author interview, June 28, 2016.

Now he was the star of The Show Gordon Hall author interview, April 28, 2016; Kevin Hall author interview, February 6, 2016.

he would adjust his work schedule to tend to him Kevin Hall letter to Meg, January 3, 1990.

eight hours, mushroom time This, of course, was likely not eight hours.

promising future with a degree in . . . French literature? Kevin Hall author interview, October 28, 2014.

Kevin was back, and that's all that seemed to matter Richard Feeny author interview, October 27, 2015.

In a mix of French and English Kevin Hall journal entry, December 26, 1989.

Quantum mechanics, in particular, drew her interest   Amanda Hall author interview, January 31, 2016; Feynman.com.

he was not meant for collaboration   Kevin Hall author interview, November 6, 2014; Kevin Hall, *Black Sails White Rabbits* (Createspace Independent Publishing Platform, 2015), 61.

confusion and stress and medical bills   Kevin Hall author interview, July 5, 2015.

doing the assignment on her own   Kevin Hall author interview, January 31, 2016.

This time, he was more receptive   Amanda Hall author interviews, February 5, 2015, and February 10, 2016.

a cartoon of a physics student   Kevin Hall, *Black Sails White Rabbits* (Createspace Independent Publishing Platform, 2015), 63.

"state of perfection we cannot achieve"   Diane Ackerman, *A National History of Love* (New York: Random House, 1994), 11.

pain in his testicle and a lump   Mike Craycraft author interview, April 18, 2017; Connor O'Leary author interview, April 21, 2017; Michael Rovito author interview, April 24, 2017. All three are testicular cancer experts and advocates who were gracious enough to walk me through and contextualize testicular cancer treatment and symptoms.

the taboos around it were high   Michael Rovito author interview, April 24, 2017; Brandon Hayes-Lattin and Craig R. Nichols, "Testicular Cancer: A Prototypic Tumor of Young Adults," *Seminars in Oncology* 36, no. 5 (2009): 432–38. *PMC*. Web. 7 May 2017. Data for testicular cancer rates can also be found on Cancer.gov.

how many days he had until his next race   Gordon Hall author interview, April 18, 2016; Kevin Hall author interview, November 6, 2014; Kevin Hall, *Black Sails White Rabbits* (Createspace Independent Publishing Platform, 2015), 65.

astounded them both   Ibid, 72.

didn't seem to be much room for anything else   Amanda Hall author interview, February 5, 2015.

had just gone through cancer treatment   Ibid.

the French horn wolf   The 1978 version of *Peter and the Wolf* narrated by David Bowie is not to be missed.

in the presence of a man in crisis   Amanda Hall author interview, February 5, 2015.

much to the amazement of his teammates   Zachary Leonard author interview, September 15, 2014.

bronze medalists are actually happier   Victoria Husted Medvec, Scott F. Madey, Thomas Gilovich, "When Less Is More: Counterfactual Thinking and Satisfaction Among Olympic Medalists." *Journal of Personality and Social Psychology* 69 (1995): 603–10, http://www.anderson.ucla.edu/faculty/keith .chen/negot.%20papers/MedvecMadeyGilovich_ContFactSatisf95.pdf. Researchers have also examined facial expressions at judo competitions to test these theories. See also David Matsumoto and Bob Willingham, "The Thrill of Victory and the Agony of Defeat: Spontaneous Expressions of Medal Winners of the 2004 Athens Olympic Games," *Journal of Personality and Social Psychology* 91, no. 3 (2006): 568–81.

Researchers first observed imposter syndrome   Joe Langford and Pauline R. Clance, "The Imposter Phenomenon: Recent Research Findings Regarding Dynamics, Personality and Family Patterns and Their Implications for Treatment," *Psychotherapy: Theory, Research, Practice, Training* 30, no. 3 (1993): 495–501, doi:10.1037/0033-3204.30.3.495.

feeling that they have failed to live up to an idealized image   Ibid. Kevin would later note in the margin of this paper near this quote, "here, my TSD in a nutshell." David Foster Wallace's "Good Old Neon" also contains a characterization of imposter syndrome, which begins: "My whole life I've been a fraud. I'm not exaggerating. Pretty much all I've ever done all the time is try to create a certain impression of me in other people."

an epic missive against loneliness and sorrow   Sanda Golopentia author interview, June 28, 2016.

"gorillas on the water"   Kevin Hall author interview, November 12, 2014.

level of precision required for Olympic competition Various author interviews with sailors; Gary Jobson, "Weighty Issues of College Sailing," *Sailing World*, December 11, 2002, sailingworld.com/how-to/weighty-issues-college-sailing.

He could never win Kevin Hall email to author, September 29, 2016.

Japan's broader efforts to bolster its sailing culture Barbara Lloyd, "Yachting; Japan's Plan for a Major Effort," *New York Times*, March 3, 1991, http://www.nytimes.com/1991/03/03/sports/yachting-japan-s-plan-for-a-major-effort.html.

an incontestable state of flow Kevin Hall author interview, February 23, 2017.

The Director wouldn't want to kill off his lead actor Kevin Hall author interview, February 11, 2016, and emails to author about backstory of The Show, February 2016.

flipped down a sun visor Kevin Hall, *Black Sails White Rabbits* (Createspace Independent Publishing Platform, 2015), 62. There's skepticism as to whether anyone actually keeps a spare set of keys above the visor. See: http://www.escapistmagazine.com/forums/read/18.829960-Poll-Car-Keys-in-the-Sun-Visor-Does-Anybody-really-do-that. A totally unofficial poll online found that 1.9 percent of people actually do this, but things might have been different (1) in Japan, (2) in the early 1990s. It's also possible that after seeing this done so often on television and in movies, people stopped doing it, realizing that it made their cars ripe for auto theft. The keys are also behind the visor in at least one episode of *Breaking Bad*.

being groomed to be his leading lady Kevin Hall author interview, February 11, 2016, and emails to author about backstory of The Show, February 2016.

a sign reading GENIUS SCHOOL When asked about the GENIUS SCHOOL sign years later, Kevin is among the first to concede that it probably wasn't there.

Real estate in Tokyo Edward Jay Epstein, "What I Lost (and Found) in Japan's Lost Decade," *Vanity Fair*, February 17, 2009, vanityfair.com/news/2009/02/what-was-lost-and-found-in-japans-lost-decade.

a post in Ridgecrest, California Gordon Hall author interview, April 19, 2016.

muttered something about sponsorships Kevin Hall author interview, February 5, 2016.

a well-regarded hospital in Pasadena   Information about Las Encinas can be found at lasencinashospital.com/about/las-encinas-about-our-facility.

Kevin's first visions were euphoric   Kevin Hall author interview, February 11, 2016.

prevention of another global conflict   Kevin Hall author interview, February 11, 2016, and emails to author about backstory of The Show, February 2016.

come to terms with strange mental events   Joel Gold and Ian Gold, *Suspicious Minds: How Culture Shapes Madness* (New York: Free Press, 2015) Location 1340 of Kindle Edition.

to help him sort through life's complexities   Edward H. Hagen, "Non-bizarre delusions as strategic deception," Washington State University, August 2007, anthro.vancouver.wsu.edu/media/PDF/Delusions_revised_Aug_2007.pdf.

lyrics from the band Styx   Kevin Hall journal entry, December 26, 1989.

hallucinogenic, drug-induced experiences   Kevin Hall and Kristina Hall author interviews, January 31, 2016.

give the people, the audience, what they wanted   This is a mild anachronism, but Kevin likened it years later to being something like the 2011 REM music video "ÜBerlin." Kevin said that being on The Show is something like the moment when the guy in the video is swaggering down the street, sees a squirrel, then has to do a performance. "Michael Stipe gets it," Kevin said. If nothing else, it's a really cool video: youtube.com/watch?v=ZITh-XIikgI.

sometimes they even packed their own lunches   Kevin Hall author interview, June 6, 2016.

exposure to the Olympic training regime   Trotman would go on to win a bronze medal in Barcelona, the first ever in the one-person dinghy.

quoting Herman Melville   Kevin Hall author interview, July 29, 2014.

If you improved on Depakote   Andrew Solomon, *Far from the Tree: Parents, Children and the Search for Identity* (New York: Scribner, 2012), 347.

"depression and the difficulty of its treatment"   William Styron, *Darkness Visible: A Memoir of Madness*, (New York: Vintage, 1992), 11.

"confident with myself and excited about the future"   Kevin Hall journal entry, September 15, 1992.

Grape Nuts with peaches   Kevin Hall letter to Amanda Rosenberg, October 5, 1992.

"differentiate between dreams and expectations"   Amanda Rosenberg letter to Kevin Hall, October 14, 1992.

everyone else could eat the sweets but him   Kevin Hall author interview, September 10, 2014.

"Please hear: I Love You."   Kevin Hall letter to Amanda Rosenberg, December 7, 1992.

It seemed implausible   Kristina Hall author interview, January 31, 2016.

well below one percent of those who had it one time   Michael Rovito author interview, April 24, 2017.

cut him from the sternum to the groin   Christine Brennan, "An Olympic Struggle," *Washington Post*, April 15, 1996.

Kevin's ability to have biological children   Amanda and Kevin Hall, author email thread, May 23, 2017.

his performance on the water was peaking   Kenneth B. Noble, "After Cancer Struggle, Olympic Nightmare," *New York Times*, February 15, 1996, http://www.nytimes.com/1996/02/15/us/after-cancer-struggle-olympic-nightmare.html.

"Unfortunately, this includes you."   Kevin Hall journal entry, undated.

150 pounds in January 1993   Kevin Hall letter to Amanda Rosenberg, January 11, 1993.

simply weren't supposed to get cancer   A handy guide to superhero vulnerabilities can be found here as a lovely chart: cbr.com/heres-a-handy-guide-to-the-weaknesses-of-superheroes-villains/.

last four or five days of a cycle   Nazem Bassil, Saad Alkaade, and John E. Morley, "The Benefits and Risks of Testosterone Replacement Therapy: A Review," *Therapeutics and Clinical Risk Management*, 5 (June 22, 2009): 427–448, https://www.ncbi.nlm.nih.gov/pmc/articles/PMC2701485/.

testosterone injections and psychiatric drugs   Michael Rovito author interview, April 24, 2017.

grief still weighed on both of them   Kevin Hall, *Black Sails White Rabbits* (Createspace Independent Publishing Platform, 2015), 82–83.

Kevin retreated to Aspen, Colorado   Kevin Hall author interview, June 6, 2016.

Jung's focus on spirituality and creativity   There's a mountain of information about Jung himself, as well as his views on psychology and culture, but a good place to start is the Jung Page: http://www.cgjungpage.org/.

rather than merely dismissing them   Kevin Hall author interview, November 6, 2014.

reaching out to Kevin in the 1990s   Kevin Hall author interview, July 18, 2016.

believed deeply in the power of coincidences   Louis Menand, "Silence, Exile, Punning," *The New Yorker*, July 2, 2012. Menand also points out that Joyce was "contemptuous of psychoanalysis" and called Jung "the Swiss Tweedledum who is not to be confused with the Viennese Tweedledee."

"one falling and the other diving"   Tara Pepper, "Portrait of the Daughter: Two works seek to reclaim the legacy of Lucia Joyce," *Newsweek International*, March 8, 2003.

"don't take the stray bullets personally"   Letter dated January 1993.

announced that the two of them were going to Boston   Amanda Hall author interview, February 5, 2015; Kevin Hall author interview, February 6, 2016.

talking more and sleeping less   Kevin Hall medical records from McLean Hospital, March 1993.

flipping through its tissue-paper pages   Amanda Hall author interview, February 5, 2015.

"I'm going to hurt you."   Kevin Hall medical records from McLean Hospital, March 1993.

Police officers picked Kevin up   Ibid.

"Mary Had a Little Lamb"   "McLean Hospital: History and Progress," *McLean Hospital*, http://www.mcleanhospital.org/about/history-and-progress.

recover from his latest episode   Ibid.

fantasizing about who he thought he might be   Kevin Hall author interview, April 16, 2015.

wandered out into the streets of Tokyo   Amanda Hall author interview, February 5, 2015.

still madly in love with Kevin   Ibid.

He had taken a job at a Coffee Bean   Kevin Hall author interview, February 5, 2016.

he had lost the love of his life   Diane Ackerman, *A Natural History of Love* (New York: Random House, 1994), 86: "Humans love sports—pitting their strength, nerve, and cunning alongside a teammate or against an opponent on a field of glory, in the hope of winning and being rewarded. Love is a demanding sport involving all the muscle groups, including the brain. The goal of love games is intense physical pleasure, and its special challenge is that the rules are always changing, there is plenty of misdirection, the goal sometimes disappears behind a fog of guilt or misgiving, other players (such as in-laws or rivals) can unexpectedly appear on the field, one's advantage can reverse at a moment's notice, a power often changes hands before the game is finished. What is chess, polo, baseball, or war compared to that?"

feeling that he needed some stimulation   Kevin Hall email to author, September 29, 2016.

"Air Jesuses" campaign   There was no Air Jesus campaign under way by Birkenstock or any other shoe manufacturer at the time. Kevin Hall interview, February 6, 2017; Kevin Hall, *Black Sails White Rabbits* (Createspace Independent Publishing Platform, 2015), 99. Note: this does foreshadow some of Toms shoe marketing by a few years, so the whole idea of shoes as a means to save the world is alive and well today.

Kevin retrieved his white Toyota truck   Suffolk Community College Campus Security Report, June 28, 1993.

have a picnic and talk things through   Kevin Hall interview, February 6, 2016.

"disoriented," according to the professor   Suffolk Community College Campus Security Report, June 28, 1993.

a talk he never wanted to have   Kevin Hall author interview, June 6, 2016.

transported him to a nearby psychiatric facility   Suffolk Community College Campus Security Report, June 28, 1993.

one of the pillars of his life   Author email to Kevin Hall.

"the way I handle the pressure."   Kevin Hall journal entry, September 15, 1994.

let the food in his refrigerator spoil   Kevin Hall journal entry, September 21, 1994.

"and yet I hoped for something from it."   Kay Redfield Jamison, *Touched with Fire: Manic-Depressive Illness and the Artistic Temperament* (New York: Free Press, 1993), 44.

"But I don't know where the start line is"   Kevin Hall journal entry, September 26, 1994.

real life heroes live 24 hours   Full actual quote is: "Heroes in the real world live life twenty-four hours a day, not just two hours in a game."

loss of his fertility and future with Amanda   Kevin Hall journal entry, October 13, 1994.

an ever reinvented, ever beautiful dance   Kevin Hall journal entry, October 16, 1994.

sight of children and infants made him weep   Kevin Hall journal entry, October 20, 1994.

they were meant to be together   Kevin Hall journal entry, October 22, 1994.

Lawyers weren't the stars   Kevin Hall journal entry, December 19, 1994; Kevin Hall author interview, June 6, 2016.

"just be peaceful and steady about it"   Kevin Hall journal entry, September 28, 1994.

not far from where she had grown up   Amanda Hall author interview, January 31, 2016.

the quintessential California couple   A request to Anne for comment was not answered.

remarkable comeback on the water   Brown Athletics, brownbears.com/excep tional_bears/hallfame/Bios/hall_kevin.

Sailing is, by nature, an escapist sport   Richard Feeny author interview, October 27, 2015; John Rousmaniere author interview, April 20, 2016; Mary Pilon, "Sailing Tries to Solve Its One-Percenter Problem," *The New Yorker*,

May 9, 2016, newyorker.com/news/sporting-scene/sailing-tries-to-solve-its -one-per-center-problem; and Mary Pilon, "The America's Cup in Manhattan, Once Again," *The New Yorker,* May 6, 2016, newyorker.com/news/sporting -scene/the-americas-cup-in-manhattan-once-again.

"waiver could not be granted" Kenneth B. Noble, "After Cancer Struggle, Olympic Nightmare," *New York Times,* February 15, 1996, nytimes.com /1996/02/15/us/after-cancer-struggle-olympic-nightmare.html.

way up over his highest budget estimates Christine Brennan, "An Olympic Struggle," *Washington Post,* April 15, 1996.

easily evading what little drug testing existed At least seven athletes tested positive for banned substances at the 1996 Games, including the Americans Mary Slaney and Sandra Patrick-Farm, for testosterone.

Kevin's war with the IOC Brennan, "An Olympic Struggle."

cameras and recorders in front of him Noble, "After Cancer Struggle."

"be on the verge of collapse" Ibid.

gleaming addition to a Southern city Savannah Sailing Center, savannah sailingcenter.org/index.php/about/.

"I enjoy the gym. My wife is a personal trainer" Angus Phillips, "Hall is on an Even Keel in Quest for Olympics." *Washington Post,* May 7, 1996.

four races that weekend "were not pretty," Ibid.

"unable to keep his mind together" Richard Feeny author interview, October 27, 2015.

his days on the junior circuit Kevin Hall author interview, June 6, 2016.

"gentrification of emotions" Olivia Laing, *Lonely City* (New York: Picador, 2016), via BrainPickings: brainpickings.org/2016/07/11/the-lonely-city-olivia -laing/.

he had to hold it all together Credit for this thought goes to Alain de Botton: "My view of human nature is that all of us are just holding it together in various ways—and that's okay, and we just need to go easy with one another, knowing that we're all these incredibly fragile beings."

having shed the old skin Alain de Botton, *The Art of Travel* (New York: Pantheon, 2002).

'89 my mind fails me   Kevin Hall journal entry, November 1997.

'94/5 fail to get accepted to law school   It's worth noting that Kevin had applied to the intensely competitive JD/MBA program at Stanford, which rejects a glut of very talented people regularly.

"My world was about 'Accomplishment,' about 'goals,'"   Kevin Hall journal entry, January 12, 1998.

something other than his mania bringing them together   Kristina Hall author interview, February 2, 2016.

The 49er had quickly captured the imagination   "The Men's 49er—A History Lesson . . . ," *World Sailing*, August 4, 2016, http://www.sailing .org/news/40415.php#.V-uwyqIrK2w; Barbara Lloyd, "The 49er Brings a Rush of Sailors to Try It Out," *New York Times*, April 20, 1997, nytimes.com /1997/04/20/sports/the-49er-brings-a-rush-of-sailors-to-try-it-out.html.

"a wild machine"   Lloyd, "The 49er."

financial setup for striving Olympians   "1998 World Championship Results," *49er*, 49er.org/event/1998-world-championships/?event_id=2727 and "McKee Brothers, Brown and Railey are Winners," *World Sailing*, January 17, 2002, http://www.sailing.org/news/19280.php#.VwzkSTYrK2w.

During the 1998 Sydney to Hobart race   BBC News, "1998: Six die as huge waves smash into yachts," *On This Day 1950–2005*, news.bbc.co.uk/onthisday /hi/dates/stories/december/29/newsid_4034000/4034603.stm and Bryan Burrough, "Storm Warning," *Vanity Fair*, May 1, 2000, vanityfair.com/culture /1999/05/yacht-race-tragedy-200005.

the 80-foot *Sayonara*   Steve Hamm, "Larry Ellison's Brush With Death Aboard Sayonara," *Bloomberg*, May 8, 2000; Burrough, "Storm Warning."

He would "not do another Hobart"   Amanda Lulham, "Larry Ellison says 'never again' to Hobart race," *News Corp Australia Network*, October 12, 2009, http://www.news.com.au/news/ellison-says-never-again/news-story/373623ae 9aabb0eccd412026bd2cdc43.

Michael Jordan, America Online, satellites   Kevin Hall journal entry, July 15, 1998.

1995 made-for-cable movie called *Harrison Bergeron* Kevin Hall author interview, July 18, 2016. The film was released on VHS in 1998.

but part of him felt freaked out Kevin Hall author interview, July 18, 2016.

he, too, could see himself on a reality TV show Kevin Hall author interview, September 10, 2014.

Kevin watched the film on his VHS Kevin Hall author email, September 29, 2016.

He felt that finally, *finally*, someone understood Ibid.

hard not to imagine being on the boat with Truman Kevin Hall author interview, September 10, 2014.

such a strong backlash Kristina Hall author interview, January 31, 2016.

"They are circling around." Malidoma Patrice Somé, *The Healing Wisdom of Africa: Finding Life Purpose Through Nature, Ritual, and Community* (New York: Jeremy P. Tarcher / Putnam, 1998).

"its energetic correspondent" Somé, *Healing Wisdom of Africa*, 23.

He looked over the edge of the building Kevin Hall author interview, September 10, 2014; Author visit to site of old Oracle building in Auckland, February 11, 2016; Kevin Hall author interview, July 29, 2014.

The bird, quite unintentionally, had saved his life Kevin Hall author interview, September 10, 2014; Author visit to site of old Oracle building in Auckland, February 11, 2016. Two weeks later, curious and confused, Kevin went back to the Oracle building. He thought the elevator from the street and his time on the roof with the bird had to have been hallucinations. He was on his meds, on Planet Earth, and felt that going back to the scene of The Show wasn't going to be a trigger. He walked up the block, one of Auckland's downtown avenues that slopes up. The building was, for sure, still there, with its large Oracle sign staring back at him. And much to his astonishment, there was an elevator from the street. Even in moments of clarity, it was hard to tell what was real and what had been imagined.

He felt amazing. Kevin Hall author interview, August 12, 2014.

described his bipolar disorder in detail Kevin Hall author interview, April 16, 2015.

The Show and was perhaps untrustworthy Kevin Hall author interview, June 6, 2016.

or if they lived merely in his head Oliver Sacks, *Hallucinations* (London: Picador, 2013).

fair amount of alcohol and missing sleep Kevin Hall, *Black Sails White Rabbits* (Createspace Independent Publishing Platform, 2015), 153.

something was amiss Morgan Larson author interview, June 1, 2016. Confirmed in Kevin Hall author interview, June 6, 2016.

He had done some kind of power slide Kevin Hall author interview, June 6, 2016; Gordon Hall author interview April 18, 2016.

physically pushed him down Kevin Hall author interview, June 6, 2016.

Gordon wasn't one to nag Kevin Gordon Hall author interview, April 18, 2016.

This aroused little sympathy from Gordon Ibid.

experience working with several Olympians Zachary Leonard author interview, September 15, 2014. Today, Zach coaches the Yale sailing program.

invitation to join the AmericaOne team Amazingly, the 2000 AmericaOne website is still up, and it is a treasure of early Web design: americaone .org/index.html.

the modern workplace water cooler Online Etymology Dictionary, etymon line.com/index.php?allowed_in_frame=0&search=scuttlebutt.

The team had a logistics operator Sarah O'Kane author interview, April 5, 2016.

knew nothing of his mental health history Ibid.

Kevin, by outward appearances, had moved on Morgan Larson author interview, June 1, 2016.

earn a living by being on a boat Zachary Leonard author interview, September 15, 2014.

"didn't mind restarting Windows twice" Kevin Hall author interview, August 15, 2014.

Kevin was not himself Sarah O'Kane author interview, April 5, 2016.

he might reconsider Morgan Larson author interview, June 1, 2016.

considered their engagement official   Kevin Hall, *Black Sails White Rabbits* (Createspace Independent Publishing Platform, 2015), 161.

making sure that Kevin remained stable   Gordon Hall author interview, April 18, 2016.

"Now Kevin is off my desk and on Amanda's."   Confirmed in three separate author interviews with Kevin Hall, Amanda Hall, and Gordon Hall, April 18, 2016.

the 2004 Athens Games   Carol Migdalovitz, "Threat of Terrorism and Security at the Olympics," *CRS Report for Congress*, April 30, 2004, fas.org/irp/crs /RS21833.pdf.

New Zealand-to-U.S.-dollar exchange rate   Kevin Hall author interview, June 6, 2016.

PART III: THE LOWS

one of the more grueling places to spend time   Paul McMullen and Candus Thomson, "State of Olympics," *Baltimore Sun*, August 13, 2004, articles.balti moresun.com/2004-08-13/sports/0408130587_1_sailing-filter-kevin-hall.

One of the top programs in the world   Ron Cassie, "Inside Shock Trauma," *Baltimore* magazine, November 2010, baltimoremagazine.net/2010/10/31/a-look -inside-the-worlds-most-advanced-emergency-room.

initially known as the "death lab"   Ibid.

There were new tactics to learn   School of Sailing, http://www.schoolofsailing .net/tacking-and-jibing.html.

the bold maneuvering lay with the Finn   Kevin Hall, *Black Sails White Rabbits* (Createspace Independent Publishing Platform, 2015), 243.

finishes anemic compared to his forceful starts   Ibid., 244.

a sideways mouse in the first place   Ibid., 246.

a show of the love of the sport   Gordon Hall author interview, April 19, 2016.

couldn't help but chuckle   Kevin Hall, *Black Sails White Rabbits* (Createspace Independent Publishing Platform, 2015), 182.

"Yes, ducks." Ibid.

wanted to be a fair partner Ibid.

Some common cases that had come up World Anti-Doping Agency, "What We Do," wada-ama.org/en/what-we-do/science-medical/therapeutic-use -exemptions.

She wrote a letter and blasted it out Rich Roberts, "Olympic Hopeful's Wife Blisters Sailing Bureaucracy," *YachtRacing.com*, sail-world.com/Australia /Olympic-hopefuls-wife-blisters-sailing-bureaucracy/13966?source=google.

the weight of their expectations Kristina Hall and Kevin Hall author interviews, February 2, 2016.

unexpected hit of sadness and grief Kevin Hall, *Black Sails White Rabbits* (Createspace Independent Publishing Platform, 2015).

the fact that I wasn't a man Kevin Hall author interview, November 6, 2014.

She was never great with faces. Kristina Hall and Bud Culbertson author interviews, January 31, 2016.

more than thirteen miles of Athens traffic Kevin Hall author interview, November 6, 2014.

a hangar-like complex Official Report of the XXVII Olympics, Athens 2004 Organizing Committee.

mix of light, medium, and heavy sailing Kevin Hall email to author, October 5, 2016.

navy blue with USA at the top Image of Kevin at the Olympics via Getty Images, gettyimages.com/detail/news-photo/american-sailor-kevin-hall-sails -during-the-mens-single-news-photo/51177461.

exhausted during her rotations Amanda Hall author interview, May 8, 2017.

Kevin finished eleventh overall. Athens Olympic Results, olympic.org/athens -2004/sailing/finn-one-person-dinghy-heavyweight-men.

reluctant to talk to the press Candus Thomson, "Hall attempts positive tack as seven-month ordeal ends," *Baltimore Sun*, August 22, 2004, articles.balti moresun.com/2004-08-22/sports/0408220081_1_kevin-hall-sailing-clearance.

comparison with Armstrong was considered a compliment Lance Armstrong has clearly had a stunning fall from grace since 2004. Among the most notable Lance Armstrong–Kevin Hall references is from the Baltimore *Sun*: Thomson, "Hall attempts positive."

$20,000 debt to show for it   Kevin Hall author interview, June 6, 2016.

They needed her.   Kristina Hall and Amanda Hall author interviews, January 31, 2016.

It was an unorthodox lifestyle   Kevin Hall author interview, October 28, 2014.

Kevin visiting the psych ward   Kevin Hall and Amanda Hall author interviews, February 5, 2016. Kevin says that ever since then, he has tried his best to avoid red wine. For more on alcohol and manic depression, seek out the Teri Cheney and Kay Redfield Jamison memoirs cited in the Note on Sources.

workouts for the Finn class   Kevin Hall email to author, October 5, 2016.

the success of starting a family   "US Sailing Trails Coverage," *Sailingworld.com*, sailingworld.com/racing/2007-us-olympic-sailing-trials-coverage.

nothing short of taxing   Kevin Hall author interview, June 16, 2015.

sliced like a loaf of bread   Sarah O'Kane author interview, April 5, 2016.

prestigious circuit standings   Quantum Racing win in Sarginia, *Yachting World*, July 6, 2008, yachtingworld.com/news/quantum-racing-win-in-sardinia-14773.

Cokes instead of his usual beer   Kevin Hall author interview, July 29, 2014.

taken off his Olympic watch   Ray Davies author interview, February 6, 2016.

to be closer to the earth   Kevin Hall author interview, September 10, 2014.

"I am a cactus/Trying to be a canoe"   "The Ascent of Man," *Around the Sun*, 2004.

stowed in Kevin's luggage   Tommy Dodson author interview, July 21, 2017.

Pink Floyd's "Comfortably Numb"   Ray Davies author interview, February 6, 2016; Sarah O'Kane author interview, April 5, 2016.

anyone's guess how long it would take   Author interview with Tommy Dodson, July 21, 2017.

from partying on the boat to being on The Show   Tommy Dodson author interview, July 20, 2017; Kevin Hall author interview, July 29, 2014.

his mission, and their role in it   Ibid.

he had made a few bad calls Ibid.

Auckland, Planet Earth, The Universe Ray Davies author interview, February 6, 2016; Tommy Dodson author interview, July 20, 2017.

version of him that he no longer recognized Kevin Hall author interview, September 10, 2014.

port of significance Tommy Dodson author interview, July 20, 2017. Kevin has told me he is "pretty sure" that during this flight he vomited into his shoe shortly after takeoff. Considering that this is virtually impossible to fact-check and his own memory is hazy, readers can draw their own conclusion.

wasn't sure how he had done it Kevin Hall author interview, July 29, 2014.

actually liked the Gucci bag Ibid.

Russian was also their best shot In 2012, Americans would be banned from adopting Russian children.

23 miles per hour 52 Super Series, "TP Class," 52superseries.com/the-52-super -series/tp52-class/.

"Mostly to be liked or admired" Stanford makes "Good Old Neon" available online for free here: stanford.edu/~sdmiller/octo/files/no_google2/GoodOld Neon.pdf.

Swedish businessman Torbjörn Törnqvist Forbes profile: Torbjörn Törn-qvist, forbes.com/profile/torbjorn-tornqvist/.

new boats were called AC72s Diane Swintal, R. Steven Tsuchiya, and Robert Kamins, *Winging It: Oracle Team USA's Incredible Comeback to Defend the America's Cup* (Camden, Maine: International Marine / McGraw-Hill Educational), 45.

unlike that of any previous regatta G. Bruce Knecht, *The Comeback: How Larry Ellison's Team Won the America's Cup* (Createspace Independent Publishing Platform), 10.

1998 Sydney to Hobart race Ibid., 14.

"people who were stronger, faster" Ibid., 10.

chain-link fencing and barbed wire Author visit to the *Artemis* site in Alameda, California, May 3, 2016.

$400 million for the 2013 cycle Diane Swintal, R. Steven Tsuchiya, and Robert Kamins, *Winging It: Oracle Team USA's Incredible Comeback to Defend the America's Cup* (Camden, Maine: International Marine / McGraw-Hill Educational), 19. Note that estimated costs of the Cup have varied wildly.

some combination of all three Knecht, *The Comeback*, 11.

No one was aware of his experiences Kevin Hall email to author, September 29, 2106.

'They *did* write about me' Dr. Joel Gold author interview, January 6, 2016.

he wondered if he wasn't alone after all Kevin Hall author interview, August 22, 2014.

likely to suffer from erotomania Joel Gold and Ian Gold, *Suspicious Minds: How Culture Shapes Madness* (Free Press / Kindle Edition, July 8, 2014), 66.

the influence of organized religion had diminished For those interested in more, there's a fascinating relic in the psychiatric Jesus canon, "The Three Christs of Ypsilanti," a 1964 psychiatric case study by Milton Rokeach in which he takes three patients with paranoid schizophrenia who each think they're Jesus and puts them in the same room.

the Cotard delusion Hat tip to Barry Newman.

"through the wrong end of a telescope" Jerome M. Schneck, "Micropsia," *American Journal of Psychiatry* 118, no. 3 (September 1961): 232–234, ajp. psychiatryonline.org/doi/abs/10.1176/ajp.118.3.232.

just about any psychotic illness Gold and Gold, *Suspicious Minds*, 11.

"it does lead to serious control issues" Dave Reed, "AC72: Designed in the Matrix," *Sailing World*, October 19, 2012, sailingworld.com/racing/ac72 -designed-matrix.

the technical edge of risk Ibid.

promote videos on YouTube "Going, going, going . . . gone—AC45 capsize," America's Cup on YouTube, https://www.youtube.com/watch?v=ddZND avV4Y4.

to the tune of at least $8 million Lisa Fernandez, "Capsized Oracle Catamaran Towed to Pier," NBC Bay Area, October 17, 2012.

the *Artemis* was arriving "Artemis Racing Changes as Hutchinson Leaves Team," *CupInfo*, November 30, 2012, cupinfo.com/en/artemis-terry-hutchin son-released-12106.php.

it had been damaged in tow-testing "Artemis Racing Launches AC72 for 2013 America's Cup." *CupInfo*, Noember 3, 2012, http://www.cupinfo.com/en /artemis-launches-ac72-catamaran-12102.php.

adding foils under a tight deadline Ibid.

headline from the blog *Sailing Anarchy* "Already Broken," *Sailing Anarchy*, October 18, 2012, sailinganarchy.com/2012/10/18/already-broken/.

driving down the road at sixty miles per hour Alexa Lyons, "Can Sailing Be the Next F1?" *Maxim*, October 19, 2014, maxim.com/gear/can-sailing-be -next-f1.

their cause for deciding to terminate him Ibid. Thanks to *Sailing Anarchy* for pointing me to the *Maxim* interview (sailinganarchy.com/tag/terry -hutchinson/). It's worth noting that Hutchinson later backpedaled from his comments. Hutchinson did not respond to a request for comment.

a new fleet of sailors "Artemis Racing Brings More Olympic Talent to Crew," *CupInfo*, February 26, 2013, cupinfo.com/en/artemis-adds-olympic-crew -13011.php.

known each other for a decade Kevin Hall author interview, August 15, 2014.

sent the *Artemis* to the shed for modifications "The Boats of America's Cup 2013: AC72," *CupInfo*, cupinfo.com/en/americas-cup-2013-ac72-catama rans.php#Artemis.

series of snaps that curdled the blood Sam Rigney, "Olympic medallists safe after fatal capsize," *Border Mail*, May 11, 2013, bordermail.com.au/story/1494 463/olympic-medallists-safe-after-fatal-capsize/?cs=2452. Outteridge mentions the crack in this interview.

entire balance of the boat careen D. R. Ibarra, San Francisco Police Department Report #130 381 063, May 9, 2013. Facts from the police report are confirmed by my interviews with people familiar with the crash as well.

marine unit responded to the call Ibid.

a mess of tangled metal   Jean Elle, "New Theory Emerges for Artemis Capsize," *NBC Bay Area*, May 12, 2013, nbcbayarea.com/news/local/New -Theory-Emerges-For-Artemis-Capsize-207026431.html.

handed him an oxygen bottle   Ibid.

the boat had simply buckled   Adam Fisher, "What Went Wrong in the Deadly America's Cup Crash," *Wired*, May 9, 2013, wired.com/2013/05 /americas-cup-crash/.

on the phone again   Gordon Hall author interview, April 19, 2016.

can be flexible and malleable   *Invisibilia*, Season 2, "The Personality Myth," npr.org/programs/invisibilia/482836315/the-personality-myth. If you aren't listening to this podcast, *Hidden Brain*, on NPR or Radiolab, get on it. The work of Walter Mischel in particular may be of interest.

"to not be victims of their biographies."   Ibid.

eyes glaze with tears   Kristina Hall author interview, January 31, 2016.

the sound of the boat snapping in his ears   Kevin Hall author interview, January 23, 2015.

stopped taking them on his own   Kevin Hall email to author, July 25, 2017.

lows were as unpredictable as his highs   Kevin Hall author interview, December 1, 2015.

Was it ever going to be enough?   Kevin Hall author interview, November 6, 2014.

It seemed utterly insignificant.   Kevin Hall author interview, December 1, 2015.

a failure of self-esteem   William Styron, *Darkness Visible: A Memoir of Madness*, (New York: Vintage, 1992), 7.

"the safety of this sport very seriously"   Jean Elle, "New Theory Emerges for Artemis Capsize," *NBC Bay Area*, May 12, 2013, http://www.nbcbayarea.com /news/local/New-Theory-Emerges-For-Artemis-Capsize-207026431.html.

their prayers are with Andrew Simpson's family   It's one of many Artemis-related pages from the America's Cup website that is now no longer available. It's unclear to me when it was removed.

out into the bay "Artemis Racing AC72 Takes First Sale," *CupInfo*, July 24, 2013, cupinfo.com/en/artemis-second-ac72-first-sail-americas-cup-13066.php and "Artemis Racing AC72 Launched, Nearly Ready to Race," *CupInfo*, July 22, 2013, cupinfo.com/en/artemis-launches-second-ac72-catamaran-americas-cup-13065.php.

financially supporting his family To be fair to Kevin, the life of a writer is, often, financially wildly unstable. His notion here is not far-fetched.

something as horrific as Simpson's death Kevin Hall author interview, January 23, 2015.

Kevin was still drinking too much Kevin Hall author interview, July 18, 2016.

she couldn't answer for him Ibid.

they weren't going to matter Ibid. For what it's worth, years later, Kevin said he didn't think there was any major evidence that his teammates or other sailing executives frowned on his decision to leave the team, but given how insular sailing's culture is, his line of thinking on this makes sense.

public remarks about Andrew's death Kevin Hall, "Legend," *Sailing Anarchy*, July 14, 2013, sailinganarchy.com/2013/07/14/legend/.

"one of the greatest comebacks" Stu Woo, "Against the Wind," *Wall Street Journal*, February 28, 2014, wsj.com/articles/SB10001424052702303393804579312803907849782.

changes to the race going forward Josh Levin, "The Miracle on San Fransisco Bay," *Slate*, September 25, 2013.

whatever he was in the mood for Kevin Hall author interview, July 29, 2014.

2001 film *A Beautiful Mind* Kevin Hall author interview, confirmed in author interview with Stephanie Gisonde-Little, January 5, 2015.

"So I took them seriously" Sylvia Nasar, *A Beautiful Mind: The Life of Mathematical Genius and Nobel Laureate John Nash* (New York: Simon & Schuster, 2001).

as untethered as Nash's At the risk of stating the obvious, these thoughts are clearly coming to Kevin in a manic upswing and in no way is he, or am I, alleging that there was some mass conspiracy cover-up surrounding the 2013 America's Cup race.

PART IV: FINALE

what they had seen while living in New Zealand   Amanda Hall and Kevin Hall author interviews, February 13, 2016. Author drive to Legoland, March 25, 2016. If you're reading this, you're in the depths of my endnotes. Bless you. Email to marypilon@gmail.com a reference to your favorite piece of pop culture that appears in this book and receive a digital hug. Keep being awesome.

Alice **book online for $9,000**   Kevin Hall author interview, February 23, 2017.

worse than she could ever remember seeing him   Kristina Hall and Kevin Hall author interviews, February 3, 2016.

fantasyland built of brick and plastic   Author visit to Legoland, Friday, March 25, 2016. A map of Legoland can be found here: legoland.com/global assets/california/downloads/resort/legoland-california-resort-park-map.pdf. Everything at Legoland is, indeed, awesome.

center of its round 128-acre grounds   The 128-acre estimate comes from Google Maps, yet one could argue it's never big enough.

The Lego models were beautiful   The Lego models really are impressive, even when one is not in a manic state.

The uniforms of the Legoland staff were beautiful   Kevin Hall, *Black Sails White Rabbits*, (Createspace Independent Publishing Platform, 2015).

as if they, too, were going crazy   Kristina Hall and Amanda Hall author interviews, February 3, 2016.

Every Love Story Is a Ghost Story   Kevin Hall author interview, February 1, 2016.

the stakes for this episode   Kevin Hall author interview, July 29, 2014.

"a different kind of bottom"   D. T. Max, *Every Love Story Is a Ghost Story* (New York: Penguin, 2012), 135.

Skin Horse tells the Velveteen Rabbit   Ibid., 233.

It was not a cheap set   Amazon Prime has it for $479, four years after the fact, so $500 is likely a generous estimate, without sales tax. https://www.amazon .com/LEGO-Creator-Expert-10234-Sydney/dp/B00EQ7LZSY/ref=sr_1_1?ie =UTF8&qid=1493726679&sr=8-1&keywords=lego+sydney+opera+house.

They compromised and settled on a book   To be fair, the *Beautiful Lego* book is really cool.

obsessed with rearranging the silverware   Kristina Hall author interview, February 1, 2016.

wreckage that his mania left in its wake   Gordon Hall author interview, April 18, 2016.

whether he liked it or not   Ibid.

environments growing up can vary widely   Frank J. Sulloway, *Born to Rebel: Birth Order, Family Dynamics, and Creative Lives* (New York: Pantheon, 1996), 150, 352.

Darwinian fights of human development   Ibid., 354.

digging deeper into the status quo   Ibid., 356.

There was no easy cure   MadnessRadio.net, "Bipolar Medication Myths," Augist 26, 2010, madnessradio.net/madness-radio-bipolar-medication-myths -joanna-moncrieff/. Hat tip to Kevin for sending this one along.

He had been faking it for years   Kevin Hall, Amanda Hall, and Kristina Hall author interviews, January 31, 2016.

a collective fib they could all agree on   Kristina Hall author interview, February 1, 2016.

the most tranquil approach might make him flee   Ibid.

where the gray had started and the black begun   Kevin Hall author interview, June 15, 2016.

thought about his battle with medication   Kevin Hall author interview, December 1, 2015.

as openly and honestly as he could   Kevin Hall author interview, July 29, 2014.

devoid of a soul or sensorial experience   Kevin Hall author interview, January 31, 2016.

as if he wasn't his real self   Kevin Hall author interview, August 15, 2014.

still had to wake up and be a dad every day   Kevin and Kristina Hall author interview, January 31, 2016.

"job, friends, or even sanity"   Kevin Hall, *Black Sails White Rabbits* (Createspace Independent Publishing Platform, 2015).

just as a problem   For more on the lack of information about SSRIs, see Robert Whitaker's *Anatomy of an Epidemic*, p. 331 (New York, 2010). Whitaker writes of a 2003 hunger strike by "psychiatric survivors" who confronted the APA about the lack of information. (The APA did not respond to my requests for comment.) Also see "Head Case" by Louis Menand (*The New Yorker*, March 1, 2010), "When it Comes to Depression, Serotonin Isn't the Whole Story" by Alix Speigel (*Morning Edition*, NPR, January 23, 2012, http://www.npr.org /sections/health-shots/2012/01/23/145525853/when-it-comes-to-depression-sero tonin-isnt-the-whole-story).

blogs chronicling their battles in detail   Colby Itkowitz, "Unwell and Unashamed," *Washington* Post, June 1, 2016, http://www.washingtonpost .com/sf/local/2016/06/01/unwell-and-unashamed/?utm_term=.542ad6f6c32b

"You are the author and the sentence is your life."   Project Semicolon, http:// www.projectsemicolon.org/.

More nuanced depictions of people   Nic Sheff, "Why Can't Hollywood Get Bipolar Disorder Right?" *Salon*, February 5, 2013, https://www.salon .com/2013/02/05/misdiagnosing_bipolar_disorder_in_tv_and_movies _partner/

Joyce played with the idea of fours   James Joyce, *Finnegans Wake* (New York: Viking, 1939). A very handy guide to the chapter can be found here: finwake .com/1024chapter24/1024finn24.htm. The four birds appear in chapter 4. A metanumerical coincidence? That is for the reader to decide.

that moderation was the goal   Kevin Hall author interview, November 6, 2014.

focused, literally, on the right channel   Kevin Hall author email, August 4, 2014.

vast majority of people can only imagine   For more, see Stephen Fry's 2006 two-part documentary, *The Secret Life of the Manic Depressive*.

entered a hospital shortly thereafter   Kevin Hall author interview, September 9, 2015.

not a competition or preparation for one   Kevin Hall author interview, January 23, 2015.

being a stay-at-home dad is more difficult   Kevin Hall, "Five Reasons Being a Stay At Home Dad Is Harder Than Being an Olympian," *The Good Men Project*, August 10, 2016, goodmenproject.com/featured-content/five-reasons-sahd-olympian-mkdn/.

"whether you ever wore the pants at all"   Nor is it that simple if you win a gold medal, or dozens of them. See Tim Layden's coverage of Michael Phelps: "After rehabilitation the best of Michael Phelps may lie ahead," *Sports Illustrated*, November 9, 2015, https://www.si.com/olympics/2015/11/09/michael-phelps-rehabilitation-rio-2016.

"I just want to be supportive"   Kevin Hall author interview, October 28, 2014.

who many scholars today believe may have had   For more on Melville and mental illness, see J. J. Ross, "The many ailments of Herman Melville (1819–91)," *Journal of Medical Biography* 16, no 1 (February 2008): 21–9, ncbi.nlm.nih.gov/pubmed/18463061 and Clare Dolman and Sarah Turvey, "The impact of Melville's manic-depression on the writing of *Moby Dick*," *Mendtal Health Review Journal* 16, no. 3 (2011): 107–112, emeraldinsight.com/doi/abs/10.1108/13619321111178050.

"There are no mysteries out of ourselves"   Herman Melville, *White Jacket*, Project Gutenberg, 2015, chapter 93. (Originally published in New York in 1850.)

AFTERWORD

misogynistic, bigoted, and xenophobic views   Marisa Lancione, "We Need to Stop Calling Donald Trump Mentally Ill," *Mad Girl's Lament*, August 8, 2016, madgirlslament.com/2016/08/08/we-need-to-stop-calling-donald-trump-mentally-ill/.

medication-free on his own   There is likely a separate book to be done on medication and bipolar disorder, and yet another to be done on how varied individual experiences with bipolar disorder can be. This was something I found in my interviews with folks who had been diagnosed with bipolar I, II, or had experienced Truman Show–like symptoms. One particularly powerful account was Linda Logan's in the *New York Times Magazine* in 2013, which also elicited some strong comments from readers that can be read in the online version of the story: Linda Logan, "The Problem With How We Treat Bipolar Disorder," *New York Times Magazine*, April 26, 2013, http://www.nytimes.com/2013/04/28/magazine/the-problem-with-how-we-treat-bipolar-disorder.html.

"We'll do it together," she said. "I love you." Kevin Hall email to author, Amanda Hall, July 25, 2017. Kevin's decision to go drug-free was over a year ago, and it has been a year of big changes and some trials: the Halls moved around the world from a place where they knew everybody to a town of strangers in a frigid locale, and family dynamics have been tested as the Halls learn more about their eldest son's gifts and challenges.

John Nash stopped taking his psychiatric medication Clare Allen, "Don't Use John Nash to Promote the Use of Anti-Psychotic Drugs." *The Guardian*, June 2, 2015, https://www.theguardian.com/society/2015/jun/02/dont-use-john-nash-schizophrenia-a-beautiful-mind-promote-anti-psychotics.

to create that perfect Instagram There is a place in hell for those who quote their own work, but if you want to know more of my thoughts about how Instagram is ruining vacations, you can find them here: "Instagram is Ruining Vacation," *Wired*, April 13, 2016, https://www.wired.com/2016/04/instagram-is-ruining-vacation/.

"fantasy machines whose use is addictive" Susan Sontag, *On Photography* (New York: Penguin, 1977).

'None of that matters.' Kevin Hall author interview, February 23, 2017.

A NOTE ON THE AUTHOR

MARY PILON is the author of *The Monopolists*, the critically acclaimed and *New York Times* bestselling history of the board game. A regular contributor to *The New Yorker, Esquire, Fast Company,* MSNBC, *Vice, Politico,* and *Bloomberg BusinessWeek,* among other news outlets, Pilon worked as a staff reporter at the *New York Times* and the *Wall Street Journal* and as an Emmy-nominated producer for NBC Sports at the 2016 Rio Olympics. She lives in Brooklyn. Visit her website at marypilon.com and follow her on Twitter at @marypilon.